NAZI-LOOTED JEWISH ARCHIVES IN MOSCOW

A GUIDE TO JEWISH HISTORICAL AND CULTURAL COLLECTIONS IN THE RUSSIAN STATE MILITARY ARCHIVE

NAZI-LOOTED JEWISH ARCHIVES

IN

MOSCOW

A GUIDE TO JEWISH HISTORICAL AND

CULTURAL COLLECTIONS IN THE

RUSSIAN STATE MILITARY ARCHIVE

Edited by
David E. Fishman
Mark Kupovetsky
Vladimir Kuzelenkov

University of Scranton Press
Scranton and London

Published in association with the
United States Holocaust Memorial Museum
and
The Jewish Theological Seminary

Published in association with the United States Holocaust Memorial Museum, 100 Raoul Wallenberg Place, SW, Washington, DC 20024–2126, and The Jewish Theological Seminary, 3080 Broadway, New York, NY 10027

The assertions, arguments, and conclusions contained herein are those of the contributors and volume editors. They do not necessarily represent the opinions of the United States Holocaust Memorial Museum or The Jewish Theological Seminary.

Library of Congress Cataloging-in-Publication Data

Nazi-Looted Jewish Archives in Moscow : a guide to Jewish historical and cultural collections in the Russian State Military Archive / edited by David E. Fishman, Mark Kupovetsky, Vladimir Kuzelenkov.
   p. cm.
  ISBN 978-1-58966-220-9 (cloth)
  1. Holocaust, Jewish (1939-1945)--Sources--Catalogs. 2. World War, 1939-1945--Jews--Sources. 3. Jews--Germany--History--20th century--Sources. 4. World War, 1939-1945--Confiscations and contributions--Germany--Sources. 5. World War, 1939-1945--Confiscations and contributions--Soviet Union--Sources. 6. Rossiiskii gosudarstvennyi voennyi arkhiv--Archives--Catalogs. 7. World War, 1939-1945--Germany--Sources. 8. Germany--History--1933-1945--Sources. I. United States Holocaust Memorial Museum. II. Jewish Theological Seminary of America. III. Title: Guide to Jewish historical and cultural collections in the Russian State Military Archive.
  Z6374.H6N39 2010
  [D804.3]
  026'.90904924--dc22

2010009619

Distribution:

University of Scranton Press
Chicago Distribution Center
11030 S. Langley
Chicago, IL 60628

The research for this volume, as well as its editing, translation, and publication, were made possible thanks to grants from:

The Conference on Jewish Material Claims Against Germany
Memorial Foundation for Jewish Culture
Joseph S. and Diane H. Steinberg Charitable Trust
The Blavatnik Family Foundation
Yad Avi Hayishuv
United States Holocaust Memorial Museum

Translation from Russian: Avram Brown

Editor of English-language edition: David E. Fishman

A publication of Project Judaica, a program of The Jewish Theological Seminary

CONTENTS

III France

Organizations

Individuals
IV. Germany

Organizations

Government Agencies

INTRODUCTION

The Russian State Military Archive (RGVA) contains a wealth of Jewish historical and cultural material currently unknown to most specialists in the field of Judaica and unused in scholarly research. It is the purpose of this guide to provide comprehensive descriptions of the RGVA collections containing such materials, some of which are of Jewish provenance, and others of which are from European state institutions and public organizations.

The volume was prepared jointly by the RGVA and Project Judaica, a program of The Jewish Theological Seminary and Russian State University for the Humanities, as part of the archival guide series *Jewish Documentary Sources in the Archives of Russia, Ukraine and Belarus*, which has published guides to Jewish documentary sources in Moscow, Belarus, Kiev, and Volhyn, to date.[1]

The collections of Jewish provenance held by RGVA are from Austria, Czechoslovakia, France, Germany, Greece, Latvia, and Yugoslavia. They were seized by Nazi German state agencies during the course of World War II, and were transported to the Soviet Union after the war.

This material includes the records of major international Jewish organizations such as the American Jewish Joint Distribution Committee

---

1 M. S. Kupovetsky, E. V. Starostin, Marek Web, eds., *Dokumenty po istorii i kul'ture evreev v arkhivakh Moskvy: putevoditel'* (Moscow: Rossiiskii gosudarstvennyi gumanitarnyi universitet, 1997). The Moscow guide includes descriptions of only 13 RGVA collections containing documents related to Jewish history and culture and is superseded by the current volume. M. S. Kupovetsky, E. M. Savitskii, Marek Web, eds., *Dokumenty po istorii i kul'ture evreev v arkhivakh Belarusi: putevoditel'* (Moscow: Rossiiskii gosudarstvennyi gumanitarnyi universitet, 2003); E. I. Melamed, M. S. Kupovetsky, eds., *Dokumenty po istorii i kul'ture evreev v arkhivakh Kyiva: putevoditel'* (Kiev: Dukh i litera, 2006); E. I. Melamed, ed., *Dokumenty po istorii i kul'ture evreev v regional'nykh arkhivakh ukrainy. Putevoditel. Volynskaia, zhitomirskaia, rovenskaia, cherkaskaya oblasti* (Kiev: Feniks, 2009).

and the World Jewish Congress, and the archives of national and local Jewish communal bodies, including the Central Association of German Citizens of the Jewish Faith, the Union of Austrian Jews, and the Jewish community of Salonika. Also deposited in RGVA are records of various Zionist organizations (including the Berlin Zionist Union), records of Jewish institutions of higher learning (such as the Israelite Theological Institute of Vienna), and the papers of major Jewish social organizations, such as the German and Austrian Grand Lodges of B'nai B'rith. Finally, the RGVA houses the personal archives of public Jewish figures, including those of the sixth Lubavitcher Rebbe, Rabbi Yosef Yitzchok Schneerson.

The guide describes RGVA collections that formerly belonged to the Central State Special Archive (*Tsentral'nyi gosudarstvennyi osobyi arkhiv*, TsGOA) of the USSR. It is therefore appropriate to review briefly the history and activity of this archive.

The TsGOA was established on 9 March 1946 in accordance with a resolution of the USSR Council of People's Commissars. It became necessary to create the Special Archive when, in the summer of 1945, the Central Archival Administration of the NKVD (*Glavnoe arkhivnoe upravlenie*, GAU NKVD SSSR) received "documents of foreign provenance (in need of sorting and description)," with "the possibility of more coming in the future." The new archive was to occupy a special position in the Soviet archival system due both to its secret status as a closed archive and to the fact that "most of the Special Archive's document collections" were to be "held temporarily."[2]

At the time of its founding, the TsGOA's core holdings consisted of Polish documents removed from western Ukraine and western Belorussia in 1939 and groups of documents discovered in the summer of 1945 by Red Army forces in Czechoslovakia (in the vicinity of Česká Lípa) and Lower Silesia, in Habelswerdt (now Polish Bystrztca Kłodzko) and Wölfelsdorf (now Polish Wilkanów).

In the course of 1946, the TsGOA received for preservation 1.5 million files of foreign provenance, as well as card catalogues and numer-

---

2 V. I. Korotaev, V. P. Kozlov, V. N. Kuzelenkov, eds., *Ukazatel' fondov inostrannogo proiskhozhdeniia i Glavnogo upravleniia po delam voennoplennykh i internirovannykh NKVD-MVD SSSR Rossiiskogo gosudarstvennogo voennogo arkhiva* (Moscow: RGVA, 2001), p. 3.

ous printed publications. The documents came to the archive in a chaotic state. Most of the collections had been broken up, there were usually no finding aids to speak of, and many files lacked headings. Documents were badly shuffled.

In 1951, a special building was constructed for the TsGOA. The Special Archive then began accepting for preservation documents from various state and departmental archives. Thus, for example, a large volume of foreign documents was transferred to the Archive from the USSR Ministry of Internal Affairs in 1954. In 1959, the Archive received approximately 30,000 files of German Ministry of Economics documents from the USSR Ministry of Foreign Trade.

In 1960, following a decision of the USSR Council of Ministers, the TsGOA began receiving documents of the USSR Ministry of Internal Affairs Main Administration on POW and Internee Affairs (*Glavnoe upravlenie po delam voennoplennykh i internirovannykh MVD SSSR*) and institutions subordinate to it from the period 1939–60, as well as documents of the Administration of the USSR Council of Ministers Commissioner on the Repatriation of Foreign Citizens from the period 1945–53.

From late 1946 to the mid-1960s, the staff of the TsGOA made significant progress in arranging, systematizing, and composing finding aids to its collections. The systematizing of a number of collections continued subsequently as well. Between 1962 and 1973, TsGOA staff prepared a three-volume guide to the archive's holdings of foreign provenance. This guide was available only for internal use. In 2001, the archive published that guide as *Index to the Russian State Military Archive's Collections of Foreign Provenance and of the USSR NKVD-MVD Main Administration on POW and Internee Affairs.*

Beginning in the mid-1950s, the Central Committee of the Communist Party of the USSR and the USSR Council of Ministers issued a number of directives stipulating the repatriation of some TsGOA holdings to Yugoslavia (four collections in 1956), Poland (in 1956 and 1963, a total of 83 collections), the German Democratic Republic (391 collections in 1957), Romania (three collections in 1960) and Czechoslovakia (two collections in 1961). In 1966 and 1968, certain sets of documents pertaining to French cultural figures and scholars, and to General de Gaulle's role in the Resistance, were transferred to France. The task of document repatriation resumed after changes in the archive's operations (in early 1992) allowed researchers considerably greater access to its collections.[3] At the same time, in 1992, the Archive was renamed the Center for the Preservation of Historical Documentary Collections (*Tsentr khraneniia istoriko-dokumental'nykh kolektsii*, TsKhIDK). In 1999, the TsKhIDK was incorporated into the Russian State Military Archive (*Rossiiskii gosudarstvennyi voennyi arkhiv*, RGVA). From 1992 to 2004, a total of 277 collections from the former TsGOA were repatriated to France, Poland, the Federal Republic of Germany, the Netherlands, Belgium, and Liechtenstein.[4] The work of determining countries of origin and of repatriating the archive's documents thereto continues at present.

---

3 The opening of the archive allowed a number of Russian and foreign researchers to publish summaries and lists of the war trophies of the former TsGOA. Among these, the following are relevant to the study of Jewish history and culture: Götz Aly, Susanne Heim, *Das Zentrale Staatsarchiv in Moskau ("Sonderarchiv"): Rekonstruktion und Bestandsverzeichnis verschollen geglaubten Schriftguts aus der NS-Zeit* (Düsseldorf: Hans-Böckler-Stiftung, 1993), 58 pages; Kai von Jena, Wilhelm Lenz, "Die deutschen Bestände im Sonderarchiv in Moskau," *Der Archivar* 45 no. 3 (1992): 457–67; B. Wegner, "Deutsche Aktenbestlinde im Moskauer Zentralen Staatsarchiv: Ein Erfahrungsbericht," *Vierteljahrshefte für Zeitgeschichte* 40:2 (1992): 311–19; Wolfgang Form, Pavel Poljan, "Das Zentrum für die Aufbewahrung historisch-dokumentarischer Sammlungen in Moskau — Ein Erfahrungsbericht," *Informationen aus der Forschung* (Bundesinstitut für ostwissenschaftliche und internationale Studien), 20 October 1992, no. 7: 1–8; George C. Browder, "Captured German and Other Nations' Documents in the Osoby (Special) Archive, Moscow," *Central European History* 24, no. 4 (1992): 424–45; T. A. Vasil'eva, A. S. Namazova, M. M. Mukhamedzhanov, *Fondy bel'giiskogo proiskhozhdeniia: annotirovannyi ukazatel'* (Moscow: Rosarkhiv, TsKhIDK, Institut vseobshchei istorii RAN, 1995), 26 pages; Gerhard Jagschitz, Stefan Karner, *Beuteakten aus Österreich: Der Österreichbestand im russischen "Sonderarchiv" Moskau* (Graz: Selbstverlag des Ludwig Boltzmann-Instituts für Kriegsfolgen-Forschung, 1996), 268 pages; *Dokumenty po istorii i kul'ture evreev v arkhivakh Moskvy*, 265–281; "Spravochnik <Kartoteka Z> operativnogo shtaba <Reichsleiter Rosenberg>: Tsennosti kul'tury na okkupirovannykh territoriiakh Rossii, Ukrainy, Belorussii 1941–42," Tsentr khraneniia itoriko-dokumental'nykh kollektsii (TsKhIDK), in Patricia Kennedy Grimsted, ed., *Archives of Russia: A Directory and Bibliographic Guide to Holdings in Moscow and St. Petersburg* (Armonk, NY; London: M. E. Sharp, 2000) 1: 225–30; Patricia Kennedy Grimsted, F. J. Hoogewoud and Eric Ketelaar, eds., *Returned from Russia: Nazi Archival Plunder in Western Europe and Recent Restitution Issues,* (Builth Wells, Britain: Institute of Art and Law, 2007), and the website http:/www.sonderarchiv.de.

4 An appendix at the end of this guide lists and describes RGVA collections that contain significant groups of documents on Jewish history and culture, returned to their countries of origin since 1991. It also notes whether RGVA holds microfilms of those collections.

The holdings of the RGVA currently include documents from state administrative and judicial institutions of the Weimar Republic and the Third Reich, Nazi occupation authorities of the WWII period, the National Socialist German Workers' Party (NSDAP), Storm Trooper detachments of the NSDAP, and the administrations of the SS and of concentration and POW camps. The archive also contains materials of various public organizations and cultural, philanthropic, scientific, and pedagogical institutions and organizations of Germany and of other countries of Central, Southeastern, and Western Europe.

Also housed in the RGVA are archives, confiscated by the Nazi occupiers, of a number of state ministries and departments of France, Austria, the Netherlands, Belgium, Poland, Czechoslovakia, Yugoslavia, Romania, Bulgaria, and Greece, as well as of various NGOs and political, religious, cultural, professional, philanthropic, and other organizations of these countries. The archive also possesses numerous personal collections, seized by the Nazis in the 1930s to early 1940s, of prominent social, religious, and political leaders, scholars, and cultural figures of interwar Europe.

A significant portion of the RGVA's collections are relevant to the study of Jewish history and culture. Several Nazi institutions and organizations were involved in the expropriation of Jewish cultural treasures, including archives. Noteworthy among these was Section B2 of Reichssicherheitshauptamt (RSHA) Department VII (the Office of Information and Counter-Propaganda), established in late 1941. Section B2 employed a group of "specialists," headed by E. Krumach, to collect, catalogue, and sort confiscated documents and materials pertaining to Jews. So far as is known, one of the principal tasks of Department VII of the RSHA was to create a voluminous card catalogue of "enemies of the Reich"— particularly, of notable Jewish and part-Jewish figures in world culture, public life, politics, and economics. (At the time of the project's cessation, the catalogue contained nearly 15,000 cards.) Most of Department VII's collection of expropriated documents were concentrated in April 1944 in the Wölfelsdorf Castle in Lower Silesia.[5]

---

5 Patricia Kennedy Grimsted, "Twice Plundered or 'Twice Saved'? Identifying Russia's 'Trophy' Archives and the Loot of the *Reichssicherheitshauptamt*," *Holocaust and Genocide Studies* 15, no. 2 (2001): 200, 204.

Another Nazi institution involved in confiscating archival documents and other cultural treasures of Jewish provenance was the Einsatzstab Reichsleiter Rosenberg (ERR)[6]. It seems likely that the fundamental motivation behind this group's efforts to amass materials on Jews was the desire to create a collection of sources for the Institute for the Study of the Jewish Question (Institut zur Erforschung der Judenfrage). On the initiative of Rosenberg, this institution was founded in Frankfurt-on-Main in March 1941 within the framework of Nazi Germany's "Higher School" (Hohe Schule). According to stated plans of the Institute for the Study of the Jewish Question, in Frankfurt, its collections were to serve as a central repository for documents pertaining to the Jews.

Numerous Nazi-confiscated Jewish archives were discovered by the Soviet army at the end of the war, were transferred to the USSR, and eventually deposited in RGVA. The majority of RGVA collections of Jewish provenance originate from three major Jewish urban centers of prewar Europe: Paris, Berlin, and Vienna. There are, however, noteworthy materials from smaller European Jewish communities (such as Bromberg, Stettin, and Graz), as well as from Greece and the former Yugoslavia (Athens, Salonika, Belgrade, Zagreb, and others).

The documents date for the most part to the period between 1860 and 1939, a time of great ferment in the socio-political and cultural life of European Jewry. It should be noted, however, that some of the collections contain materials that are considerably older. The RGVA houses collections of Jewish educational and scholarly institutions — for instance, the Israelite Theological Institute of Higher Learning (Vienna) and the Central Archives of German Jews — that include historical documents and Hebrew manuscripts from medieval and early modern times, as well as rabbinic writings from the eighteenth and early nineteenth centuries. Therefore, this guide will be of interest not only to students of modern Jewish history, but also to researchers specializing in pre-modern Jewish history, philosophy, kabbalah, and rabbinic literature.

In the mid-1960s, documents housed in the TsGOA pertaining to Jewish history and culture were partially systematized and arranged in files. More detailed systematizing of these documents did not begin until the

6   Donald E. Collins and Herbert P. Rothfeder, "The *Einsatzstab Reichsleiter Rosenberg* and Looting of Jewish and Masonic Libraries during World War II," *Journal of Library History* 18 (Winter 1983): 21–36.

mid-1990s. As a result, even in the case of those Jewish-origin collections at TsGOA that had inventories, up to half of the file headings were blank as late as the mid-1990s. The headings of some files, moreover, did not match their contents. In a number of other cases, documents of undetermined collection provenance were arranged in files marked "Material in Hebrew, Author Unknown" or "Compositions of an Unknown Author." Preparation of the current guide required the direct examination of many files, and the project involved the cataloguing of previously unregistered materials.

The present volume came about through the efforts of a team of RGVA archivists and Project Judaica specialists, who, during the period 1998–2003, worked on identifying, systematizing, and describing those RGVA collections containing documents relevant to the study of Jewish history and culture. This team was composed of the following scholars: Anna Simonova (group director), Tatiana Vasil'eva, Yulia Danilkova, Liubov Kudriavtseva, Alexei Kornilov, Leonid Lantsman, Ivan Pichugin, and Pavel Tarutin. A previous Russian-language version of this guide was published in Moscow in 2005. The current volume contains corrections and additions to the Russian edition.

Preparation of this guide is based on the previous work of the project *Jewish Documentary Sources in the Archives of Russia, Ukraine and Belarus*. The first step was to establish precise criteria for selecting the broadest possible array of collections to be annotated and described. Presumptions about the existence of documents on Jewish history and culture in archival collections were based upon analysis of the collection originators' activities; in the case of consolidated collections, we relied upon the direct examination of files. As for the private collections of individuals of Jewish origin, the guide includes those collections that the course of annotation showed to contain documents pertaining to Jewish history and culture.

Naturally, the list of collections to be annotated included those originating from Jewish communities and from Jewish political, philanthropic, cultural, scholarly, pedagogical, and other organizations. If a collection was of non-Jewish provenance, the research group took it into account only if its originator's activities suggested it might contain Jewish subject matter. These include collections of governmental, social, and other agencies, one of whose areas of activity was Jewish affairs. The private collections of individuals of non-Jewish origin were included if the individual dealt with Jewish issues.

Among the tasks taken up by the specialists of Project Judaica and RGVA in preparing this guide was the individual annotation, file by file, of Fond 1427k (The Jewish Community of Athens) and Fond 1428k (The Jewish Community of Salonika).

During the annotation of Fond 672k (The Union of Austrian Jewish War Veterans [Vienna]) and Fond 707k (The Jewish Religious Community of Vienna), it was discovered that both contained significant quantities of documents properly belonging to other collection originators. The former contains documents of the Israelite Theological Institute of Higher Learning in Vienna (Fond 717k) and the latter contains documents by Y. Y. Schneerson and his ancestors (Fond 706k).

In a similar instance, in Fond 1325k (Collection of Documents on the History and Culture of European Jewry), alongside documents of various Jewish religious communities, social, political, and cultural organizations of interwar Europe, were found eighteenth- and nineteenth-century manuscripts from the library of The Jewish Theological Seminary in Breslau (Wrocław). The editors of this guide considered it necessary to include the description of the misplaced materials in the collections as they are currently arranged.

Because several collections include materials of other provenance (that is, not from the collection creator given in its title), it is essential that users of this guide consult the index under the name of the person or organization of interest to them.

For the researcher's convenience, the collections described in this volume have been arranged in the following sections: (1) International Jewish Organizations and Personalities; collections from (2) Austria, (3) France, (4) Germany, (5) Greece, (6) Romania, and (7) Yugoslavia; and (8) Mixed Collections (from more than one country). Each section has subsequently been divided into as many as three parts: the collections of organizations, government agencies, and individuals.

The description of each entry gives the following information: collection title, collection number, chronological parameters of the collection's contents, number of storage units in the collection, the history of the collection originator (in the case of private collections, a brief biography), the system of the collection's organization, whether there is a finding aid, the description of the collection's contents, the language(s) in which the documents are written, and whether there are microfilm copies at RGVA and the United States Holocaust Memorial Museum.

The title of each collection is given in two or three languages. The Russian and French or German titles of the collections follow the current nomenclature of the RGVA. The English titles follow conventional English spelling and usage for the names of the organizations, and omit some of the extraneous (and often erroneous) information given in the Russian titles.

Transliteration of the names of various Jewish organizations, Jewish first and last names, and other Jewish terminology from Hebrew and Yiddish into Roman characters follows, whenever possible, standard academic conventions.

An appendix at the end of the guide lists and describes collections with significant materials on Jewish history and culture that were repatriated to their countries of origin since 1991.

Information on the contents of collections given in this guide is of uneven thoroughness, a fact that reflects the collective nature of this project. And given the voluminous nature of the collections at RGVA, and the fact that some collections are not yet fully catalogued, the editors do not exclude the possibility of future discoveries.

We should note, by way of conclusion, the complex and tragic history of the materials described in this guide.

This has to do, first of all, with possible losses incurred during the confiscation and subsequent sorting and transport of these documents during the Second World War. A certain portion of the materials may have been lost even before they were transferred to the USSR in 1945–46. Second, a significant portion of these captured collections were first sent to various Soviet state and ministerial archives, and by no means all of the materials they received were sent on to the TsGOA. Under such circumstances, losses and rearrangements were inevitable. And the rearrangement of collections continued at the TsGOA itself.

One also should bear in mind that other parts of the groups of documents described in this guide are held in archives in the United States, Israel, and Western Europe. For example, the archive of the YIVO Institute for Jewish Research in New York holds collections of the European offices of HICEM (RG 740) and the Jewish Community of Salonika (RG 1428).

The editors of this guide would like to express their gratitude to the Conference on Jewish Material Claims Against Germany, Yad Avi Ha-

Yishuv, the Memorial Foundation for Jewish Culture, and the Joseph S. and Diane H. Steinberg Charitable Trust for their financial support of the research project that made this volume possible. We are also deeply indebted to the Center for Advanced Holocaust Studies of the United States Holocaust Memorial Museum for co-sponsoring the translation, further editing, and publication of this guide in English. We hope that it will occupy a worthy place among reference works on the history and culture of the Jewish people.

David E. Fishman
Mark Kupovetsky
Vladimir Kuzelenkov

INTRODUCTION TO THE ENGLISH-LANGUAGE EDITION

This volume is based on the Russian-language edition, *Dokumenty po istorii i kul'ture evreev v trofeinikh kollektsiakh Rossiiskogo gosudarstvennogo voennogo arkhiva: Putevoditel'* (Russian State University for the Humanities Press, 2005), which has undergone extensive correction and revision.

Tatiana Vasil'eva, senior archivist at the Russian State Military Archive, has corrected the inaccuracies that crept into the previous text, with regard to the names of certain collections, inclusive dates, and number of files.

Several annotations on collection creators have been expanded or rewritten, and the descriptions of the collections themselves have been revised. Most descriptions have been reorganized to make them more readable; similar materials have been grouped together in the text, and redundancies have been removed. We also have been able to provide more accuracy and detail on the Hebrew manuscripts contained in these archival collections, thanks to the collaboration of Dr. Shimon Yakerson of the Institute of Oriental Studies, Russian Academy of Sciences, who kindly shared his research notes on those materials.

This edition also refers readers to finding aids on the website www.sonderarchiv.de, when such exist, and indicates the availability of microfilms at the United States Holocaust Memorial Museum Archives. Interested researchers may also wish to consult with the Central Archives for the History of the Jewish People and the Central Zionist Archives (both in Jerusalem), which hold microfilms of many of the collections contained in this guide.

Errors in the Russian edition were meticulously pointed out, in private communication, by Dr. Patricia Kennedy Grimsted, the foremost authority on the Nazi plunder and Soviet seizure of archives. Her volume *Returned from Russia: Nazi Archival Plunder in Western Europe and Recent Restitution Issues*, co-edited with F. J. Hoogewoud and Eric Ketelaar (Leicester: Institute of Art and Law, 2007), is an invaluable guide to the subject, and readers interested in the full migratory history of the collections described in this volume are urged to consult it.

11

Thanks to Ms. Vasil'eva and Dr. Grimsted, the list of collections returned to their countries of origin has been corrected, and information about their precise current location is included. In this edition, the collections returned to their countries of origin constitute a separate appendix to the guide. We have provided descriptions of most such collections, even though they are no longer held by RGVA, because there usually are no publicly accessible finding aids or descriptions for most of them. The descriptions were based on visual examination of the collections prior to their return, or on inventories that remain at RGVA. When new, fuller descriptions have appeared since a collection's return to its country of origin, we have referred the reader to them (rather than reproduce the description found in the Russian edition of the guide).

Mr. Avram Brown translated the Russian edition ably and gracefully. He also offered numerous valuable editorial comments and corrections that have been incorporated into this edition.

Mr. Brown and I have made considerable efforts to present the correct spelling of the names of individuals mentioned in the descriptions. This has proven difficult because the original inventories and the notes of the research team were kept in Russian. Accordingly, a process of retransliteration was required, supplemented by searches in historical literature for the names of the individuals in question. The names of organizations have also been challenging. We tried to avoid the phenomenon of "broken telephone," due to the translation of the names of organizations from French and German to Russian in Moscow, and from Russian to English for this edition. Again, we consulted available literature to determine the correct English names. While major organizations were easy to identify, some smaller ones have eluded us, and their names may have been mistranslated.

Researchers will note that the word *propaganda* appears occasionally in the descriptions of collections of Jewish origin. Jewish and other organizations commonly used this term before World War II, when it was not yet a term of opprobrium, to mean the public dissemination of information and ideas.

I would like to express my gratitude to Benton Arnovitz, Director of Academic Publications at the United States Holocaust Memorial Museum, and Jeffrey Gainey, Director of the University of Scranton Press, for their editorial advice and collegial friendship. While their names do not appear as editors of this volume, they played an invaluable role in shaping the final book as it now appears. Anthony Zannino and John P. Hunckler meticuolously reviewed and corrected the manuscript.

Finally, on a personal note, I view this guide as fulfilling (albeit only partially) the mitzvah of *hashavat aveida*, of returning lost objects to their owners. These collections, which long were deemed to be lost, and which even after their discovery were largely unknown and inaccessible to scholars, are part of the cultural legacy of European Jewry. They belong to Jewish history. Now that they have been described, the materials they contain can be more easily studied and used for Jewish historical scholarship.

David E. Fishman

I

INTERNATIONAL JEWISH
ORGANIZATIONS AND PERSONALITIES

ORGANIZATIONS

Evreiskii natsional'nyi fond — Keren kaiemet leizrael'

Jewish National Fund — Keren Kayemeth LeIsrael (Paris)

Fond 44k, 1909–1940. 932 storage units.

The Jewish National Fund (Keren Kayemeth LeIsrael) for the purchase of land in Palestine was founded in 1901 by the Fifth Zionist Congress. The organization's bylaws were ratified by the British government in 1907. The JNF was led by a committee of nine members elected by the general assembly of the World Zionist Organization. The JNF was headquartered in Vienna until 1907, later relocating to Cologne, the Hague, and, in 1922, to Jerusalem. The Jerusalem central bureau was the main executive body of the JNF. It included departments of land, finance, and organization/propaganda. The first president of the JNF was Johann Kremenetzky; later, starting in 1914, Max Bodenheimer; and from 1920, Menahem Ussishkin. The Fund engaged in the large-scale collection of charitable contributions, setting up ubiquitous collection points (charity boxes) for donations (the little blue box of the JNF); it also helped organize soirees, festivals, and lectures for the purpose of collecting donations; it issued stamps, produced other promotional products, and made films. Since it was — along with the Keren Hayesod fund — the main financial organ of the WZO, the JNF directed most of its resources to the purchase of land in Palestine, as well as irrigation projects, forestation, and the like. On the eve of the Second World War, more than a third of the Jewish-held land in Palestine belonged to the JNF. Demarcation of these two funds' functions was taken up, starting in 1936, by the Commission of Three: representatives of the executive committee of the WZO, the JNF, and Keren Hayesod. (The president of the commission was L. Bernheim.)

15

The official organ of the JNF was the journal *Karnenu*; in France, the journal *La terre retrouve* was published. The central commission of the JNF in France was based in Paris; its president was M. Mirtel, its general secretary J. Fisher, and its board of directors included H. Stourdze, M. Segal, S. Zack, M. Steinberg, and A. Levy.

The collection's contents are described in three inventories. The inventories are arranged by document type, systematically, and geographically. The sections of inventories no. 1 and 2, entitled "Documents in Hebrew," catalogue items of correspondence in Hebrew and Yiddish, in large part between members of the central French commission and representatives of the Fund's central Jerusalem bureau.

The collection contains documents reflecting the functions and aims of the JNF as a whole: historical information on the founding and functioning of the Fund; pamphlets on the JNF's activity in acquiring plots of land, and related activities; materials on JNF commissions' charitable fundraising activities; instructions to employees organizing events in this regard; invitations to charitable fairs, soirees, and lectures, and lists of their participants; subscription forms; correspondence by Fund employees on the conduct of charity drives, in particular the "Balfour Campaign" of 1930; and bookkeeping documents. The collection also contains the minutes of individual meetings of the Fund's board of directors, in particular for 1930 and 1938; the minutes of sessions of the French central commission for 1931–40; and reports of the Fund's central French commission and its subordinate local commissions in various cities of France and French colonies of North Africa. The collection contains lists of commissions and authorized officers of the JNF in various cities.

Items of correspondence included in the collection illustrate the interaction of the JNF's central French commission with leaders of the World Zionist Organization (WZO); with the Jerusalem bureau of the JNF; with various Jewish entities: Mizrachi, Hashomer Hatzair, Hechalutz, Hitachdut, Tzeirei Mizrachi, et al.; with officers of Keren Hayesod, in particular its director in France, N. Herman; with members of the Commission of Three; with representatives of local commissions of the JNF in various cities of France and its colonies; with the Austrian, Hungarian, Italian, Bulgarian, and other bureaus of the JNF; and with commissions in London, Brussels, Berlin, and other cities.

The collection's printed publications include informational bulletins issued by American and British bureaus of the JNF for 1935–37; and collections of stories about Jewish tradition and holidays, and songbooks, in particular a book of stories and songs dedicated to J. Trumpeldor. The collection also contains individual issues of the JNF publications *Karnenu* and *La terre retrouve*.

The documents are in French, English, Hebrew, and Yiddish.

Microfilms are held by the United States Holocaust Memorial Museum Archives.

Fond rekonstruktsii Palestiny "Keren khaesod"

Fonds de Reconstruction de la Palestine. Keren Hayessod de France (Paris)

Keren Hayesod, Palestine Foundation Fund of France (Paris)

Fond 115k, 1924–1940. 121 storage units.

Keren Hayesod was established by the World Zionist Organization (WZO) at the London Conference of 1920. The goal of the fund was to collect donations to assist in Jewish settlement and absorption in Palestine. Until 1926, Keren Hayesod was headquartered in London; thereafter, in Jerusalem. Keren Hayesod remained the primary financing organ of WZO activities in Palestine even after the establishment of the expanded Jewish Agency. Its mission included financing Jewish agricultural settlements, transportation infrastructure, and housing construction; and supporting the Jewish community's professional courses, schools, and health care system in Palestine. Keren Hayesod had branches in various countries, including France. The French national branch of Keren Hayesod was founded in 1922 (with B. Weill-Halle as president), and was called the Palestine Foundation Fund of France. The French fund was headquartered in Paris, but it was also active in North Africa (Tunisia, Algeria, and Morocco).

The collection's contents are described in two inventories. In inventory no. 1, documents are systematized as follows: documents reflecting the organization, functions, and activities of the Palestine Foundation Fund; documents reflecting the activities of various Jewish organizations in France, North Africa, and other countries; lists and subscription forms; documents reflecting the Fund's collaboration with the Jewish National Fund; financial documents; and printed publications. In inventory no. 2, documents are catalogued by type: minutes, reports, correspondence, lists, and informational bulletins.

The collection contains minutes of meetings of the Keren Hayesod central committee for 1934 and 1937–38; documents of Keren Hayesod conferences, including the ones held in Antwerp in September 1938, in London in February 1939, and others; correspondence with Fund bureaus in various cities of France and North Africa, and with the national branches of other countries, on taking measures to stimulate Zionist propaganda, and on organizational issues; with L. Herrmann, the general secretary of Keren Hayesod in Jerusalem, on organizing the Palestine Pavilion at the Paris World's Fair of 1937; with various Jewish organizations such as the Jewish National Fund, the Jewish Telegraphic Agency, the World Federation of Sephardic Communities, and others, on coordinating and collaborating with private individuals, corporations, and other entities to raise funds for the Palestine Foundation Fund; and notifications of funds received.

The collection also includes lists of members of the central committee of Keren Hayesod in France; lists of delegates to Fund congresses and conferences; subscription forms for contributing funds to the Palestine Foundation Fund; financial documents of the Fund (financial statements for 1937–39, expense statements, Keren Hayesod's insurance policy); and printed publications: informational bulletins, copies of newspapers, and books.

The documents are in French, English, German, and Hebrew.

Evreiskoe telegrafnoe agentstvo (ITA)

Jewish Telegraphic Agency (JTA) (Paris)

Fond 674k, 1918–1940. 197 storage units.

The Jewish Telegraphic Agency (JTA), originally named the Jewish Correspondence Bureau, was founded in 1919 by Jacob Landau and Meir Grossman. The JTA brought together six bureaus — in New York, London, Berlin, Paris, Warsaw, and Jerusalem. It subsequently opened bureaus in Prague and Geneva. The JTA published daily news-report bulletins in English, German, French, and Polish, as well as the *Jewish Daily Bulletin* (from 1924). Its reports dealt with the situation of the Jewish population of various countries, in particular Nazi Germany, and the activities of Zionist and other Jewish organizations. From 1924 to 1968, Boris Smolar served as editor in chief. The Berlin bureau of the JTA existed from 1922 until November 1937, when it was shut down by the Gestapo. After the banning of the JTA in Germany, the Berlin bureau was transferred to Paris, where it continued its work until the Nazi occupation of that city in June 1940.

The collection's contents are described in three inventories. Documents are catalogued in the inventories for the most part chronologically, and with geographical and chronological indexes.

Copies of informational bulletins of the JTA published in Berlin, London, Prague, and Paris constitute the bulk of the collection's documentary materials. The collection also has copies of bulletins and journals published in Palestine and Switzerland; articles, accounts, reports, and newspaper clippings on the situation of the Jewish population of various countries, on the activities of Zionist and other Jewish organizations, and on the holding of Zionist congresses.

The documents are in English, German, French, and Hebrew.

Microfilms are held by the United States Holocaust Memorial Museum Archives.

Amerikanskaia ob"edinennaia vosstanovitel'naia organizatsiia.
Upravlenie delami

American Joint Reconstruction Foundation (Paris)

Fond 723k, 1922–1940. 1,305 storage units.

The American Joint Reconstruction Foundation was established in 1924 by the American Jewish Joint Distribution Committee and the Jewish Colonization Association (JCA). The organization was created primarily to improve the economic situation of Eastern European Jewish victims of the First World War by developing cooperative credit, and supporting Jewish agricultural colonies, trade schools, and related initiatives. In 1936, the Reconstruction Foundation supported 672 loan funds (*kassas*) with 200,000 members, the majority of them small craftsmen and merchants. Starting in 1933, it helped sponsor Jewish refugees from Germany, including their settlement in Palestine. The American Joint Reconstruction Foundation was headed by an administrative council made up of representatives of the JDC, the Jewish Colonization Association (JCA), and Jewish organizations of the countries of Central and Eastern Europe.

The Reconstruction Foundation's day-to-day operations were managed by an administrative department located, until 1933, in Berlin; thereafter, in Paris. Its directors were Bernhard Kahn representing the JDC and, on behalf of the JCA, Louis Oungre. Upon the advance of Nazi troops in 1940, the administrative department was evacuated from Paris to Bordeaux. Before the Second World War, branch offices of the American Joint Reconstruction Foundation were in operation in many countries of Europe and South America.

The collection's contents are catalogued in three inventories. Each of these contains three sections: secretariat documents, documents of the finance department, and printed materials.

The collection contains the JDC charter of 1924; the JDC's assignment of legal rights to the newly created American Joint Reconstruction Foundation; listings of transferred bonds, promissory notes, bills of exchange, and other securities (1924); and accounts of the Reconstruction Foundation's activities for 1924–26 and 1937–39.

The collection also has minutes of meetings of the Reconstruction Foundation's board of directors for 1924–26 and 1929–40, of meetings of members of the executive committee for 1925–31, and of meetings of the its administrative council with managers of Jewish loan *kassas* in Poland, Romania, and Bulgaria (1924–32); reports by the Reconstruction Foundation's inspectors on the state of Jewish credit institutions in Germany, Poland, and Lithuania, on the legal position of Jewish pawnshops in the countries of Eastern Europe and in Palestine, and on audits of Jewish credit institutions in Salonika and Istanbul; an alphabetical index of correspondents of the Joint Reconstruction Foundation for 1924–38; and lists of addresses of members of the Joint Reconstruction Foundation administrative council and of Jewish credit organizations in Germany, Bulgaria, Romania, Poland, and Lithuania.

The collection also contains regulations; financial and statistical reports on Jewish pawnshops and loan *kassas*; audit materials; summary statistical information on the state of small business in Austria, Belgium, Bulgaria, Czechoslovakia, Estonia, Finland, France, Germany, Greece, Hungary, Latvia, Lithuania, the Netherlands, Palestine, Poland, Romania, Turkey, and South Africa; minutes of sessions and financial statements of the Foundation's board of inspectors in Warsaw (1932–34); lists of Jewish cooperatives and pawnshops in Poland (1935–39) by city; a draft petition to rescind edicts aimed at liquidating Jewish loan *kassas* in Romania; and information on the state of Jewish *loan kassas* in Warsaw after Nazi Germany's seizure of Poland.

There are financial statements of the JDC for 1924–39 and the JDC cashbook for 1939–40; budget projections for 1939; financial statements of Foundation branches in Berlin (1924–34) and Warsaw (1932–39), of the Warsaw Cooperative Bank (1935–36), of the Central Jewish Bank in Kaunas (Kovno) (1929–31), and of the Central Jewish People's Bank in Vilna (Wilno/ Vilnius) (1929–40).

The collection also contains correspondence of JDC administrative council members with branches of Jewish social organizations and banks on allocating credit among Jewish savings and loan associations of Eastern Europe; on drawing up guidelines for Jewish pawnshops; on auditing the work of Jewish banks in Poland, Lithuania, Latvia, and Romania; on merging and liquidating banks, and carrying out financial audits; on bank account operations; on setting up Jewish credit cooperatives in Latin America; and on the situation of European Jewish émigrés in Shanghai; with the administration of Keren Hayesod on credit and currency operations in the financing of Jewish immigration to Palestine; and with the Polish section of the JDC on the liquidation of the Warsaw Cooperative Bank.

The collection also has printed materials: instructions to Foundation inspectors on rules for auditing loan *kassas* (1933, 1934); issues of the journal *Poradnik Spółdzielni* (Poland) for 1933–36 and 1939; *Wiadomości statystyczne* for 1935–38; *Folkshilf* (Poland, in Yiddish) for 1933–38; *Der Deutscher Economist* (Germany) for 1933–35; *Cuvant Cooperativist* (Romania) for 1934–36; and issues of the JDC informational bulletin for 1937.

The documents are in Hebrew, English, German, Polish, French, and Romanian.

Komitet po delam evreiskoi emigratsii GITsEM

HIAS-JCA Emigration Association (HICEM) (Paris)

Fond 740k, 1906–1941. 2,483 storage units.

HICEM was the Jewish emigration association founded in April 1927 by HIAS (the Hebrew Immigrant Aid Society, New York), the JCA (the Jewish Colonization Association, Paris), and Emigdirect, an organization founded jointly by HIAS and the JCA and headquartered in Berlin. The acronym HICEM contains the first letters of the above-mentioned three organizations. HICEM's mission was to provide information as well as legal, material, and practical aid to Jewish émigrés. On the eve of the Second World War, HICEM had 51 committees (branch offices) in 23 countries. HICEM's administrative council and central directorate were located in Paris. The central directorate consisted of ten members, five each from HIAS and the JCA. HICEM was active in every country that admitted Jewish immigrants, with the exception of the United States, Germany, and Palestine, where these functions were under the competence of HIAS, the German Jewish Aid Society, and the Jewish Agency, respectively. The first president of HICEM was James Simon, who occupied the post until his death in 1932. The leadership was comprised of three executive co-directors: Aaron Benjamin (HIAS), Edouard Oungre (JCA), and Miron Kreinin (Emigdirekt).

The collection's contents are catalogued in three inventories. The inventories are arranged according to structure.

The collection contains the HICEM charter (January 1935); accounts of HICEM activities for 1926–39; circulars to HICEM branch offices (1933–40) on rules for filling out a central card file of émigrés; on conditions of emigration to Uruguay, Ecuador, Haiti, and other countries, and on procedures for statistical calculation of émigré data; minutes of sessions of the HICEM administrative council for 1930, 1934–39, as well as of the HICEM commission on émigré doctors for 1934–35, the HICEM commission on the distribution of émigré grants for 1935–36, and the League of Nations Commission for Refugees for 1934–36; information on the personal composition of the HICEM central bureau in Paris (1937–40); lists of members of the HICEM administrative council and their addresses (1936); lists of association's branch offices, of Jewish organizations in

Europe, America, Australia, and Africa that worked with HICEM (1938), and HICEM representatives and agents of transportation companies in the United States, Bolivia, Brazil, Chile, Columbia, and other countries in the Americas (1939); the HICEM secretariat's case list; personal files of émigrés (1,198 individuals, arranged alphabetically by last name); and registers of incoming correspondence for 1937–39.

The collection includes various internal reports: reports by the director and officers of HICEM on their trips to Hungary, Czechoslovakia, Italy, Poland, Romania, Germany, and the USSR, and on the situation of Jews in these countries; a report by Lazar Epstein on his trip to Manila and on prospects for Jewish emigration to the Philippines (1938) and regions of southwestern China; a report on the situation of Jewish émigrés in Fascist Italy; a report on Jewish settlements in Argentina, and on a trip to Brazil by representatives of Jewish organizations to Brazil regarding prospects for emigration to that country (1937); a report by the director of the JCA on climate conditions in Brazil and on prospects for emigration to that country; a report on prospects for emigration to Albania, Bolivia, Guatemala, Mexico, and other countries; a report on prospects for establishing Jewish settlements on Madagascar and Cyprus; and a report on trips to the Union of South Africa, Rhodesia, and Kenya.

The collection contains various HICEM correspondence: correspondence with League of Nations High Commissioner for Refugees Neill Malcolm on the situation of Jewish refugees from Germany in Czechoslovakia, Austria, and Portugal, and on the opening of a HICEM branch in Zagreb (1937); correspondence with the Harbin branch and the Jewish health association OZE on helping Jewish doctors emigrate from Germany to the USSR and to the Americas (as well as lists of Jewish doctors who emigrated from Nazi Germany to the USSR).

The collection also contains correspondence of the HICEM central bureau with the organization's European branches regarding delegate elections and preparations for the 1936 Paris Conference on Jewish emigration; with the editors of Jewish newspapers and with the Jewish Telegraphic Agency (JTA) on press coverage of the above-mentioned event; with the German Jewish Aid Society and the JCA on prospects for establishing Jewish settlements in Abyssinia, China, Mozambique, Tasmania, and the Philippines; with the consulates of Argentina, Belgium, and other countries on the issuance of entry visas and loyalty certificates for Jewish émigrés; with the League of Nations High Commission for Refugees on the activities of emigration committees in France, on submitting HICEM annual reports to the League of Nations, and on HICEM representatives' participation in meetings of League of Nations Committee of Experts (1933–36); and with members of the HICEM administrative council regarding the coordination of dates and agendas for meetings called to approve balance sheets, and analogous documents (1931–39).

The collection has documents of HICEM representative offices in Australia, Albania, Belgium, Brazil, Bulgaria, Canada, Chile, China, Columbia, Cuba, Czechoslovakia, Denmark, the Dominican Republic, Ecuador, Egypt, Estonia, France, Germany, Great Britain, Greece, Haiti, Hungary, Italy, Latvia, Lithuania, Luxembourg, Mexico, the Netherlands, Norway, Paraguay, Poland, Portugal, Romania, Spain, Switzerland, Syria, Turkey, the United States, Uruguay, Venezuela, and Yugoslavia. These documents contain reports and financial statements regarding branch offices and their various subcommittees; and correspondence with other Jewish social and charitable organizations on admission and settlement opportunities for Jewish immigrants, on obtaining entry visas, acquiring tickets, and related concerns.

Finance department materials include HICEM budget projections for 1930–40; balance sheets for 1939; financial statements for 1928–35 (some of the financial statements have statistical indicators attached); HICEM fund expense statements for 1939–40; and audit reports of the association's budget for 1938–40.

Documents of the statistics bureau include statistical information on the number of German and Austrian Jews who emigrated to Brazil in 1937 and 1938, on Jewish emigration from Poland (1939), on Jewish émigrés in transit from Trieste bound for Palestine and the Americas in 1939–40, on the number of Jews in various countries of the world (1926), on the number of Jewish émigrés arriving in the United States in 1937–38, and on Jews emigrating from Poland to the countries of North and South America in 1919–36; and a list of Jewish refugees who departed for the United States from German ports in 1939.

The collection also has minutes of sessions of the international Evian Conference on Jewish refugees from Germany and Austria (July 1938); and printed materials: JTA bulletins on the activities of emigration organizations in America and Palestine in 1935–36; *Korrespondenzblat* bulletins (1935–36) on Jewish emigration issues; bulletins of the Czechoslovak League Against Antisemitism (1935–38); the journal *L'Univers Israelite*; articles by Mark Wischnitzer on the history of the Jews of

Poland; and a collection of statements by representatives of Christian churches on the persecution of Jews in Nazi Germany (published by the Swiss Union of Jewish Communities).

The documents are in French, German, English, and Hebrew.

Microfilms are held by the United States Holocaust Memorial Museum Archives.

Amerikanskii evreiskii ob"edinennyi komitet po raspredeleniiu fondov (Dzhoint). Evropeiskoe ispolnitel'noe biuro

American Jewish Joint Distribution Committee, European Executive Bureau (Paris)

Fond 772k, 1922–1941. 685 storage units.

The American Jewish Joint Distribution Committee (JDC) is an American Jewish charitable organization founded in November 1914 at the initiative of Jacob Schiff. The JDC was formed by uniting three American Jewish organizations: the American Jewish Relief Committee, the Central Relief Committee, and the People's Relief Committee. The organization's original title was the Joint Distribution Committee of American Funds for the Relief of Jewish War Sufferers; the name American Jewish Joint Distribution Committee was adopted in 1924. The JDC's aim is to provide material assistance to Jewish communities throughout the world.

The European bureau of the JDC was created in late 1920 in Berlin, and was headed by Dr. Bernard Kahn. When the Nazis came to power in Germany in 1933, the bureau was transferred to Paris. Kahn was responsible for JDC activities in Central and Eastern Europe, and the bureau supported medical care, schools and education, social welfare, loans, vocational training, and other services, particularly in Poland, Romania, Czechoslovakia, Hungary, and Lithuania. After 1933, it provided relief to Jews in Nazi Germany.

Upon Nazi Germany's invasion of France in 1940, the European bureau was evacuated to Angers and Bordeaux.

For the most part, the collection reflects the activities of the JDC European Executive Bureau in Paris during the period 1933–40. The collection includes the JDC charter (1931); accounts of JDC activities (1932–38); minutes of sessions of the presidium of the JDC executive committee in New York (1929–33, and 1938), of the JDC managing committee in New York (1937–38), and the JDC presidium and executive committee (1938); reports by members of its managing committee and board of directors (1938–39); minutes of the meeting of subsections of the European Executive Bureau in Paris (April 1935). Among subjects most discussed are these: the adoption of budget items for the fiscal year in question; Jewish emigration; and support for Jewish social, educational, religious, and commercial organizations.

Materials of the JDC's finance department include budget projections and action plans for 1939; JDC balance sheets for 1937–39; expense statements for 1938–39; JDC directors' receipts for funds received (1938–40); the JDC's main account book for 1938; the log of credit extended to Jewish refugees bound for Shanghai and the Americas; lists of refugees; a log of credit extended by the JDC to German Jews emigrating to the United States, Brazil, Argentina, and Chile; a card index of credit allocated by the JDC to Jewish organizations in Latvia, Lithuania, and Poland in 1940; financial statements of the Union of German Jews and the Committee to Aid Refugees in France for February–May 1940, of the Swiss Union of Jewish Communities for January–May 1940, and of JDC branch offices in London (March–April 1940), Budapest (1940), and other cities.

The overwhelming majority of the collection's documents are connected in one way or another with the emigration and subsequent settlement of Jewish refugees from Germany and Austria. These include, in particular, minutes of sessions of the League of Nations emigration committee and subcommittees (1937–38), and of the international Evian Conference on Jewish emigration from Germany and Austria (1938); a petition by the Jewish delegation to the Council of the League of Nations protesting German laws discriminating against Jews; information on the legal and political situation of Jews in Germany (1933–38); reports of an expert commission presented to the League of Nations; lists of émigrés and refugees receiving financial aid; reports by JDC inspectors on the situation of European Jews; a statistical survey on German Jewish emigration to the countries of North and South America and to Palestine; an analysis of conditions for Jewish emigration to New Caledonia, Madagascar, Brazil, and other countries; statistical tabulations of Jewish emigration to the countries of Europe, Asia, and America in 1933–39; financial statements of committees to aid Jewish refugees and émigrés in Antwerp, Brussels, Vienna, London, and other cities; documents of the London branch offices of the Union of Jews from Germany and the Central Council of Jewish Refugees on plans to resettle Jewish refugees in Northern and Southern Rhodesia, on the results of emigration to Palestine, and on the legal position of Jewish refugees and émigrés in Britain; a report by Simon Marks at a meeting of the Zionist Federation of Great Britain on the activities of Jewish committees in German cities; and Bernhard Kahn's correspondence with the administration of Hebrew University in Jerusalem on helping Jewish scholars in Germany leave for Palestine and on financing their emigration.

The collection also contains documents of the JDC's representative offices, and of organizations subordinate to the JDC, in Albania, Bulgaria, China, Czechoslovakia, Finland, France, Germany, the Netherlands, Hungary, India, Italy, Latvia, Lithuania, Luxembourg, Morocco, Poland, Portugal, Romania, Switzerland, Turkey, Yugoslavia, and countries of South America; and also of the United Jewish Appeal. These include lists and addresses of Jewish organizations and philanthropic societies active in these countries; financial statements and statistical reports of the German Jewish Aid Society (Hilfsverein), the Central Committee of German Jews for Relief and Reconstruction, the Reich Representation of Jews in Germany, the Committee to Aid Refugees in France, the Federation of Jewish Communities of France, the Brussels Committee to Aid Émigrés, the Jewish Émigré Information Bureau in Basel, and the Geneva Job Placement Bureau for Learned Immigrants; information on the situation of the Jewish population and the activities of Jewish communities in Bombay, Genoa, Trieste, Bologna, Shanghai, Tangier, Zagreb, Durrës, Sofia, Bucharest, and other cities, and on the activities of Jewish credit cooperatives and Jewish educational institutions in Eastern and Central Europe; statistical information on the course of emigration and the settlement of Jewish colonies in locations admitting émigrés; information on the activities of the Jewish medical institutions of Warsaw in 1939, on economic aid extended to the Jews of Poland by the JDC, on anti-Jewish pogroms in Poland in 1936–39, on the founding of the Central Committee of Polish Jews in Warsaw, and on the awarding of individual grants.

A set of documents pertaining to the USSR contains information on the financing of Jewish agricultural colonies in the Crimea and the Ukraine, on the work of foreign specialists in Birobidzhan, and on the course of Jewish resettlement in Birobidzhan; an account by Joseph Rosen on the work of Agro-Joint, 1924–34; a report by the chairman of the Union of Jews from Germany on the conditions of German Jewish immigration to the USSR; lists of German Jewish immigrant doctors working in the USSR; and copies of letters of the Soviet ambassador in London Ivan Maisky to the League of Nations high commissioner for refugees, Neill Malcolm, on the Soviet government's granting of permission to Jewish émigrés from Nazi Germany to enter the USSR.

The collection also contains correspondence from the European Executive Bureau in Paris to board members in New York on drawing up reports for international conferences on Jewish emigration from Italy and

Germany, on setting up the Council for German Jewry and endowing the committee with an investigative bureau to counter German spies, on raising and allocating funds, on the activities of the HICEM organization, and on planning Jewish emigration to the United States and other countries; with the firm Mavrich-Muzevich on setting up Jewish colonies in Bolivia and Brazil and on conditions for Jewish émigrés' admission to the Dominican Republic; with Jewish community and charitable societies, businesses, and private individuals on aiding the departure and resettlement of, and on providing material assistance to, Jewish émigrés from Europe; with the German Grand Lodge of the Order of B'nai B'rith, the National Coordination Committee, and the Jewish religious community of Vienna on helping Jewish refugees and émigrés obtain American visas; and with the writer Sholem Asch on his trips to Poland in 1933–39 and the publication of his essays on Polish Jewish life in the JTA's *Press-Service* bulletin.

Printed materials deposited in the collection include an illustrated Zurich magazine on the Evian Conference (July 1938); the pamphlet *Die Geschichte der Juden in Deutschland*, published by the Union of German Jewish Youth (1935); a directory of Jewish emigration organizations and educational institutions in Germany; newspaper clippings on the economic situation in Palestine and the settlement of Jewish colonies in Chapar (Brazil); issues of the journal *Folkshilf* (Poland) for 1934–39; and other periodicals from Romania, Bulgaria, and Poland (1934–36).

The documents are in English, Hebrew, Yiddish, German, French, and Russian.

Tsentral'noe biuro ispolnitel'nogo komiteta Vsemirnogo evreiskogo kongressa

World Jewish Congress, Executive Committee (Paris)

Fond 1190k, 1896–1940. 948 storage units.

The World Jewish Congress (WJC) is an international Jewish organization founded by resolution of the First World Jewish Congress, which took place in August 1936 in Geneva. This organization's goal is to defend the political, social, and economic rights of Jews throughout the world. Its governing bodies were elected at the First World Jewish Congress: the executive committee, headed by Stephen Wise (also the organization's chairman), an administrative committee, headed by Nahum Goldmann, and a central council headed by Louis Lipsky. At the first session of the executive committee (6 September 1936), it was decided to establish regional offices of the WJC in Geneva, New York, and London, and a central bureau in Paris. The central bureau coordinated the WJC's work, collected information on the situation of Jews in various countries, published materials, and also lobbied at the League of Nations. In 1940, with the Second World War under way, the central bureau was transferred to New York, and a European office was established in London.

The collection's contents are described in two inventories. The inventories are systematized by structure. Materials are catalogued in the following sequence: documents on preparations for the First World Jewish Congress; documents of the First World Jewish Congress; documents of the secretariat; documents of the organizational section; documents of the political section; documents of the economics section; documents of the Jewish youth section; documents of the information section; and documents of the WJC archive.

The collection includes documents (1931–36) on preparations for the First World Jewish Congress. These are circulars and informational letters from the organizing committee on the convening of the First World Jewish Congress; minutes of an executive committee meeting on the calling of the Congress; pamphlets and articles on the calling of the Congress, its aims, and goals; an account of the activities of the executive committee with regard to the convening of the First World Jewish Congress; correspondence of the secretariat and the executive committee chairman, Nahum Goldmann, with members of the executive committee and with Jewish organizations of various countries on the course of preparations for the Congress, on the situation of Jews in various countries, and on financial issues.

The collection contains minutes of sessions of the WJC central bureau and executive and administrative committees, accounts of the activities of the WJC central bureau in Paris and its secretariat, and accounts and informational letters on the WJC's political and organizational activities.

Documents of the political section include correspondence with the League of Nations on Jewish refugee issues and on the situation of Jews in various countries; petitions, memoranda, and press releases on the persecution of Jews and the introduction of anti-Semitic laws in various countries; and correspondence with statesmen, politicians, and public figures on the Jewish question. Organizational section documents consist mainly of correspondence with Jewish organizations on the founding and functioning of local WJC committees. The collection also contains lists of local WJC committee members and of leaders of Jewish organizations in various countries, as well as lists of Jews from France and the Netherlands who aided in the establishment of the WJC information center. Deposited in the collection are informational bulletins of the WJC for April–July 1940, newspapers, journals, and pamphlets.

The documents are in Hebrew, French, Serbian, Dutch, English, German, and Romanian.

Microfilms are held by the United States Holocaust Memorial Museum Archives.

Postoiannoe predstavitel'stvo palestinskogo evreiskogo agentstva vo Frantsii

Permanent Office of the Jewish Agency for Palestine in France (Paris)

Fond 1226k, 1924–1940. 48 storage units.

The Jewish Agency for Palestine was founded in August 1929. Its aims included establishing lasting contacts between the Palestinian Yishuv and Diaspora Jewry. The Jewish Agency was governed by a council of 224 members, and by executive and administrative committees that included representatives of various Zionist as well as non-Zionist Jewish organizations. At the time of its founding, the Jewish Agency's president was Chaim Weizmann (head of the World Zionist Organization); its executive director was Louis Marshall (head of the American Jewish Committee). Baron Edmond de Rothschild was honorary chairman, and Felix Warburg was chairman of the administrative committee. The executive body of the Jewish Agency was the executive committee, which had two headquarters: one in Jerusalem and the other in London. The London headquarters was represented at the League of Nations in Geneva by a permanent office. The Paris office was administered by Nahum Goldmann and general secretary A. Cohen.

The collection's contents are described in one inventory. Documents are catalogued according to type.

The collection comprises documents on the history, structure, and personal composition of the Jewish Agency. It contains correspondence and memoranda of the Paris office: correspondence with the British high commissioner for Palestine, with Jewish Agency president Chaim Weizmann, with director of the Jewish Agency political department Moshe Shertok, and with the permanent office of the Jewish Agency at the League of Nations in Geneva. It also includes correspondence with the headquarters of the Jewish Agency executive committee in Jerusalem, the Jewish National Fund, the Palestine Reconstruction Fund, and HICEM on the state of Jewish immigration to Palestine and on financing the activities of the Jewish Agency office in France; with the French Ministry of War and National Defense on the creation of a Jewish Legion; and with the French Ministry of Foreign Affairs on Jewish emigration issues.

The collection also has minutes of a discussion between a representative of the Jewish Agency's London headquarters and officials of the British Colonial Office regarding Jewish immigration to Palestine, and a memorandum by Jewish Agency president Chaim Weizmann to the British high commissioner for Palestine and the Secretary-General of the League of Nations regarding Jewish refugees and the founding in Palestine of a Jewish national home.

The collection contains a financial statement of the office of the Jewish Agency in France for 1939–40, and copies of journals and informational bulletins, posters, articles, and newspaper clippings.

The documents are in German, English, French, Flemish, and Hebrew.

Vsemirnyi soiuz evreiskogo studenchestva

World Union of Jewish Students (Vienna)

Fond 1230k, 1924–1936. 74 storage units.

The World Union of Jewish Students (WUJS) was founded in May 1924 in Antwerp. It comprised Jewish student organizations of Great Britain, Germany, Austria, Belgium, Hungary, Romania, and other countries. The World Union of Jewish Students was created primarily to consolidate the efforts of Jewish student organizations of various countries toward solving social problems among Jewish students, combating antisemitism, and preserving and studying Jewish religious traditions and the Jewish historical and cultural heritage.

The collection's contents are catalogued in one inventory. The inventory is arranged by document type.

The collection includes the WUJS charter; resolutions adopted at the First World Congress of Jewish Students in Antwerp (1924); lists of Jewish student unions in Czechoslovakia, Germany, Italy, and other countries belonging to the World Union; resolutions of the WUJS executive committee in Vienna for April–May 1925; minutes of meetings of the WUJS central council for January 1929; minutes of meetings of the union's subcommittee on preparations for a scholarly conference on the Jewish question (November 1930); and a report on a meeting of the union's executive committee (Geneva, March 1935).

The collection contains correspondence with Jewish student unions in Austria, Belgium, Germany, Great Britain, Hungary, the Netherlands, Palestine, Poland, Romania, South Africa, Switzerland, and Yugoslavia; with Jewish students in Denmark, Finland, Latvia, and Lithuania; and with the executive committee of the Judäa Union of Jewish Students in Austria on holding congresses and conferences, on uniting Jewish student organizations into a single union, on providing material aid to Jewish students in need, on fundraising, on setting up hostels for Jewish students and developing student tourism, on Jewish student emigration from Germany and Poland, on the Jewish quota at Hungarian universities, and on Jewish student trips from Bratislava to Palestine. It also includes correspondence with

Albert Einstein, Julian Mack, and Stephen Wise on measures to reduce unemployment among Jewish university graduates, on providing material aid to the World Union of Jewish Students, and on organizing protests against the persecution of Jews in Nazi Germany; and correspondence by WUJS leaders E. Pachtmann, Z. Lauterpacht, A. Steinig, and A. Teich on the holding of the Second Congress of the union in Great Britain.

The collection includes correspondence with Jewish and other public organizations: the World Jewish Congress, American Jewish Congress (AJC), the League of Nations International Institute of Intellectual Cooperation, the World Student Christian Federation, the International University Federation for the League of Nations, the International Student Relief Organization, and others.

There are documents on the Union's participation in the work of international conferences, meetings, and congresses: minutes of a meeting of the World Union's delegation at a conference of the International Student Relief Organization in Oxford (1930); agendas of the Eleventh Congress of the International Confederation of Students (1929) and the Twelfth Congress of the International University Federation (1935); minutes of meetings of the executive committee of the International Student Relief Organization (Paris, February 1932; Geneva, January 1933); resolutions of the First Conference of Representatives of Youth Organizations in Geneva (August 1930) and the Conference of Jewish Students of Palestine (April 1932); materials of the Eleventh Conference of the International Student Relief Organization in Brno (July–August 1932).

Printed materials include bulletins of the International Student Relief Organization (1920, 1930, 1933), the Union of Jewish Students in Germany (1927), and the Jewish Telegraphic Agency (JTA); and the pamphlet *The International Student Relief Organization: A Brief Survey of its History, Goals, and Plans for the Future.*

The documents are in German, French, Polish, English, and Hebrew.

Microfilms are held by the United States Holocaust Memorial Museum Archives.

INDIVIDUALS

Margulis Emil', prezident Evreiskoi partii v Chekhoslovakii, advokat

Emil Margulis

Fond 705k, 1913–1930. 9 storage units.

Emil Margulis was an attorney and Zionist leader born in 1877 in Sosnovets (Austro-Hungary). He published his first Zionist pamphlet in 1904. In 1923, he was one of the founders of the radical faction of the WZO. In 1927, Margulis became one of the founders of the Jewish State Party of Czechoslovakia, and was elected to parliament. In 1939, he emigrated to Palestine, where he passed away in 1943.

The bulk of the documents in Emil Margulis's archive were transferred to Czechoslovakia in 1961.

The collection's contents are catalogued in two inventories. The inventories are arranged by document type.

The collection's documents were collected and systematized by the collection's originator. They include bylaws, circulars, minutes of meetings, financial statements, and other documents of Keren Kayemeth LeIsrael and Keren Hayesod for 1929–30; Jewish Agency overviews of the situation in Palestine and the activities of Zionist organizations; minutes of meetings of the presidium of the Jewish State Party central committee and of the office of the World Zionist Organization (WZO) in London; correspondence with members of the organizing committee and with members of Zionist organizations on the calling of and conduct of the 20th World Zionist Congress and on coverage of the activities of Zionist organizations in the press; materials on the conduct of the election campaign in the run-up to the 20th Zionist Congress; letters from the director of a regional committee of Zionists in Vienna; letters from the International Council for the Rights of Jewish Minorities to Margulis inviting him to take part in a session of the Council's executive committee, and informing him about the situation of Jews in Romania (1928); circular letters of the Union of Radical Zionists in Berlin on organizational matters, on working out an action plan, and on establishing a Jewish state in Palestine (1928–29); letters from the Zionist Regional Committee for Inner Austria to its members on calling a special congress (1931); preparatory materials for the 4th Congress of Jewish Minorities of the Countries of Europe in Geneva, and declarations by Congress delegations; a memorandum of the Russian Zionist Center (1929); a memorandum and reports by the commerce and industry section of the Organization of Creditors of the Russian Zionist Center; declarations by delegations of Zionists to the Congress of Jewish Minorities of the Countries of Europe; and other materials.

The collection also contains informational bulletins of the International Council for the Rights of Jewish Minorities in Geneva, of the Jewish Agency for Palestine in London, and of the WZO on the activities of Jewish organizations, current events, and the situation in Palestine; surveys of the press, newspaper clippings and items with notes by Margulis; and Margulis's article, "Against the Partition of Palestine."

The documents are in English, German, and French.

Shneerson Iosel'-Itska – glavnyi ravvin g. Rigi

Yosef Yitzchok Schneerson

Fond 706k, 1907–1935. 98 storage units.

Yosef Yitzchok Schneerson (b. 1880, Lubavichi — d. 1950, New York) was the sixth Rebbe of Lubavitch Hasidism (Chabad). He became head of the Lubavitch Hasidim upon the death of his father Sholom Dov Ber Schneerson in 1920. Unlike other Jewish religious leaders, Y. Y. Schneerson did not choose to emigrate from the USSR, and in 1922 became head of the Committee of Rabbis of the USSR, established on his initiative. In 1924 he settled in Leningrad and initiated the creation of a Jewish religious educational network throughout the USSR, including underground yeshivas in Moscow, Leningrad, Minsk, Vitebsk, and Nevel. In June 1927, Schneerson was sentenced to death by firing squad for "counterrevolutionary activities," but, due to protests in the West, his sentence was commuted, first to three years' exile in Kostroma, and then to expulsion from the USSR.

From 1927 to 1934, Y. Y. Schneerson lived in Riga, Latvia, where he organized a new Chabad center, and from 1934 to 1940, in Warsaw, Poland — where, on his initiative, a number of yeshivas were founded. In 1940, he emigrated to the United States and established the Chabad Center in Crown Heights, Brooklyn. He played an important part in the strengthening of Orthodox Judaism in the United States.

[Materials of this collection also are deposited in Collection 707k, "Jewish Religious Community (Vienna)", and Collection 1326k, "Jewish Religious Community (Berlin)."]

The collection's contents are described in one inventory, arranged by document type.

The collection contains Y. Y. Schneerson's sermons on Jewish holidays, ethics, and religious rituals; Schneerson's manuscript commentaries on the Torah, and his mealtime discourses on religious subjects; a book containing the typewritten texts of Schneerson's sermons and commentaries on individual passages of the Torah (bound together are sermons read in Lubavitch, Riga, and other cities); manuscripts, typescripts, and page proofs of Y. Y. Schneerson's articles on issues of Jewish religious education

(1930s) and on issues of faith and ritual; articles and sermons on halakhah and other religious topics: "The Crown of the Torah," "The Taxation of Kosher Meat" (1930); "The Essence of Things" (1930s); a draft of his father, Sholom Dov Ber Schneerson's, manuscript of commentaries on the Torah (written in the early twentieth century); and handwritten texts of sermons on Biblical themes (1906).

The collection also contains documents, articles, and memoirs on the history of Lubavitch Hasidism: Y. Y. Schneerson's manuscript and typewritten texts entitled "The Fathers of Hasidism" on the lives of Hasidic rabbis in the late eighteenth to early nineteenth centuries; notes with Hasidic traditions regarding the activities of Lubavitch tsaddikim in the nineteenth century, their trips to Mezherich and studies at the Nezhin yeshiva (as well as their crossing the Dnieper with Russian forces during the war with Napoleon in 1812); reminiscences of the life of Sholom Dov Ber Schneerson in the late nineteenth century (1902, original); a typewritten text of reminiscences (from the 1930s) about the Lubavitch-led collection of matzo and Passover goods for Jews fighting in the ranks of the Russian Army during the Russo-Japanese War of 1904–05; and reminiscences of life in Lubavitch.

The collection also contains materials on the situation of Jews in the USSR and on the Soviet authorities' policies with regard to the Jewish religion; it also contains a list of rabbis of Eastern Europe, with notes and descriptions by Y. Y. Schneerson (original, 1930s).

Also of note is the correspondence deposited in the collection. There is correspondence between Y. Y. Schneerson and various Jewish charitable organizations, including the JDC, on providing material aid to religious Jews in the USSR; correspondence regarding arrangements for Schneerson's trips to the United States, France, and other countries.

There is Y. Y. Schneerson's correspondence with relatives, followers, and constituent organizations of Lubavitch Hasidism: R. Samarius Gurary, Riga; Kolel Chabad in Palestine, and the Tomchei Temimim yeshivas in Vilna and Warsaw; The Lubavitch Library, Riga; Shlomo Zalman Havlin (Jerusalem); Shneur Zalman Shmotkin and Feivish Zalmanov (Poland); Rabbi Elijah Simpson (Congregation Anshe Lubawitz, Borough Park, New York); Agudas Chasidim Anshe Chabad, Philadelphia; Agudas Chasidei Chabad of Chelsea, Massachusetts; and Rabbi Shneur Zalman Slonim, Tel-Aviv-Jaffa. Also included is correspondence with followers in the Soviet Union: Krugliak of Boguslav, Belkin of Arkhangelsk, Schapiro of Belaia Tserkov', Yanovskii of Nikolaev, and others.

There is correspondence with various Jewish religious organizations and rabbinic figures: Agudath Israel, Zeire Agudath Israel of Latvia; World Union for Keeping of the Sabbath; the Society of Friends of the Berlin Rabbinical Seminary for Orthodox Judaism (Dr. Emil Hirsch); R. Chaim Ozer Grodzienski, Vilna; Chief Rabbi Avraham Kahana Shapiro of Kaunas (Kovno), Lithuania; Rabbi Meir Shapiro in Lublin; Rabbi Israel Meir Kagan ("The Chofets Chaim"), Radun; R. Ahron Kotler, Kletsk; Rabbi Abraham Isaac Kook, Jerusalem; Dr. Meir Hildesheimer, Berlin; and Rabbi Jacob Lind, Libau.

The collection also contains correspondence with various Jewish communities and organizations: the Jewish Community Council of Riga; the Moscow Jewish religious community; the American Jewish Committee, and others; Jewish communal leaders Cyrus Adler (New York), Hillel Zlatopolsky (Paris), and others.

The collection also includes congratulatory telegrams to Y. Y. Schneerson from rabbis of various Jewish communities of the USSR; typewritten copies of individual letters from the Hebrew-language correspondence of Lubavitch Hasidic rabbis. There are also letters from an earlier period, by Sh. Zalkind, Persitz, Gurevich, written during the years 1905–09.

The collection includes photo materials, including photocopies and photographs of Y. Y. Schneerson's manuscript works and letters (from the 1900s to the 1930s). The collection also contains Y. Y. Schneerson's pamphlet *Colloquy: "Simchas Torah at the Table"* (New York, 1930s, in Yiddish) and clippings from the Russian-language Riga newspaper *Segodnia*.

The documents are in Hebrew, Yiddish, Russian, and English.

II

AUSTRIA

ORGANIZATIONS

Vsemirnaia organizatsiia bor'by protiv rasovoi nenavisti i nuzhdy (g. Vena)

Weltorganisation gegen Rassenhass und Menschennot (Wien)

World Organization Against Racial Hatred and Poverty (Vienna)

Fond 520k, 1897–1938. 639 storage units.

The World Organization against Racism and Poverty was founded in October 1933 by Irene Harand, an Austrian Catholic housewife. On the eve of the Austrian Anschluss in March 1938, its supporters numbered 40,000 (of whom only 3,500 were Jews) with branches in 27 countries. From January 1934 through March 1938, the organization, also known as Harand-Bewegung (the Harand Movement), published the weekly newspaper *Gerechtigkeit*, with a circulation (in 1936) of 20,000 copies. As a Christian, Harand saw the point of her struggle against antisemitism not so much that of defending Jewish interests, but rather of "keeping Christians from turning into animals." In 1969, Yad Vashem bestowed upon her the title of Righteous among the Nations.

The collection's contents are catalogued in two inventories. The inventories are arranged by document type.

The collection contains bylaws, memoranda, platforms, minutes, instructions, and appeals of the World Organization; biographical information on the organization's leader, Irene Harand; applications to join the organization; correspondence with subscribers to the newspaper *Gerechtigkeit* (by country); lists of subscribers to the newspaper *Gerechtigkeit*; correspondence on providing aid to the Jewish population of Vienna; letters of invitation to Harand; proposals for publication in the newspaper *Gerechtigkeit*; orders for journals and books; articles on the situation of Jews; a card file of members of the World Organization against Racial Hatred and Poverty; membership cards; leaflets; and photographs of Organization members.

The documents are in German and English.

Microfilms are held by the United States Holocaust Memorial Museum Archives.

Soiuz avstriiskikh frontovikov-evreev

Bund jüdischer Frontsoldaten Österreichs

Union of Austrian Jewish War Veterans (Vienna)

Fond 672k, 1915–1938. 359 storage units.

The Union of Austrian Jewish War Veterans was founded in July 1932; it was established in response to the creation of the Austrian Nazi Party. Until 1934, the
Union was headed by Generalmajor E. Sommer (1869–1947) — and from 1934
to 1938, by Captain S. Friedman. The key points of the union's program, adopted
in October 1933, were Austrian patriotism and Jewish self-defense. The organization was nonpartisan; it included supporters of the Habsburg monarchy as well as
liberals, Zionists as well as assimilationists. The union called for unity among Jews
in the face of growing antisemitism in Austria. It supported Austrian chancellor
Dollfuss's assumption of emergency powers in 1933 and the ban on the Social
Democratic Party in 1934 — and favored Dollfuss's and von Schuschnigg's policies generally. The union, which in 1935 numbered 20,000 members, was one of
the largest Jewish organizations in Austria. In 1937, it comprised 17 branches in
Vienna and 20 in Austria's provincial cities, including Baden, Linz, Graz, Eisen-
stadt, and Innsbruck. The union published the journal *Jüdische Front* (December
1932–February 1938), which began as a monthly, but later became a bimonthly.
From 1935 on, the union had departments of communications, publications, social
measures, Jewish self-defense, sports, and personnel. In the first years of its existence, the union attracted significant public attention due to its members' clashes
with Austrian Nazis in the streets of Vienna (September 1932) and its organization
of a demonstration to protest antisemitism (attended by 2,000 people in January
1933). Also among its primary undertakings were the unveiling of a monument to
Austrian Jewish soldiers who died in the First World War (attended by some 30,000
people) in September 1934 and the holding of the Second International Congress
of Jewish War Veterans in June/July 1936. The union ceased its activities after the
Austrian Anschluss in March 1938, although it was formally closed by the Gestapo
4 October 1938.

The collection's contents are described in one inventory arranged
by document type. The inventory has a geographical index.

The collection contains the charter of the Union of Austrian Jewish
War Veterans and the Jewish Front association; a list of the administrative

duties of the union leadership; lists of union members (in the form of a register of typewritten cards); the circular of the union's Jugendbund; a report by union director Friedman on the defense of the rights of Jews; A. Kundert's pamphlet *Warum immer die Juden*; and printed publications of the union.

The collection also has documents, presumably from the library of the Israelite Theological Institute of Higher Learning in Vienna (see Fond 717), accumulated in the course of Abraham Epstein's and Simhah Pinsker's research. There are manuscripts of works by Abraham Epstein: *Targumim*, which examines the reasons that translations of Biblical texts from Hebrew to Aramaic arose in the period of the Second Temple, and peculiarities of the language of *Targum Onkelos* and *Targum Jonathan*; the introduction and index to Simhah Pinsker's work *Likutei Pardes*; a draft of a work on the grammar of Biblical Hebrew; an excerpt of a manuscript examining the narratives in the first two chapters of the Book of Genesis; a description of Hebrew grammar; and an index to the names of rabbis mentioned in the Talmud. There is also a commentary (author unknown) on the Pentateuch (1918), and an excerpt of a manuscript by the same author on kosher food (written in the first quarter of the twentieth century).

The documents are in German, Hebrew, and Yiddish.

Evreiskoe blagotvoritel'noe ob"edinenie Izraelitishe al'ians

Israelitische Allianz (Vienna)

Fond 675k, 1872–1939. 783 storage units.

The Israelitische Allianz was created as a branch of the Paris-based Alliance Is-raélite Universelle. However, the decision to open the branch was held up by Aus-trian officials and put off for many years; permission was finally granted in 1873. The Israelitische Allianz subsequently functioned as an independent charitable or-ganization. Joseph Ritter von Wertheimer (1873–87), David Ritter von Guttmann (1888–1912), Alfred Stern (1912–18), A. Kuranda (1919–33), and J. Ornstein (1933–37) served as Allianz presidents. The Allianz aided Jews who were being oppressed by the authorities in the Austro-Hungarian and Russian Empires, and Jews in the Balkan countries struggling for equal rights. The Allianz was also active in countering the blood libel in the city of Tisza-Eslar (1883) — and later in other cities of the Habsburg Empire. The Allianz maintained German-language Jewish schools in Lvov, Brody, and other cities in Galicia and Bukovina. For a period after 1881, the Allianz focused its efforts primarily on aiding Jewish émigrés from Russia and Romania. In 1891, the Allianz set up aid centers in Austro-Hungarian cities near the Russian border to receive and resettle Jewish refugees and émigrés from Russia. Financial assistance was provided to victims of pogroms in Russia (1903–06) in conjunction with other Jewish charitable organizations: the German Jewish Aid Society (Hilfsverein), the French Alliance Israélite Universelle, and the Jewish Colonization Association (JCA). After the First World War, the Allianz focused mainly on receiving (in Vienna) Jewish émigrés from the countries of Eastern Europe. The organization was liquidated after the Austrian Anschluss in 1938.

The collection's contents are catalogued in two inventories. The inventories are arranged by document type, and have a geographical index.

The collection's documents include charters of the Israelitische Al-lianz, of other Jewish organizations, educational institutions, committees, and unions; reports on the activities of the Israelitische Allianz, and of Jew-ish communities; financial statements; and minutes of meetings of the or-ganization's board.

The collection contains letters and correspondence with other Jew-ish organizations — the Jewish Literary Association (Vienna), the Jewish

Society to Aid the Jewish Population of Romania, the Palästina-Amt, the Zionist youth organization Akiba, the Zionist Union of Deaf-Mutes, the Jewish National Council of Eastern Galicia, Poale Zion, Keren Kayemeth LeIsrael, and Betar — and with the authorities and private individuals on aiding various categories of the Jewish population; lists of members of the Israelitische Allianz organization, and of persons receiving grants; as well as files on donations and estate bequests to the organization, and on the purchase and rental of plots of land.

Also contained are instructions by the Austro-Hungarian Ministry of Internal Affairs on rules for allocating funds among refugees from Galicia and Bukovina in connection with the outbreak of the First World War in 1914; memoranda by Jewish communities and organizations to the League of Nations; appeals by Jewish communities to the authorities of various countries requesting aid for communities and Jewish refugees.

Printed materials include clippings from newspapers and journals; issues of Jewish journals, newspapers, bulletins, books, pamphlets, and the like. There are also manuscripts of works on historical, philosophical, and theosophical subjects, originating from the collections of other institutions.

The documents are in German, English, French, Hungarian, Italian, Hebrew, and Yiddish.

Microfilms are held by the United States Holocaust Memorial Museum Archives.

Evreiskii sportivnyi klub Gakoakh

Jüdischer Sportklub *"Hakoah"* (Graz)

Jewish Sports Club *Hakoah* (Graz)

Fond 676k, 1929–1938. 32 storage units.

The Jewish Sports Club *Hakoah* was founded in Graz in 1919; it brought together Jewish youth sympathetic to Zionism. In 1931, the club had more than 400 active members. *Hakoah* had soccer, handball, chess, gymnastics, tennis, swimming, and winter sports sections. The *Hakoah* club in Graz closed after the Nazi Anschluss of Austria in 1938.

The collection's contents are catalogued in two inventories. The inventories are arranged by document type, and have a geographical index.

The collection contains the club's charter (1936); a financial statement of the club, and a report on its functioning (1937); an appeal to the Jewish population requesting material aid to the club; letters from the Invalids' Union, sports clubs in Vienna and Czechoslovakia, and the Footballers' Union of Styria on collaboration, and on the club's participation in soccer competitions and in the report and election meeting of the Union of Austrian Jews; the club's cashbook for 1926–30; letters from the Graz police department and district court regarding the club's creditors; membership and identification cards of club members; applications for club membership; notifications from Vienna insurance companies to club members on insurance conditions; correspondence between club members on personal matters and on organizing sporting events; issues of the club bulletin for 1936–38; and an issue of the Vienna sports magazine *Stadion* (1933).

The documents are in German.

Microfilms are held by the United States Holocaust Memorial Museum Archives.

Redaktsiia evreiskogo zhurnala Di Varkhait

Editorial Offices, *Die Wahrheit* (Vienna)

Fond 677k, 1924–1938. 30 storage units.

Founded in 1899, *Die Wahrheit* was initially a biweekly newspaper with a liberal political outlook, which reported on Jewish communal affairs. After the First World War, *Die Wahrheit* was acquired by the Union of Austrian Jews and became a weekly. The newspaper espoused the position that the roots of Judaism lay in religion, and it opposed both Jewish nationalism and socialism. Edited by Oskar Hirschenfeld, *Die Wahrheit* declared that its most important task was to fight against antisemitism and defend the legal rights of Austrian Jews. It was closed following the *Anschluss* in 1938.

The collection's contents are catalogued in two inventories. The inventories are arranged by document type.

The collection contains correspondence with members of the Union of Austrian Jews and with subscribers on newspaper subscription terms, on sending subscription fees, and on subscription renewals; with correspondents of the newspaper on submitting and publishing articles, and on the payment of fees; with religious communities, Jewish organizations, and the JTA branch office in Prague; with Hungarian parliament deputy J. Vasony on the newspaper's publication of his speech (delivered 5 May 1937) on the Jewish question; and with the book publisher and printing house Ignaz Spitz and Sons regarding payment of accounts for the publication of the newspaper *Die Wahrheit*, and regarding settlement of the newspaper's creditors' complaints about nonpayment of accounts.

The collection contains the editorial office's cashbook for 1937–38 and the register of subscribers to *Die Wahrheit*; a card file of organizations and individuals having placed advertisements in the newspaper; issues of the newspapers *Der Morgen*, *Der Wiener Tag*, and *Gemeindeblatt*; clippings from German newspapers on clashes between Arabs and Jews in Palestine; manuscripts of articles by various authors on the situation of Jews in the countries of Europe and America. The collection includes issues of the newspaper *Die Wahrheit* for 1937.

The documents are in German.

Microfilms are held by the United States Holocaust Memorial Museum Archives.

Evreiskaia religioznaia obshchina (g. Vena)

Israelitische Kultusgemeinde (Wien)

Jewish Religious Community of Vienna

Fond 707k, 1782–1940. 281 storage units.

In 1852, the Austrian authorities gave de facto recognition to the Jewish Religious Community as the sole organization authorized to conduct religious, educational, and charitable operations among Jews in Vienna. The community's charter was ratified in 1867 and revised in 1890. The community oversaw the maintenance of various components of Jewish religious life — including the rabbinate, religious education, synagogues, cemeteries, kosher food, and charity — and oversaw the keeping of birth registers. The community was the unofficial representative of Jewish interests vis-à-vis state entities and the city authorities. The community's budget consisted of dues paid by its members. The number of actual dues-payers, however, was small. In 1895, out of a Viennese Jewish population of 133,397, only 12,797 paid the 10-florin community tax, giving them the right to vote in community council elections. By 1924, with a general Viennese Jewish population of 201,000, the number of payers had increased to 53,000.

The community council typically represented the wealthiest and most successful segment of the Jews of Vienna. For most of its existence, the community was dominated by adherents of liberal, Reform Judaism. Before the First World War, Orthodox Jews generally abstained from community council elections, and Zionist candidates were unsuccessful. Among its presidents in the imperial period were Ignaz Kuranda, Wilhelm Ritter von Guttmann, Heinrich Klinger, Joseph Ritter von Wertheimer, and Alfred Stern (1903–18). From 1920 to 1932, the president of the community council was Alois Pick, who represented a Liberal-Orthodox alliance. In 1932, the Zionist slate of candidates received the majority of votes, and Desider Friedmann became president.

After the Nazi Anschluss of Austria on 13 March 1938, the Jews of Vienna, numbering by that time 115,000, fell victim to the Nuremberg Laws. During Kristallnacht (9–10 November 1938), 49 synagogues in Vienna were destroyed, Jewish property was looted, and several thousand Viennese Jews were deported to the Dachau concentration camp. Between the fall of 1939 and September 1942, the Jews of Vienna were systematically deported to ghettos in Nazi-occupied Poland, and, after the German invasion of the Soviet Union, to occupied territories there, including the Baltics. The Jewish Community was officially dissolved in November 1942.

The collection's contents are catalogued in three inventories. The inventories are arranged by structure and document type.

The collection has charters of the Jewish religious community of Vienna — and of affiliated organizations: the Union to Aid Jewish Students, the Union for the Care of Orphans, Jewish Literary Association, the Mendelssohn Jewish Literary Union, and others. It contains the minutes of meetings of the community board for 1891–1938 as well as community financial documents — statements, estimates, summaries, income statements, cashbooks for 1928–37, and tax tables.

The collection contains reports on communal election preparations, and on auditing the community's finances; a historical survey, composed by Biedermann, of the activities of the Jewish religious community of Vienna for fifty-eight years; and lists of Vienna synagogues.

Among the documents found in the collection, there is an agreement between the Jewish religious community of Vienna and the Orthodox Jewish religious party Agudath Israel on dividing responsibilities between them; documents on the structure of the community board; a report by the community board presidium on the conduct of the winter 1935–36 charity drive initiated by the Austrian government; a report by community vice president B. Rappaport and the architect J. Gartner on the construction of a Jewish cemetery (with plans enclosed); an announcement by the community denying Hitler's statements connecting Jewish and communist organizations; and congratulatory letters, addresses, and telegrams from the Jewish religious community of Vienna to the Jewish religious communities of Graz, Fünfkirchen, Gross-Kanischa, and Ehrendorf.

The collection contains correspondence from the Jewish religious community of Vienna, including letters to various individuals: community president Kuranda, Rabbi Zecharias Frankel, Chabad leader Y. Y. Schneerson, Austrian Chancellor K. Schuschnigg; a letter to the Vienna consulate of Czechoslovakia expressing condolences upon the death of the Czechoslovak president Tomáš Masaryk; correspondence with publishing houses on publishing Jewish literature; with the Austrian Ministry of Education and the Israelite Theological Institute of Higher Learning in Vienna on apportioning plots of land for this educational institution; with Hechalutz and the European headquarters of the JDC in Paris on providing aid to Austrian Jews; and correspondence with the journalist B. Freistedt, with H. Klee, and T. Rappaport.

The collection also has correspondence for the period 1828–83 on the subject of collecting materials on Jewish history and literature. These documents may very well be connected in origin with the archive of the Israelite Theological Institute of Higher Learning (see Fond 717, "Israelite Theological Institute of Higher Learning, Vienna"). These include letters from Solomon Rosenthal to Abraham Geiger on the subject of exchanging books; letters from M. Kann to J. Rosenthal (7 August 1828); and a letter (author unknown) to H. Satanover on the subject of collecting materials on Jewish history. The collection contains minutes of meetings of the board of the Israelite Theological Institute of Higher Learning for 1893; personnel files and documents of instructors at the Israelite Theological Institute of Higher Learning; lists of teachers and students at the Jewish religious school Beth Hamidrash in Vienna; as well as class registers, schedules, and student progress reports.

The collection includes the minutes of sessions of the Rabbinate of Breslau for 1828–48; it also houses draft studies by Leser Landshuth: notes of a biographical nature, and short biographical sketches of medieval rabbinical authorities in Germany, northern France, and Eastern and Central Europe. There are also documents on the plans to establish, in Berlin, the Hochschule for Jewish Studies. It is possible that part of this archival set originated in the archive of the Berlin Jewish religious community (Fond 1326).

Documents of the library of the Jewish religious community of Vienna include these: manuscripts in Yiddish and Hebrew, Psalms, catalogues of Biblical manuscripts, bibliographic indexes, directories, dictionaries, essays, lectures, dissertations, and articles. The library books contained in the collection may be divided into several document categories: commentaries on the Hebrew Bible and Talmud; rabbinical treatises; copies of responsa of well-known rabbis; works on history, philosophy, ethics, and culture; and bibliographic lists. The collection includes a large number of Hebrew manuscripts. Because virtually none of the Hebrew-language manuscripts have been thoroughly examined by scholars, file headings in the inventory do not reflect the files' contents.

Among the identified older manuscripts, the following are noteworthy: sections of Nahmanides's commentary on the Torah, written in Sephardic script, from the fifteenth century; a fifteenth-century Hebrew medical manuscript, in Sephardic script, which refers to a medical manual prepared for the King of Aragon; a fifteenth-century manuscript of Hasdai Crescas's *Or Adonai* copied in Aragon in 1410; a fifteenth-century manuscript, in Sephardic script, of Profiat Duran's work of Hebrew grammar, *Ma'aseh Efod*. Other identified manuscripts include these: pages from a seventeenth-century kabbalistic manuscript, written in Oriental script; a poem by Abraham Ibn Ezra written in Oriental script; an Oriental manuscript of comments on the Talmudic tractates of Ketubot, Berakhot, and Hulin by R. Isaac b. Moshe, probably from the seventeenth century; a large manuscript collection of piutim, in Oriental script; a Karaite treatise *Sefer sha'ar yehudah* by Yehudah Puki, on Biblical sexual prohibitions, copied in Constantinople in 1582; selections from the book *Even sapir* written in Karaite script; and other manuscripts of Karaite origin.

The following are among the manuscripts of unknown dating: a manuscript copy of the unfinished work of ethics *Baal Iter (Takanot Aharon)*; the manuscript book *Sefer Hishtalmut ha-Olamot*, said to be authored by Isaac Luria (the Ari); a manuscript of the medieval anti-Christian polemical work *Toledot Yeshu*, entitled *Ma'aseh Yeshu*; a notebook containing a manuscript copy of the treatise *The Rotation of Heavenly Bodies*; and a manuscript copy of a commentary *Vayaged Moshe* (author unknown) on Jacob ben Solomon Ibn Habib's compilation of aggadot *Ein Yaakov*.

There are also numerous nineteenth-century handmade copies of older manuscripts: a copy of the Paris manuscript of the Midrash *Bamidbar Rabbah* (copying completed in December 1885); the commentaries to *Sefer yetsirah* by R. Sa'adah Gaon and R. Jacob b. Nisim, copied by Rabbi Zalman Werbluner of Munich (nineteenth century); *Beraita de-Yosef ben Uziel*, copied from a Paris manuscript in 1893; an eighteenth- or nineteenth-century manuscript of *Sefer Nehmad Ve-na'im* by R. David Ganz of Prague; a commentary on the Song of Songs by R. Shemaia Ha-Shoshani, copied in the late nineteenth century; a copy of a manuscript commentary on the Jethro section of the Book of Exodus with an introduction by the Viennese Rabbi A. Jellinek (presumably from the 1890s); and a hardcover notebook containing a copy of *Sefer ha-Olam*, Ezra ben Shlomo's commentary on difficult passages in Abraham ibn Ezra's Torah commentary (the copy was made by Mordechai ben Shlomo Drann, 1887).

The collection also contains a variety of Ashkenazic Hebrew manuscripts from the eighteenth and nineteenth centuries: an eighteenth-century Ashkenazic kabbalistic manuscript entitled *Atzei te'enah*; numerous eighteenth- and nineteenth-century rabbinic works, some of which are quite lengthy, on the Talmud and halakha, including one dealing mainly with laws of ritual slaughtering; a number of manuscript poems by Rabbi Aaron Khorin; and a treatise devoted to Jewish medicine, including dietology, from the late eighteenth and/or early nineteenth century. There is also a Samaritan manuscript (with sections in Arabic) from the modern period.

The collection contains draft materials and notes for a monograph on the historical formation of the *Yelamdenu* collection of Midrashim. There are documents on the history and culture of the Jews of Europe, including an article in German (author unknown) on the role of Jews in the intellectual life of Austria and their contribution to Austrian scholarship, and a fragment of a manuscript monograph on the organization and everyday life of the traditional Jewish community.

The collection contains several bibliographic descriptions: the handwritten bibliographic listing (undated) of Jewish manuscripts in the collections of the Biblioteca Casanatense, the Biblioteca Nazionale Centrale "Vittorio Emanuele II," the Biblioteca Angelica in Rome, in the Palatino collections in Florence and the Vatican, in Jewish book depositories of Rome; and also in the collection of Leon Vita Saraval of Trieste. There are also fragments of a bibliography of codices of Hebrew Bible manuscripts in the Abraham Firkovich collection.

The collection under discussion also includes materials originating from Y. Y. Schneerson, whose documents are for the most part deposited in Fond 706k ("Y. Y. Schneerson"). These include Hasidic and halakhic works by previous rabbis of the Schneerson dynasty. Among them: halakhic writings on matters of religious divorce and ritual slaughter, and the Talmudic tractate *Baba Kamah*, possibly by the third Lubavitcher Rebbe, R. Menachem Mendel Schneerson [The "Tzemach Tzedek"] (1789–1866); manuscript discourses by the latter, written down by his son and successor, R. Shmuel Schneerson (1834–82); discourses by fourth Lubavitcher Rebbe, Rabbi Shmuel Schneerson delivered in 1879–80, written down by his son and successor, R. Sholom Dov Ber Schneerson (1860–1920); a discourse delivered by Sholom Dov Ber Schneerson on the occasion of his bar mitzvah in 1873; discourses by Sholom Dov Ber Schneerson, the fifth Lubavitcher Rebbe, delivered in 1884; the draft of a sermon by Sholom Dov Ber Schneerson delivered on Rosh Hashanah in 1891; the text of the sermon "Ma Rabbo Maasei Ya", devoted to the nature of Hasidism and issues of Jewish piety (1894); and letters by Sholem Dov Ber Schneerson to Shneur Zalman of Slonim (1888, 1889, 1890, 1899, 1903).

Several documents relate directly to the sixth Lubavitcher Rebbe, R. Yosef Yitzkhok Schneerson (1880–1950): the text of a discourse delivered by the thirteen-year-old Y. Y. Schneerson at his bar mitzvah; part of a sermon delivered by Y. Y. Schneerson as a child, and presumably written by his father, Sholem Dov Ber Schneerson; a responsum by Y. Y. Schneerson on female ritual impurity. There are also sermons by Y. Y. Schneerson delivered in Riga in 1931, and the text of a sermon he delivered in 1933. Also deposited in the collection is a color blueprint of a house made of stone for Sholem Dov Ber Schneerson, with signatures in Russian.

The collection also contains materials on Jewish emigration; these documents may originate from the archive of HICEM (see Fond 740, "HIAS-JCA Emigration Association, HICEM"). These include lists of Jewish émigrés from Austria, Poland, Latvia, and the Soviet Union; personal documents of émigrés; bulletins on emigration conditions for Jews from Austria, Switzerland, Luxembourg, and Poland; queries from Jewish organizations on the whereabouts of Jewish migrants from Belgium, the Netherlands, the United States, and other countries; and maps and statistical surveys of the Jewish population and of Jewish emigration from Austria and from Vienna.

The collection also contains printed publications: a pamphlet (1896) with a report by Alfred Stern on the founding of the Jewish religious community of Vienna, and analyzing of the religious community's system of governance (council and presidium), as well as the rights and duties of Jewish religious community members; glossaries for the school edition of M. Abraham's fable *Le-yelodeinu* (*For Our Children*). The collection also has sets of the Hebrew-language newspapers *Hatsefirah* and *Hamagid*, and clippings from these and other newspapers.

The documents are in German, Hebrew and Yiddish.

Microfilms are held by the United States Holocaust Memorial Museum Archives.

Evreiskaia religioznaia obshchina (g. Grats)

Israelitische Kultusgemeinde (Graz)

Jewish Religious Community of Graz

Fond 709k, 1871–1938. 45 storage units.

Jews began settling in Graz no later than the late thirteenth to early fourteenth centuries, living in a particular quarter of the city. In 1496, the Jews were expelled from Graz and forbidden to live there, except temporarily, until 1861. In 1865, a community prayer house was opened in Graz, and in 1892, a synagogue. The Jewish religious community of Graz was established in 1869. The community numbered 250 members in that year; 1,971 in 1910; and 2,500 on the eve of the March 1938 Anschluss. During 1908–14, it published the monthly *Grazer Israelitischer Gemeindebote*, and during 1926–34, the bimonthly *Bulletin of the Graz Jewish Community*. The president of the community in the 1930s was R. Sonnewald. The synagogue was destroyed during Kristallnacht (9–10 November 1938). By the middle of 1939, virtually the entire Jewish population of Graz had emigrated.

The collection's contents are catalogued in two inventories. The inventories are arranged by document type.

The collection features documents of the Jewish Religious Community of Graz, the community's committee for the social security of Jewish émigrés, the Graz chapter of Hashomer Hatzair, and other Jewish organizations of Graz; community circulars for 1933; minutes of community meetings for 1922–38; correspondence with the Vienna taxation and revenue board, Jewish charitable organizations, community members, and lawyers regarding the election of board members and officers of the community; documents on the founding of the committee for the social security of Jewish émigrés, on the provision of material aid to Jewish émigrés and community members in need, on the payment of taxes and membership dues, and on taking possession of real estate and financial assets bequeathed by community members; community financial statements and balance sheets, cashbooks, budget projections, and logs of dues-paying members; a card file and lists of members of the community and of the central committee for social security; community council voter lists; questionnaires for individuals joining the committee for social security; an article by community secretary L. Lemberger on the history of Jewish religious communities in Austria; a report by community secretary L. Lemberger with proposals on amending certain articles of the community charter; catalogues of books in the library of Rabbi S. Müsam; and informational bulletins of the community for 1936–37.

The collection also has documents of the central committee for the social security of Jewish émigrés for 1930, as well as of the Central Association of Jewish Communities in Austria for 1937; and reports from the Jewish communities in Augsburg and from various Jewish educational institutions, including reports on their academic programs.

The documents are in German and Hebrew.

Microfilms are held by the United States Holocaust Memorial Museum Archives.

Evreiskoe obshchestvo pomoshchi bol'nym Bikur kholim (g. Grats)

"Bikur Cholim" Jüdischer Krankenbesuchs- und Unter-stützungsverein (Graz)

"Bikur Cholim" Society for Visitation and Support of the Ill (Graz)

Fond 710k, 1919–1938. 22 storage units.

The Bikur Cholim society of Graz was founded in 1921. Despite its name, it aided not only the sick, but also the poor and needy, including Jewish refugees finding themselves in Graz during the First World War. The society conducted a yearly *Kinder auf Land!* (Children to the Country!) campaign, which allowed children from poor Jewish families to spend vacations at summer camp. It ceased activities after the Nazi Anschluss of Austria on 13 March 1938.

The collection's contents are described in one inventory. The inventory is arranged by document type.

The collection has the society's charter; appeals by the society's preparatory committee and board to the Jews of Graz urging them to join the society; correspondence with society secretary J. Teller in connection with his announcement of his leaving that office, with the Jewish religious community of Graz on the Bikur Cholim society's joining the community, and with the Jewish National Fund Keren Kayemeth LeIsrael, the Emunah union of employees in Vienna, local branches of the Order of B'nai B'rith, the Jewish sports club *Hakoah*, the Graz Union of Jewish War Veterans, and other Jewish organizations and charitable societies. The collection also contains correspondence with members of the Bikur Cholim society and with private individuals — regarding payment of membership dues owed and payment of accounts, the provision of financial assistance to the needy, the arrangement and financing of children's vacations, and applications for society membership. The collection also contains lists of society members and donors; parents' applications to the society's boardinghouse for their children; society financial statements, cashbooks (1926–38), and member accounts; and copies of the Jewish newspapers *Die Stimme* and *Der Jude* for 1937.

The collection also holds society director E. Grunschlag's personal correspondence with his wife and son.

The documents are in German and Yiddish.

Microfilms are held by the United States Holocaust Memorial Museum Archives.

Evreiskoe ob"edinenie Kharitas (g. Grats)

Jüdische Verbindung "Charitas" (Graz)

Caritas Jewish Society (Graz)

Fond 711k, 1908–1938. 29 storage units.

The Jewish youth organization Caritas was established in 1897 to represent the economic, spiritual, and social interests of Jewish students. It was a successor to the Humanitas Society of Jewish Students, closed by the authorities in 1897. From 1904 on, the Caritas Jewish Academic Union, as it was officially called, was affiliated with the Maccabee Jewish youth organization. It was closed by the authorities in 1922, and was reactivated once more in 1929. Under the aegis of the society, classes were held Monday through Friday on Hebrew, Zionism, fencing, and singing. The society worked closely with the local Graz Zionist organization.

The collection's contents are catalogued in two inventories. The inventories are arranged by document type.

The collection contains a draft charter, and charters of Caritas; minutes of meetings for the period 1929–38; reports on the activities of Caritas in Graz for 1931–33; instructions on procedures for settling personal conflicts among Caritas members. Much of the collection consists of correspondence with the Graz police department, the university in Prague, the sports club *Hakoah*, the Jewish State Party, the Union of Revisionist Zionists of Austria, the Jewish religious communities of Graz and Prague, various Zionist organizations and societies, members of Caritas, and private individuals. The collection also contains lists of members of Caritas in Graz, the text of a speech by society member Herzog at the unveiling of a monument to society members who perished during the First World War, the society's cashbooks for 1931–38 and statements of membership dues paid, a register of incoming and outgoing correspondence, an inventory of the books in the library of Caritas in Graz, a register of Graz Caritas member fencing duels for 1907–12, and clippings from newspapers.

The documents are in German and Hebrew.

Ispolnitel'nyi komitet ob"edinennogo soiuza evreiskikh studentov Avstrii Iudeia (g. Vena)

Exekutive des Gesamtverbandes jüdischer Hochschüler Österreichs "Judeja"

Judäa **Union of Jewish Students in Austria, Executive Committee (Vienna)**

Fond 712k, 1904–1938. 103 storage units.

The *Judäa* Union of Jewish Students in Austria, founded in Vienna in February 1919, was a nonpartisan organization representing the economic, cultural, and group interests of Jewish students in Austria.

The collection's contents are described in one inventory. The inventory is arranged by structure.

The collection has the charters of the Judäa Union of Jewish Students and the Union of Jewish High School Students in Austria; circulars of the World Union of Jewish Students and instructions of the Austrian Administration on Institutes of Higher Learning on procedures for organizing student unions; minutes of meetings of the executive committee for 1921–34, and of Judäa's regular delegate meetings for 1927–36; and resolutions of the delegate meetings, including an appeal to Jewish public opinion calling for the creation of a university tuition fund for Jewish students in need.

Much of the collection consists of correspondence: with the World Union of Jewish Students, the World Jewish Congress, the banking houses of M. S. Rothschild and the Gutmann Brothers in Vienna, newspaper editors, and professors — W. Knepfmacher, K. Natanson, H. Levy, E. Herzmann, L. Spitzer, S. Reismann, and Dr. M. Leventhal. The collection also contains internal correspondence with local branches of Judäa on holding regular yearly delegate meetings and electing executive committees. There is also correspondence with Jewish student unions in Poland, Hungary, and Czechoslovakia on the calling of the First World Jewish Congress in Geneva (1936) and Judäa's representation thereat, and on preparations for the Second Congress of Jewish Students. There is correspondence with professors Sigmund Freud and D. Baumgarten on organizing lectures for participants of the 14th World Zionist Congress in Vienna (1925).

Also contained are balance sheets and cashbooks of the organization's executive committee for 1925–37; personal documents, lists, and receipts from members receiving short-term loans; statistical information on Jewish students at the University of Vienna; and a speech by Rabbi Zvi Chajes, Chief Rabbi of Vienna, at a Judäa delegate meeting. Also deposited in the collection are documents of the organization's branches, including announcements about reports and lectures, and Judäa informational bulletins for 1933–38.

The collection also contains documents from other organizations: minutes of meetings of the executive committees of the Academic Union of Jewish Doctors for 1933–36, and minutes of the Academic Union of Jewish Lawyers for 1931–35.

The collection also contains S. Hirschfeld's monograph *Michel Ezofowicz* (typewritten text), bulletins of the World Union of Jewish Students, and a list of books held by Judäa's Law Library in Vienna.

The documents are in German.

Microfilms are held by the United States Holocaust Memorial Museum Archives.

Soiuz avstriiskikh evreev (g. Vena)

Union österreichischer Juden (Wien)

The Union of Austrian Jews (Vienna)

Fond 714k, 1903–1938. 134 storage units.

The Union of Austrian Jews was formed in 1886 and, until 1919, was called the Austrian Israelite Union; it was renamed the Union of German and Austrian Jews and, in 1931, the Union of Austrian Jews. The union was the first Jewish organization in Central Europe to defend the interests of Jews. Predominant in the union were Vienna Jewry's social elites and liberal circles. Over the course of its existence, the union waged legal battles against the dissemination of slanderous material about Jews and against manifestations of antisemitism. The union supported politicians and parties (primarily of a liberal orientation) that opposed antisemitism, and it lobbied to include its candidates in their party rolls. Contending that, as citizens of Austria, Jews could be reliably defended by generally accepted political and judicial methods, the union opposed Zionism and Jewish nationalism more generally. In the 1890s, the union was headed by Sigmund Mayer. On the eve of the First World War, the union had 7,900 dues-paying members.

In interwar Austria, the union acted as a multipurpose organization. It put forward candidates for election to the council of the Jewish religious community of Vienna; it published the weekly liberal newspaper *Die Wahrheit* and financed a women's club and sections for students and youth. The latter sponsored organizations of the union organized various lectures, courses, and social events. In the 1930s, the union opened a credit bureau to support Jewish small business. From 1919 to 1934, the president of the union was Jakob Ornstein; the office was later held by Hermann Oppenheim.

In the 1930s, the union's popularity declined markedly. In elections to the Vienna Jewish religious community council in 1932, the union lost its previous majority to the Zionists. By 1938, its membership fell to 3,000.

The collection's contents are described in two inventories. The inventories are arranged by document type.

The collection contains union charters for 1903–37; minutes of sessions of the union's central presidium for 1936–37, of its executive committee for 1935–37, and its general assembly and local Vienna chapter for

1937; and the union's platform for elections to the boards of Jewish religious communities of Austria.

Much of the collection contains correspondence with local chapters of the Central Association of German Citizens of the Jewish Faith in Berlin and Munich; the Union of Austrian Jewish War Veterans; Keren Hayesod; the Union of Jewish Legitimists of Austria; the organization *Keren Hayishuv*; Jewish communities in Austria, Bulgaria, Hungary, and Romania; the general secretary of the Fatherland's Front, leaders and members of local union chapters; newspaper editors; and banks. Letters relate to election of the union presidium and executive committee; election of the boards of Jewish religious communities; collaboration with Austrian Zionist organizations to mobilize forces for a joint campaign against antisemitism; the political and economic situation in Palestine in connection with Jewish emigration thereto; the holding of union meetings, admission of new members, and organizing of lectures and reports on the aims and goals of the union; financial issues, including the granting of credit and fundraising for elections and charitable purposes; the payment of membership dues; as well as the forwarding of announcements and material for the newspaper *Die Wahrheit* and subscriptions to it.

The collection also contains congratulatory letters and telegrams from various organizations and private individuals, including autograph letters of congratulation from R. N. Kudenhof and the Austrian rabbis D. Herzog, F. Kirein, and M. Grunwald on the occasion of the union's fiftieth anniversary; congratulatory letters to members of the union on the occasion of family celebrations, and letters of condolence on the deaths of relatives; lists and record cards of members of the union's executive committee and its local chapters; and the union's cashbook and logs of membership dues payments.

Also deposited in the collection are circulars on rules for electing boards of Jewish religious communities, and accounts of the activity of the Jewish religious community of Vienna for 1925–28. There are brochures, including *Festschrift zur Feier des 50 jährigen Bestandes des Union Österrreichischer Juden* (1937), and issues of the Jewish newspapers *Jüdische Welt, Jüdische Rundschau, Die Wahrheit*, and *Jüdische-liberale Zeitung*. There are also issues of the Nazi newspapers *National Zeitung* and *Reichspost*, and informational bulletins and journals.

The documents are in German.

Microfilms are held by the United States Holocaust Memorial Museum Archives.

Avstriiskii evreiskii molodezhnyi soiuz Berit Trumpel'dor (g. Vena)

Austrian Jewish Youth Association, *Brit Trumpeldor* (Vienna)

Fond 715k, 1929–1938. 45 storage units.

The Austrian section of Brit Joseph Trumpeldor (Betar) was founded in December 1926 as a branch of Betar, the international youth organization of Revisionist Zionists, headed from its inception by Vladimir Jabotinsky. Betar's ideology stressed that the only solution to the Jewish question was the creation of a Jewish state in Palestine on both banks of the Jordan River. Toward this end, they prepared for settlement activity and trained in the use of weapons to defend Jewish settlements in Palestine. The Austrian *ken* ("nest," the local Betar group) was headed by E. Wolf and Otto Seidmann. The Betar section in Graz, which is often mentioned in the collection's files, was led by B. Fleisig. The organization was of a paramilitary nature, structured on the principle of strict hierarchical subordination. An important aspect of Betar's activity in Austria was the creation of youth camps where organization members engaged in agricultural work and military training.

The collection's contents are described in one inventory arranged by document type.

The collection's documents include charters of the Austrian section of Brit Joseph Trumpeldor (Betar) and its local entities; correspondence of the central and local leadership, including correspondence with rank-and-file members; circulars, instructions, and orders on the conduct of internal organization and propaganda; and reports on work done.

A large portion of the documents comprises correspondence with Betar divisions in Germany, and also with other Zionist organizations: the Jewish Youth Front of Austria, the youth organization of the Jewish State Party, Keren Tel Chai, Brit Hakana'im ("The Union of Zealots"), Mizrachi of Austria, the Jewish academic organizations Bar-Giora and Caritas, the Revisionist Zionist Party, Betar Hatzair (Betar's wing for younger youth and children), Maccabee, Betar of Yugoslavia, Betar of Czechoslovakia, the Union of Jewish War Veterans, the Jewish National Youth Organization, the Revisionist Zionist Land Union, Hechalutz HaLeumi, Hechalutz Hatzioni Haklali, Chalutz Mizrachi, Brit Hahayal, Hakhshara Kibbutzit, the Jewish State Party of Brazil, the youth section Otzar Hanoar, the New

Zionist Organization, and Haganah. Included are lists of members of organizations and Betar documents on military training. The work of the summer camps is described in detail.

The documents are in German and Hebrew.

Microfilms are held by the United States Holocaust Memorial Museum Archives.

Sovet Evreiskogo bogoslovskogo uchebnogo zavedeniia (g. Vena)

Kuratorium der Israelitisch-Theologischen Lehranstalt (Wien)

Administration of the Israelite Theological Institute of Higher Learning (Vienna)*

Fond 717k, 1623–1938. 304 storage units.

The Israelite Theological Institute of Higher Learning of Vienna was founded in 1893 on the model of the Jewish Theological Seminary of Breslau (Wrocław). The institute trained rabbis and religious teachers for Jewish schools in Austria, the Czech and Moravian lands, and Galicia. The institute was financed by Jewish communities and the Austrian government. Subjects studied included Talmud, Bible and Biblical exegesis, Jewish history, Jewish religious philosophy, codes, *midrashim*, and others. Until 1931, its rector was Adolf Schwarz, and the institute was headed by a council (curatorium) of fifteen. The council supervised the educational process, oversaw the institute's finances, and worked on issues of graduates' job placement. Among the institute's teachers were the well-known scholars Abraham Büchler, Samuel Krauss, and Viktor Aptowitzer. The institute had an excellent library and published an annual bulletin, *Jahresbericht der Israelitisch-Theologischen Lehranstalt*, which published scholarly works by researchers and teachers. Among its graduates were Chanoch Albeck, Shalom Spiegel, and Salo W. Baron. The Israelite Theological Institute of Higher Learning of Vienna ceased to exist after the Nazi Anschluss of Austria in 1938.

The collection's contents are catalogued in three inventories, which are arranged by structure and theme.

The collection contains the charter of the Israelite Theological Institute of Higher Learning of Vienna, minutes of curatorium sessions for 1893–97, lists of students, student and employee questionnaires, graduate

---

*   The Israelite Theological Institute of Higher Learning manuscripts found in this collection are catalogued in *Manuscripts and Archival Documents of the Vienna Jewish Community Held in Russian Collections: Catalogue/ Rukopisi i arkhivnye dokumenty evreiskoi obshchiny goroda Veny v rossiiskikh sobraniiakh: Katalog* (Moscow: "Rudomino," 2006; All-Russian State Library for Foreign Literature).

certificates for 1894–1931, lists of graduates for 1893–1916, progress report registers for 1893–1927, courses of study, job descriptions of institute
teachers, and reports by members of the curatorium on the state of Jewish
education in various cities of Austria.

Institute financial accounting documents include annual reports for
1917–20, balance sheets for 1921–35, financial statements for 1893–1935,
and income statements for 1921–22.

The collection has the correspondence of the Israelite Theological
Institute of Higher Learning of Vienna with students regarding the subjects
of their written projects and admittance to exams; with teachers and employees on appointments to new positions and on everyday issues pertaining to their work; with lawyers on registering bequests to the institute by
deceased members of the Jewish religious community of Vienna; with leaders of the Jewish religious communities of Lvov, Berlin, and Prague on financial issues and on appointing rabbis to the cities of Austria-Hungary;
with the Viennese religious community on elections to the institute's curatorium, on holding joint events, and on the transfer of part of the manuscript
legacy of Simhah Pinsker to the institute library; with the Austrian Ministry
of Education and Culture on the publication of Dr. Abraham Weiss's book
on the history of Judaism; with the Vienna tax authority on the payment of
taxes; with the Jewish religious community of Lvov on establishing a seminary to train teachers for Jewish religious schools; with the Vienna magistrate on the Austrian Ministry of Education's granting of financial
subsidies to the institute; with the library of The Jewish Theological Seminary of New York; and with representatives of Jewish religious communities and private individuals on matters of book acquisitions.

Also deposited in the collection are numerous works on Jewish
history and the Jewish religion: Israel Weinstock's dissertation "Versuch
eines Grundrisses der Sozial- und Wirtschaftsgeschichte der Juden in
Mähren, von ihren Anfängen bis zum 17. Jahrhundert"; works by D. Kagan
on Jewish themes in nineteenth-century Polish literature; Astlen's *Oliver
Cromwell and the Jews*; I. Glitzenstein's economic history of the Jews of
Latvia in the seventeenth and eighteenth centuries; Bergenbaum's study of
Jewish colonies in Tsarist Russia; a study on Russian sources on the history
of the Khazars; Ch. Astel's study of Rashi as Grammarian; E. Deutsch's
study on the formation and development of Sabbath liturgy; an outline for
a work by Tenzler, "Moritz Lazarus als Jude"; a bibliography of works on
M. Lazarus; a notebook containing draft notes in preparation for a commentary on the text of the Hebrew Bible; a notebook containing excerpts

from Abraham Epstein's introduction to *Sefer Ha-Pardes* and A. Weiss's discourses and commentaries on Halakhah; M. Krieg's dissertation on the third and fourth parts of the treatise *Ikkarim* (1935); Sh. Lilienfeld's dissertation on Papal attitudes toward the Jews from Clement V to Gregory XI; B. Klar's work (1931) on Samuel Ibn Tibbon's translation of Saadia Gaon's *Sefer ha-Emunot ve-De'ot*; I. Heitner's commentary on Seder Nashim (1932); Dr. Sh. Lilienfeld's commentary on Midrash Bereshit Rabba (early 1930s); Aron Eisenstein's *Die Stellung der Juden in Polen im XIII. und XIV. Jahrhundert* (1930); the draft of a work (by Abraham Epstein?) on the history of the Jews during the Talmudic period; a notebook containing excerpts from *Shaar Hashamayim*; research (author unknown) on the grammatical structure of works by Abraham Ibn Ezra; a collection of 188 Jewish proverbs in Yiddish (Latin transliteration; in alphabetical order); an eighteenth-century Hebrew-Yiddish dictionary; and a list of Yiddish books in the library of Rabbi Adolf Jellinek.

Among Israelite Theological Institute of Higher Learning of Vienna library books are *Seder Korban Todah*, Mantua, 1623; a 1796 edition of Jacob ben Asher's treatise *Tur Hoshen Mishpat*; an 1802 edition of Joseph Caro's *Shulhan Arukh*; M. A. Ginsburg's *Dvir*; Abraham ben Chaim's commentary on Genesis (Salonika, 1826); A. Kristianpoller's collection of commentaries on the Book of Isaiah (Jerusalem, 1893); and issues of the journal *Zion* for 1840–41.

The collection also holds copies of manuscripts and historical documents including a seventeenth-century manuscript of Moshe Zakuto's commentary to the Zohar, written in Italian script; a notebook containing the general code of statutes (administrative, criminal-procedural, and commercial) in force with regard to Moravian Jewry starting in 1754 (in German, Hebrew script); fragments of responsa and Talmudic commentaries, Purimspiel verses, and songs; a homily by Abraham Ibn Ezra copied from a Bodleian Library manuscript; and fragments from *Pugio Fidei* in Hebrew.

The documents are in Hebrew, Yiddish, Aramaic, and German.

[Materials of this collection are deposited in Fond 707k, "Jewish Religious Community (Vienna)" and Fond 1326k, "Jewish Religious Community (Berlin)."]

Soiuz avstriiskikh sionistov (g. Vena)

Verband der Judenstaatszionisten Österreichs (Wien)

Union of Austrian Jewish State Zionists (Vienna)

Fond 727k, 1915–1938. 11 storage units.

The Union of Austrian Jewish State Zionists was the Austrian branch of the Jewish State Party (JSP). In 1933, criticism of Vladimir Jabotinsky gave rise to a schism in the Revisionist Zionist movement. Within the World Zionist Organization, the JSP represented the wing of radical Zionists opposed to Jabotinsky's revisionism. It rejected the plan for the partition of Palestine proposed in 1937 by the Peel Commission. Headed by M. Grossman, the party in 1938 numbered 8,000 members. Its most outstanding leader in Austria was Robert Stricker. The Union of Austrian Jewish State Zionists published an informational bulletin and the newspaper *Die Neue Welt*. It included the youth movement Brit Hakana'im ("The Union of Zealots"), which split from the Revisionist Betar in 1933, and was led by J. Kagan.

The collection's contents are catalogued in one inventory arranged by document type.

This collection houses a range of heterogeneous materials of various Zionist entities. Most of the materials do not relate directly to the Union of Austrian of Jewish State Zionists, whose records are contained in Fond 1193k below ("Austrian Organization of the Jewish State Party").

The collection contains the Jewish State Party platform; an informational letter explaining the Zionist educational program of the Brit Hakana'im organization; platforms of the American Jewish Congress (AJC); reports on the activities of the WZO for 1934 and of the Graz branch of the Women's International Zionist Organization (WIZO); minutes of meetings of the executive committee of the Zionist Organization of Holland (March 1916) and informational bulletins of the Copenhagen bureau of the Zionist Organization for 1915–17; an informational circular of the Hashomer Hatzair movement in Austria (1937); a circular of the central bureau of Jewish Agricultural Aid Societies (1933); a 1937 financial statement and a list of members (as of March 1938) of the Graz Chevra Kadisha burial society; annual reports for 1934–37, a financial statement, and a list of members (about 300) of the Graz Women's Zionist Organization (1937); lists of members of various Zionist groups in Graz; the 17th Zionist Congress (Lucerne) attendee identification of D. Grünschlag; the draft of an article (author unknown) entitled "Why We're Going to the Moshav"; the text of H. Schwarz's report "The Tactics of the World Zionist Organization" (Graz, January 1935); materials on the holding of a Zionist conference in Warsaw (13–15 September 1916) and on instances of aid to Jewish settlements in Palestine; an article on the functioning of the Brit Hakana'im summer camp; and the case file regarding union members Schwarz and Goldman, accused of personally insulting M. Later.

The collection also contains printed materials: two issues of Brit Hakana'im's journal *Haruah Hahadasha* (for April 1936 and January 1938); periodicals, including issues of the newspapers *Die Neue Zeit* (1918), *Die Stimme* (1928), *Die Wahrheit* (1938), *La Rassegna Mensile di Israel* (1935); an issue of the *Karnenu* (1937); and various Zionist pamphlets.

The documents are in German, Danish, and Hebrew.

Microfilms are held by the United States Holocaust Memorial Museum Archives.

Avstriiskii soiuz evreiskikh legitimistov (g. Vena)

Verband der jüdischen Legitimisten Österrreichs

Union of Austrian Jewish Legitimists (Vienna)

Fond 1189k, 1930–1938. 55 storage units.

The Union of Austrian Jewish Legitimists was an organization of Austrian Jewish supporters of constitutional monarchy in Austria, who called for remaining loyal to the Habsburg dynasty and to Crown Prince Otto von Habsburg. The organization collaborated with the Iron Ring, the Austrian association of legitimist parties and unions. From 1935 on, the union was part of the Fatherland's Front. Together with the Imperial Union of Austrians and other organizations, the Union of Austrian Jewish Legitimists came out in early 1938 against Germany's Anschluss of Austria. The organization was disbanded by the Nazis in March of that year.

The collection's contents are catalogued in two inventories arranged by structure.

The collection contains materials connected with the activities of the Union of Austrian Jewish Legitimists, its board, and departments: the youth group, the Legitimist Union of Jewish Women, the Legitimist Jewish War Veterans organization, and the editorial office of the newspaper *Legitimist*, the organ of the Union of Austrian Jewish Legimitists.

Deposited in the collection are charter documents; minutes of general assemblies of the union and of meetings of its board; correspondence with affiliated Jewish organizations and with organizations of war veterans and other organizations; financial documentation; as well as lists, photo albums, and the like.

The documents are in German.

Microfilms are held by the United States Holocaust Memorial Museum Archives.

Soiuz evreiskikh kuptsov i remeslennikov (g. Vena)

Verband jüdischer Kaufleute und Handwerker (Wien)

Union of Jewish Merchants and Manufacturers (Vienna)

Fond 1191k, 1928–1935. 13 storage units.

The Union of Jewish Merchants and Manufacturers was founded in 1928 with the aim of coordinating the Austrian Jewish business community's efforts in various areas of the economy and public life. Unaffiliated with any political party, the union called for unity among Austrian Jewry, believing that, given the frequent economic crises and increasing nationalist tendencies in the economy, only broad cooperation could keep Jewish manufacturers and distributors from ruin. In 1934, the Yad Harutzim (Hand of the Diligent) Society of Jewish Craftsmen, founded in 1908, joined the union on an autonomous basis. The union published the journal *Die Wirtschaft*; its chairmen were Joseph Jolles and A. Taub. The organization's activities ceased after the Nazi Anschluss of Austria.

The collection's contents are described in one inventory.

The documents comprise minutes of meetings of the Union of Jewish Merchants and Manufacturers of Vienna; minutes of meetings of the board of the officers' assembly and of the general assembly of this organization; as well as bills, receipts (including receipts for funds received), and other financial documents.

The collection consists largely of the union's correspondence: with individuals regarding their admission to the union; with the Vienna magistrate and police department regarding publication of the union's journal *Die Wirtschaft*; with the presidium of the Jewish religious community of Vienna on joint statistical works; with Robert Stricker regarding a mutual loan society to have been organized by the union; with the bureau of the Levant Fair in Tel Aviv and its representative in Vienna, B. Rabinovich, on preparations for the 1932 Fair; with the Austrian Museum of Trade on coordinating efforts with regard to foreign commerce; with the board of the Jewish religious community of Vienna regarding a meeting of the board of the community-organized pawnshop; with Austrian chancellor von Schuschnigg on the assassination of chancellor Engelbert Dollfuss; with

Desider Friedmann on his election to the Austrian State Council; and with the Yad Harutzim Society of Jewish Craftsmen regarding its members' joining the Union of Jewish Merchants and Craftsmen.

The collection also holds questionnaires about union members' professions; issues of the Vienna commercial and industrial newspaper and of the Czechoslovakian economic bulletin *Vestnik*; and informational bulletins of the Austrian Chamber of Exports.

The documents are in German.

Microfilms are held by the United States Holocaust Memorial Museum Archives.

Zhenskaia sionistskaia organizatsiia Avstrii (g. Vena)

Organisation "Zionistische Frauen Österreichs"

Women's Zionist Organization of Austria (Vienna)

Fond 1192k, 1898–1938. 26 storage units.

The Women's Zionist Organization of Austria was established in 1898; in 1920, it became the Austrian branch of the Women's International Zionist Organization (WIZO). The organization's primary goals included dissemination of Zionist information, educational work among Jewish women, and fundraising in support of Jewish settlers in Palestine. In the 1930s, the organization was led by Sophie Löwenherz. The organization had commissions on propaganda, culture, Keren Hanashim (the women's fund), the Keren Kayemeth LeIsrael fund, Totzeret Haaretz, youth affairs, and kibbutzim, as well as an economics section. There were three regional groups of WIZO in Austria in the 1920s and 1930s.

The collection's contents are catalogued in one inventory. The inventory is arranged by document type. There is a geographical index to the collection's contents.

Documents of the Women's Zionist Organization of Austria include charters of the organization; minutes of meetings of its assembly, board, and district councils; platforms, accounts of activities, reports, and lists of members (in Vienna, Innsbruck, and Graz); as well as bulletins, pamphlets, newspaper clippings, and copies of books and articles. There is also a notebook containing addresses of Zionists in Vienna (1920s–30s); a collection of quotations and passages from works by Zionist theoreticians (Theodore Herzl, Moses Hess) on women's issues and the role of the mother in Jewish tradition and culture; an appeal by the Women's Zionist Organization of Vienna to the Jewish women of Vienna encouraging them to join the organization; an application form to join the Women's Zionist Organization; and correspondence with other Zionist organizations.

The documents are in German.

Microfilms are held by the United States Holocaust Memorial Museum Archives.

Avstriiskaia organizatsiia Evreiskoi gosudarstvennoi partii (g. Vena)

Austrian Organization of the Jewish State Party (Vienna)

Fond 1193k, 1920–1938. 72 storage units.

The Union of Austrian Jewish State Zionists was the Austrian branch of the Jewish State Party (JSP). In 1933, criticism of Vladimir Jabotinsky gave rise to a schism in the Revisionist Zionist movement. Within the World Zionist Organization, the JSP represented the wing of radical Zionists opposed to Jabotinsky's revisionism. It rejected the plan for the partition of Palestine proposed in 1937 by the Peel Commission. Headed by M. Grossman; the party in 1938 numbered 8,000 members. Its most outstanding leader in Austria was Robert Stricker. The Union of Austrian Jewish State Zionists published an informational bulletin and the newspaper *Die Neue Welt*. It included the youth movement Brit Hakana'im ("The Union of Zealots"), which split from the Revisionist Betar in 1933, and was led by J. Kagan.

The collection's contents are described in one inventory in two parts. The first part of the inventory, organized by theme, has the following sections: "Governing organs," "Materials inherited from an earlier organization," "The editorial office of the newspaper *Die Neue Welt*," "The Party Court," "The Youth Group," "The Jewish People's Union," and "Printed Materials." The second part of the inventory is arranged by document type and contains foundational documents, minutes of meetings, reports, correspondence, and printed materials.

The collection's contents illustrate the history of the JSP's founding (an announcement on the Revisionist Zionists' schism and the declaration of the founding of the JSP, 1933) and various aspects of the activities of the party's organizational committee: minutes of meetings 1933–36; minutes and resolutions of party conferences; as well as materials on the JSP's preparations for taking part in the 19th Zionist Congress; on coordinating efforts with regional party branches in Poland, Romania, Czechoslovakia, Latvia, Lithuania, and elsewhere; and on interaction with the party's executive committee in Tel Aviv. The collection has materials on the activities of Zionist youth groups such as the Union of Zionist Democratic Youth, Brit Hakana'im, and the Hakoah and Maccabee sports clubs. Also deposited in the collection are materials on the work of the editorial office of the party's newspaper, *Die Neue Welt*: correspondence of the editorial office and its editor in chief, Robert Stricker, with various correspondents; manuscripts of articles; and clippings from the journal.

There are minutes of the JSP council from 25 December 1933 and 16 February 1936; minutes of the first session of the JSP's political commission (24 December 1933); lists of members of the Leopoldstadt district council of the JSP; a resolution (8 January 1936) of the Union of Zionist Organizations of Austria against British policy in Mandatorial Palestine; a joint proclamation to the Jews of Austria by the Union of Austrian Zionists, the organization Binyan Haaretz, the JSP, the Union of Revisionist Zionists of Austria, and the Austrian section of the Mizrachi party of religious Zionists against British policy in Palestine; and election commission instructions on selecting delegates to the 19th Zionist Congress.

The collection contains correspondence, arranged in alphabetical order, between the JSP secretariat in Vienna and various organizations and private individuals. Among the latter, the following are noteworthy: correspondence with the bureau of the 19th Zionist Congress in Lucerne (July 1935); with Keren Hayesod and Keren Kayemeth LeIsrael (1935); with the editors of the bulletin *Mizrachi* (1935); with the Maccabi World Union on the organizing of the Maccabiah Games (February–March 1935); and with the Austrian Zionist Committee (1934), the Union of Revisionist Zionists of Austria (1934), and JSP branches in Bessarabia, New York, and elsewhere. The collection also contains correspondence by Robert Stricker regarding JSP tactics and various current issues (1936–38). These include a letter by David Ben-Gurion (dated 21 November 1935) to Robert Stricker on WZO tactics and letters by Vladimir Jabotinsky to Stricker during the years 1933–35.

The collection contains a list of JSP faction members from various countries (F. Rosenstein, R. Stricker, J. Machover, S. Soskin, F. Sborowitz, et al.) and a summary of T. Grubner's report at the 19th Zionist Congress.

The documents are in German, Hebrew, Yiddish, and English.

Microfilms are held by the United States Holocaust Memorial Museum Archives.

Soiuz evreiskikh gumanitarnykh ob"edinenii Avstrii ordena "Bnei-Brit" i ego mestnye organizatsii

Union of Jewish Humanitarian Associations B'nai B'rith of Austria

Fond 1221k, 1919–1938. 97 storage units.

The Independent Order of B'nai B'rith (Sons of the Covenant) was established in New York in 1843 by a group of German Jews headed by Henry Jones. B'nai B'rith was established to help raise the moral, spiritual, and social level of Jews, espousing philanthropy, charity, and fraternity. The order was free of any particular political or religious ideology. To administer its affairs, a charter was drawn up and, in 1851, the first Grand Lodge was established in New York.

B'nai B'rith of Austria was founded in 1894 and designated District no. 10 of the International Order of B'nai B'rith. Its jurisdiction comprised the entire Habsburg Empire, including the lodges of Moravia and Galicia. After the First World War, B'nai B'rith was structurally reorganized to match Europe's new territorial divisions: District 10 became the Federation of B'nai B'rith of Czechoslovakia, while District 12 was created in Austria under the leadership of S. Ehrmann. Officially named "Verband der Israelitischer Humanitäts-Vereine B'nai B'rith für Österrreich," the B'nai B'rith union in Austria numbered six lodges with 862 members in 1932. It published a bulletin *Bnai Brith Mitteilungen für Österreich*, edited by Dr. Arnold Ascher.

The collection's contents are described in one inventory, in which documents are catalogued by type.

The collection contains documents on the organizational, publication, and financial activities of B'nai B'rith. Among materials on the activities of the general committee are the bylaws of the "Union of Jewish Humanitarian Associations B'nai B'rith" (1928), minutes of union meetings for 1928–34, and documents on admitting new members into the organization.

The collection also houses directories of Austrian lodges of B'nai B'rith and their personnel, as well as lists of members of lodges in Austria and a 1932 address book of members who served on the library committee, the finance committee, the propaganda committee, and the art committee. Also included are accounts of the union's financial activities for 1919–34, including the union cashbook for 1928–34. Also deposited in the collection are the bylaws of the Graz lodge for 1928–30, as well as minutes of Graz lodge meetings for 1928–37; accounts of financial and publication activities of the Graz lodge for 1928–37; information on the financial and publication activities of the Vienna lodge, the "Wahrheit" lodge (Vienna); lists of members of the Graz lodge for 1928–33; and an account of the activities of the Graz lodge by its secretary, Bernhard Biller. There are lists of members of the "Wahrheit" lodge (Vienna) for 1924–35; correspondence (1928–37) of the Graz lodge with Jewish lodges in Czechoslovakia, Austria, Zagreb, and Troppau regarding personnel changes, the holding of conferences, the election of lodge officers, and the financing of Jewish hospitals and schools in Europe and of Jewish schools in Palestine; instructions on the duties of Graz lodge officers; and personal files of its members (1928–34).

The documents are in German.

Microfilms are held by the United States Holocaust Memorial Museum Archives.

Mestnaia gruppa Zhenskoi sionistskoi organizatsii Avstrii (g. Grats)

Organisation "Zionistische Frauen Österreichs" Ortsgruppe Graz

Women's Zionist Organization of Austria, Graz Chapter (Graz)

Fond 1245k, 1929–1938. 8 storage units.

The Women's Zionist Organization of Austria was established in 1898; in 1920, it became the Austrian branch of the Women's International Zionist Organization (WIZO). The organization's primary goals included dissemination of Zionist information, educational work among Jewish women, and fundraising in support of Jewish settlers in Palestine. In the 1930s, the organization was headed by Sophie Löwenherz. The organization had commissions on information, culture, Keren Hanashim (the women's fund), the Keren Kayemet Leyisrael fund, Totzeret Haaretz, youth affairs, kibbutzim, and an economics section. There were three regional groups of WIZO in Austria in the 1920s–30s — among them, one in Graz.

The collection's contents are catalogued in one inventory. The inventory is arranged by document type.

The collection includes the organization's charter (1937), minutes of meetings of its executive committee for 1936–37, minutes of the organization's general assembly for 1938, membership cards, and applications for membership in the organization.

The collection contains correspondence with the leaders of the Women's Zionist Organization of Austria (Vienna), with the chairman of the Hakoah sports club, and with the local Graz chapter of the Union of Jewish War Veterans, on organizing the women's movement among the Jewish population, on relations with international Jewish organizations, on propaganda work, on reports, on admission of new members, and on the awarding of honorary titles.

The collection contains official and financial documents: a message to the Graz police department on the makeup of the organization's executive committee elected by the constituent assembly (7 December 1936), and financial statements and lists of members for 1933 and 1936. It also holds reports on sessions of the World Conference of Jewish Women in

Hamburg and the Jubilee Conference of the Jewish Women's League in Berlin, and a draft resolution on antisemitism by the Jewish Women's League delegation to the 25th World Pacifist Congress (Berlin, 1929).

The documents are in German.

Evreiskoe bogoslovskoe uchilishche "Bet kha-midrash" (g. Vena)

Beth Hamidrash (Vienna)

Fond 1273k, 1726–1892. 15 storage units.

"Beth Hamidrash lilmod ve-lelamed" was opened at the initiative of Rabbi Adolf Jellinek in 1862 in the new synagogue building in Vienna's Leopoldstadt district. The Beth Hamidrash trained teachers of Jewish religion for state schools in Austria, Bohemia, and Moravia. Its instructors included the well-known Talmudists Isaac Hirsch Weiss and Joseph Samuel Bloch. Although the Beth Hamidrash did not confer the title of rabbi upon graduates, for many students in upper classes of gymnasiums wishing to become rabbis, the Beth Hamidrash was an important educational step on the way to this goal. The Beth Hamidrash's best-known graduate was Solomon Schechter, one of the greatest Hebraists of the late nineteenth and early twentieth centuries.

The collection's contents are described in one inventory. The documents are catalogued chronologically.

Deposited in the collection are a transcription of sermons by Abraham Geiger; manuscripts of studies by Prof. M. Lazarus (1891–92) and Meir Friedmann; commentaries on the Hebrew Bible (late nineteenth century); a study of the origin of traditions regarding Abraham, Isaac, and Jacob (late nineteenth century); the play '*Ahavah koveshet kesilut, o 'ahavah meviah le-hokhmah* (1726); and H. Englander's textbook of Hebrew.

The documents are in Hebrew and German. ·

INDIVIDUALS

Alfred Israel Grotte

Fond 608k, 1857–1940. 23 storage units.

Alfred Israel Grotte was born in 1872 in Prague. In 1897, he graduated the Vienna Technical School. A professor at the Academy of Architecture in Breslau, Grotte was a scholar whose main research interests were the design features of synagogue architecture and Jewish tombstones. In 1914, Grotte received his doctoral degree from the Imperial Technical Academy in Danzig with the dissertation *Deutsche, böhmische und polnische Synagogentypen vom XI. bis Anfang des XIX. Jahrhunderts*. His later works include *Alte schlesische Judenfriedhöfe* (1927) and *Synagogenspuren in schlesischen Kirchen* (1937). In addition, Grotte was himself an architect; synagogues were built in Tachau and Pinne according to his designs.

The collection's contents are catalogued in two inventories; the inventories are arranged by theme.

The collection contains personal documents of Alfred Grotte: his family tree; his notebook; correspondence with family members and members of the Mayer family on personal matters, and with regard to drawing up Grotte and Mayer family trees. Other materials include Grotte's guest book for 1914–39 and his sketchbook.

The collection contains rough drafts of works by Grotte, as well as a number of his articles: "Zur Genealogie der Familie Grotte," "Jakob Hermann Mayer von Kuttenplan," "Old Synagogues of Galicia," "A Document of Stone and Cement," "The Significance for Science of Excavations of Galilean Synagogues," "The Excavation of a Medieval Synagogue in Breslau," and others.

The collection also includes documents collected by Grotte: photographs of Jewish cultural figures and of architectural monuments in Jewish shtetls; photocopies of manuscripts and landmarks of Jewish culture; articles from the journal *Breslauer Jüdisches Gemeindeblatt* on Jewish history; and an inventory of items found during excavations in the Valley of the Kings.

Documents in file 130 of Fond 1326 (the Jewish Community of Berlin) relate thematically to Grotte. There are 196 photographs and illustrations, which are bound in the file. These include views of Jewish towns in Bohemia, and also of Breslau, Poznan, Lvov, Glogau, Kurnik, Floss, and other communities. There are separate photos of the interior décor of synagogues and yeshivas, as well as of synagogue implements. It is possible that the photographs were systematized by the professor. Most of the inscriptions on them contain information on the date of construction (in the case of synagogues) and the object's location.

The collection also includes images of eighteenth-century wooden synagogues in Eastern European shtetls. Also deposited in the collection are numerous illustrations: photographs of members of Grotte's family and his personally thematized selections of photographs. These latter include photographs of Jewish religious and public leaders, of inhabitants of Eastern European Jewish shtetls and landmarks of Jewish wooden architecture, and photographic copies of medieval Jewish manuscripts. Most of these were catalogued by Grotte.

The documents are in German, Polish, and Hebrew.

Gertsog David, semitolog, professor universiteta v g. Gratse, chlen soveta ravvinov evreiskoi obshchiny v g. Gratse

David Herzog

Fond 1204k, 1810–1938. 30 storage units.

David Herzog (1869–1946) received his rabbinical ordination in Berlin and his doctoral degree at Leipzig. In 1908, he became the rabbi of Graz. During the First World War, he served as a chaplain in the Austrian Army, and in 1925 was named Landesrabbiner of Styria and Carinthia. Beginning in 1909, Herzog taught Semitic languages (Hebrew, Arabic, and Aramaic) and classical Jewish texts at Karl-Franzens University in Graz. After the Anschluss, in April 1938, he was expelled from the ranks of university teachers. In November 1938, his house was attacked during an anti-Jewish pogrom in Graz, and Herzog subsequently emigrated to England.

The collection's contents are catalogued in one inventory. The inventory is arranged by theme.

These documents were collected and systematized by David Herzog. They include his correspondence with publishing houses, editorial offices of journals, and various persons regarding the publication of his articles; with the Union of American Hebrew Congregations in Cincinnati, The Jewish Theological Seminary of America in New York, the Society for the Advancement of Jewish Scholarship (Gesellschaft zur Förderung der Wissenschaft des Judentums) in Berlin, and other Jewish organizations regarding his philological and publishing activities; and correspondence with the editorial offices of the journals *Monatschrift für Geschichte und Wissenschaft des Judentums* (Berlin), *Judaica* (Berlin), and *Zeitschrift für die Geschichte der Juden in der Tschechoslowakei* (Prague) regarding their publication of Herzog's works.

There are items of correspondence with Jewish educational institutions and libraries, including The Jewish Theological Seminary of America, Hebrew Union College (Cincinnati), the library of Hebrew University in Jerusalem, and the library of the Jewish religious community of Vienna on matters of book lending, as well as on issues of Jewish history, religion, and culture; and also with leaders of the Jewish community of Graz on the functioning of the Jewish community of that city — also discussed is the issue of preserving the archive of the community's vital records.

The collection also contains Herzog's scholarly monograph *Beitrage zur Geschichte der Juden in der Steiermark* (1936) and manuscripts of the texts of his sermons. The collection also houses a listing of Herzog's published works prepared for the biographical handbook *Wer ist wer in Österreich*; a letter from the president of the Jewish religious community of Graz to Herzog congratulating him on the thirtieth anniversary of his rabbinical career and the payment of his fees.

The collection also contains materials of the Jewish society to aid the poor "Matnot Aniyim" in Graz — including the society's cashbook for 1929–33, stubs of receipts for grants issued to the poor in Graz for 1937, information on taxes for 1931, David Herzog's report on fifty years of the society's activity (1881–1931), and lists of the society's members.

The collection also contains materials of the International Order of B'nai B'rith, including a report on meetings of the Graz B'nai B'rith lodge; address books of the lodges *Bohemia* and *Prague*; the bulletins *Der Orden Bne Briss: Mitteilungen der Großloge für Deutschland* for 1925 and *Bnai Brith Mitteilungen für Österreich* for 1936–37; and pamphlets of B'nai B'rith and other Jewish organizations. Also included are the bulletin of the Austrian section of the Jewish National Fund for 1937, and the bulletin of the Zionist Organization of Vienna for 1937.

The documents are in German, English, and Hebrew.

III

FRANCE

ORGANIZATIONS

Assotsiatsiia pol'skikh evreev vo Frantsii (g. Parizh)

L'association des juifs polonaise en France

Association of Polish Jews in France (Paris)

Fond 45k, 1938–1940. 17 storage units.

The Association of Polish Jews in France was established in 1933. The organization's goal was to unite Polish-Jewish immigrants to France. Tasks taken up by the association included providing material and legal aid to Polish Jewish immigrants and sponsoring Jewish soldiers who served in the Polish Army in France. The association published a weekly in Yiddish, *Di vokh*, in 1939–40.

The collection's contents are described in one inventory. The documents are catalogued by type.

Featured among the collection's documents are reports on association activities for 1933–40, as well as reports of the constituent session of the association's finance commission for 28 November 1939; minutes of the general assembly of association members from 4 February 1940; lists of members of the Association of Polish Jews in France; association membership application forms; cashbooks for September 1939–April 1940; as well as correspondence with the Polish Consulate General in Paris and with Polish Jews on the issuance of passports and identification cards to the latter, on improving their material situation and providing legal aid, and on arranging support for Jewish soldiers. Also included among the collection's documents is the text of instructions for carrying out the law of the German occupation authorities in Poland on compulsory labor conscription of the Jewish population.

The documents are in French, Yiddish, German, and Polish.

Microfilms are held by the United States Holocaust Memorial Museum Archives.

INDIVIDUALS

Simon Leo, evreiskii zhurnalist, obshchestvennyi deiatel', nemetskii emigrant vo Frantsii

Leo Simon

Fond 642k, 1890–1939. 39 storage units.

Leo Simon (1870–1940) owned the large Pomeranian metalworks Dübelwerke until 1933. In 1933, he emigrated to France, were he worked actively with the Jewish Agency and the Jewish emigration and colonization association "Eshkol."

The collection's contents are catalogued in one inventory. The inventory is arranged by theme.

These materials were collected and systematized by Leo Simon and include his personal documents (notebooks, a copy of his citizenship application to the French Minister of Justice, and others).

The collection contains primarily documents from Simon's years in France. It includes his correspondence: with the Jewish emigration and colonization association Eshkol and the Jewish Agency in Paris, with WZO leaders David Ben-Gurion and Chaim Weizmann, as well as with Goldsmith, B. Gurevich, the economist Neimann, the lawyer Kunzer, the banker Hirsch, and other individuals, on Jewish emigration, on the activities and economic situation of Jewish emigration organizations, on the economic and political situation of Jews in the United States, Palestine, and France, and on organizing aid to Jewish refugees in Poland and Romania. There are letters to N. Rothschild, P. Renault, and Felix Warburg on financial and political-economic aspects of the Palestine issue, and letters to Professor Lichtenberger and the journalist d'Ormesson thanking them for their help with the Zionist movement;

The collection also contains documents on the activities of Jewish organizations and on the situation of Jews in Germany and other countries: accounts and resolutions of a conference of the Joint Distribution Committee, and reports by delegates; a draft plan for the publication of a Jewish émigré newspaper in Paris; information on the economic and political situation of Jews in Syria and Lebanon; and printed publications collected by Simon. Other documents include Simon's articles "The Role and Tasks of Judaism in Modern Conditions," "On Jewish Colonization in the Southwestern Departments of France," "Jews and Arabs," and "A Draft Arab-Jewish Friendship Pact."

The documents are in French and German.

Tal'geimer Zigfrid – izdatel' sionistskogo zhurnala "Ordo" v Germanii

Siegfried Thalheimer

Fond 646k, 1916–1941. 92 storage units.

Siegfried Thalheimer (1899–1981) published the daily newspaper *Düsseldorfer Lokalzeitung* during the period 1928–33. After emigrating to France in 1933, he edited the independent German-language Paris weekly *Westland* in 1933–34. In 1938, he edited the Jewish German-language journal *Ordo*, published in Paris. Eleven issues were published between 1 April and 15 October 1938. *Ordo* was published for the purpose of disseminating information on Jews and Jewry, as well as "to aid in understanding the essence of the Jewish question." The journal supported the Zionist program of Jewish colonization of Palestine and summoned Jews to active struggle against Nazi persecution. At the same time, many Zionist leaders came in for criticism in its pages for insufficient decisiveness in the fight against Nazism and for pursuing partisan interests. Contributions to the work of the journal were also made by University of Frankfurt sociology professor Gottfried Salomon, president of the Jewish Committee for Political Research, and by H. Hirsch, secretary of this committee. The journal was closed in early 1939.

The collection's contents are catalogued in two inventories. The inventories are arranged by theme.

The collection was systematized by Thalheimer himself, and contains mainly documents that he collected during his years in France. It include documents on the activity of the Zionist movement: the program of the Zionist movement drawn up by the permanent committee of the Zionist Congress (1924), the platform of the Jewish State Party (1933), a report of the executive committee of the 20th Zionist Congress in Zurich (1937), as well as minutes of meetings of the permanent presidium of the Zionist Congress (1938), and of the Committee to Aid Jewish Settlers in Palestine (1938). It also contains a report on the work of the World Jewish Congress in Geneva (1936).

The collection contains Thalheimer's correspondence, including correspondence with Jewish organizations in the Netherlands on a trip by their members to Palestine (1939), letters to the American Chamber of Commerce urging support for plans to create a Jewish state in Palestine, and correspondence with the Jewish Committee for Political Research in Paris and with Zionist organizations in France.

There are documents on Thalheimer's activities as publisher of the journal *Ordo*: correspondence with political figures, journalists, and private individuals on publishing activities and on financial and personal matters (1935–39); bank documents on the publishing house's bank account; and lists of subscribers to the journal *Ordo* (1938–39).

The collection contains articles and reports on the situation of Jews in the Saar, Tsarist Russia, and countries of Europe, Asia, and America, and on the creation and political structure of a future Jewish state; an outline of the book *The Jewish Revolution*, and chapters from the book on the situation of Jews in Germany; issues of the journal *Ordo* (1938) and of other periodicals; and informational bulletins of Zionist organizations.

There are documents of a personal nature: a passport, personal identification documents, notebooks, personal correspondence, and photographs of Thalheimer and his family.

The documents are in German, French, and English.

IV

GERMANY

ORGANIZATIONS

Ob"edinenie "neariiskikh khristian" (g. Berlin)

Paulus-Bund Vereinigung nichtarischer Christen (Berlin)

St. Paul Alliance of Non-Aryan Christians (Berlin)

Fond 565k, 1927–1939. 11 storage units.

The "Reich League of Christian-German State Citizens of non-Aryan or not Completely Aryan Origins" (Reichsverband christlich-deutscher Staatsbürger nichtarischer oder nicht rein arischer Abstammung) was founded in July 1933, and was renamed the "Reich League of Non-Aryan Christians" in 1934. In September 1936, the group adopted the name Paulus-Bund, Vereinigung nichtarischer Christen, the appellation by which it was most popularly known.

    The organization consisted of persons of ethnically mixed German-Jewish origin, and of Jewish- origin persons, who had accepted the Evangelical faith. Following the September 1935 adoption of the Nuremburg laws regarding persons of "non-Aryan origin," a policy of social segregation and isolation by "race" was consistently enforced vis-à-vis persons of such origin. The St. Paul Alliance of Non-Aryan Christians published a monthly newsletter, sponsored mutual aid among its members, and petitioned the Nazi authorities on their behalf for job placement, education, and other matters. It undertook efforts to settle its members in the former German South West Africa and in Latin America (primarily Brazil and Ecuador). The organization was dissolved by governmental decree on 10 August 1939.

    The collection's contents are described in one inventory, to which there is a geographical index. Certain documents catalogued in inventory no. 1 were transferred to the German Democratic Republic in 1957.

The collection contains Alliance correspondence with Nazi German authorities defending the rights of "non-Aryan Christians," as well as correspondence with members of the organization on helping them find work, matriculate in programs of study, and travel abroad.

The documents are in German and English.

Berlinskoe sionistskoe ob"edinenie

Berliner zionistische Vereinigung

Berlin Zionist Union*

Fond 713k, 1915–1938. 33 storage units.

The Berlin Zionist Union (BZU), a local chapter of the Zionist Federation of Germany, was founded in 1897 at the initiative of Heinrich Löwe. According to its charter, the BZU aimed to support the creation of a Jewish national home in Palestine. The union sought to assist in the settlement of Palestine, strengthen Jewish national self-consciousness, and propagate Zionist ideology in Germany. Membership in the BZU was open to any Jew who in his or her application indicated agreement with the basic principles of the Basel Platform. The BZU was led by a board, composed of a chairman and between five and seven board members and elected by a delegate assembly (Vertretersammlung). Together with the delegate assembly, the board decided the personal composition of the finance committee, the Palestine committee, the committee on the Hebrew language and cultural work, the propaganda committee, the committee on work with Jews from the countries of the East, and the committee on youth work. The BZU was reorganized in 1932. The union was led in the interwar period by B. Cohen, S. Chertok, and A. Schwarz. It published the weekly newspaper, *Nachrichtenblatt der BZU* (1922), and the weekly *Berliner Jüdische Zeitung* (1929–30). The BZU was disbanded in 1938 soon after Kristallnacht.

    The collection's contents are catalogued in one inventory; the inventory is arranged by document type.

    The collection includes the charter of the BZU; minutes of meetings of the BZU board for 1937; minutes of sessions of electoral caucuses, and materials on the election of delegates to the delegate assembly; minutes of the 1936 twenty-fifth congress of the Zionist Federation of Germany; minutes of pre-election meetings of BZU members for 1938; circulars on

---

* A finding aid to this collection is available at http://www.sonderarchiv.de/fonds/fond 0713.pdf.

admitting new members and on improving the work of Hebrew language courses; membership cards; and instruction booklets for new members. There is also a report of the editorial board of the newspaper *Jüdische Rundschau* for 1938.

The collection contains BZU financial documents: balance sheets for 1930–38; statements of membership dues paid, income statements, and logs of dues-paying members for 1936–38; resolutions of the finance commission regarding property issues; a financial statement of the Zionist newspaper/organ *Jüdische Rundschau* from 9 November 1938.

The collection contains extensive correspondence of the BZU during the period 1915–39: with the Keren Kayemeth LeIsrael office in Tel Aviv on BZU participation in the fund; with the Zionist Federation of Germany and with BZU members on aiding their emigration to Palestine; and with the Youth Aliyah organization, other Zionist organizations and publishing houses, and union members, on organizational and financial issues. Letters deal with the Berlin Jewish community's orphanage in Pankow, and with providing assistance in obtaining entry visas to Palestine, publishing and disseminating Zionist literature, organizing lectures and reports, and admitting new members.

Materials of the BZU youth movement include information on the number and age structure of youth groups, on their financing, and on events held by them; the program of a BZU educational seminar that took place 21–27 October 1935; documents on teaching in BZU groups, including the BZU cultural work committee's circular no. 1 (6 August 1937), "On work toward the propagation of the Hebrew language"; a report, marked "confidential," on a joint meeting of representatives of the Jewish community of Berlin and representatives of the BZU on transferring BZU courses to the jurisdiction of the Jewish community in connection with the Nazi authorities' demand that some BZU courses be shut down (7 April 1937); an undated note on the budget of BZU courses, and containing information on 42 courses, 14 teachers, and 340 students; and a report by the board of the Culture Center for Jewish Youth in Germany to the Reich Representation of Jews in Germany on the state of, and programs in, Jewish youth education.

The collection also contains miscellaneous Zionist documents: a report on the work of Keren Kayemeth LeIsrael for 1930 and documents of Zionist congresses, assemblies, and conferences. These include a bulletin, "On Measures in Preparation for the 19th Zionist Congress" (30 April 1935), issued by the central bureau of the World Zionist Organization

(WZO) in London, and regulations on holding elections for delegates to the congress; instructions on the election of delegates to the 20th Zionist Congress; documents of the German Zionist Congress of 1936 (attendee reports and minutes); a report by David Ben-Gurion at a meeting of the WZO executive committee on the commencement of activities by the British Royal Commission in Palestine (1937); and indexes to the record-keeping and archival documents of the Zionist Organization in Germany. It also contains a report on the activities of the Vienna chapter of Agudath Israel for the period of 10 May–31 December 1938.

There is also correspondence of unrelated provenance, by University of Berlin librarian H. Löwe with Jewish book publishers, institutions, parties, and private individuals on matters of book acquisitions.

The collection also has printed materials and periodicals. These include pamphlets and informational bulletins of the Zionist Federation of Germany and the central bureau of the WZO in London. Also deposited in the collection are a set of the newspaper *Kongresszeitung* for 1923–31 and clippings from Jewish newspapers.

The documents are in Hebrew, German, and English.

Microfilms are held by the United States Holocaust Memorial Museum Archives.

Sinagogal'naia obshchina (g. Bromberg)

Synagogen-Gemeinde, Bromberg

Synagogue Community of Bromberg*

Fond 716k, 1844–1939. 66 storage units.

Jews settled in Bydgoszcz (Bromberg) in the mid-fourteenth century, when that city was a possession of the Polish king Casimir III. In 1555, Jews were banned from permanent residence in Bydgoszcz. The city became part of Prussia with the first partition of Poland in 1772, and many of the restrictions on Jews were lifted in 1773. In 1802, Jews received the right to live in Bromberg. The charter of the local Jewish community, which numbered 250 persons, was finalized in 1833. New community bylaws were adopted in 1867; charitable and educational institutions developed rapidly. A large community synagogue was built in 1884. In the early twentieth century, more than 2,000 Jews lived in Bromberg. The Jewish religious community of Bydgoszcz ceased to exist after the Nazi deportation of the local Jewish population in late 1939.

The collection's contents are described in two inventories arranged by structure and document type.

The collection contains community charter documents for 1834, 1836, 1842 and 1907; minutes of sessions of the community executive for 1911–26; agendas and minutes of meetings of the community council for 1844–1924; instructions on procedures for holding sessions of the community executive; information on meetings of the community council; resolutions of the community council concerning the establishment of the Louis Aronson Charitable Fund; lists of members of the community executive and council; applications to and resignations from the community; the register of results of elections to the community council for 1868–1920; and

---

*   A finding aid to this collection is available at http://www.sonderarchiv.de/fonds/ fond0716.htm.

minutes of meetings and resolutions of the community school commission for 1887–1924.

The collection contains correspondence of the Bromberg community: with the Bromberg police department on elections of the community board and community council; with the Central Archives of German Jewry in Berlin on storing community documents there; with the Bromberg magistrate and Bromberg synagogues on elections to the community executive and council; and with Jewish organizations and communities — Alliance Israélite Universelle (Paris), the Central Committee of Russian Jews in Germany (Berlin), the Union of German-Jewish Communities (Berlin), and the Union of Synagogue Communities of Westphalia and Bielefeld. It includes correspondence with community members on elections to the community's governing bodies, on charity drives to benefit the community, and on receiving material aid; there is also correspondence with Jewish shelters and retirement homes.

Among the financial documents found in the collection are edicts by the Bromberg magistrate on the community's collection of taxes; community tax rolls for 1900–1914; audit commission reports on the state of community funds for 1865–1919; community cashbooks for 1868–1937; community income statements for 1855–1932; registers of community tax assessment among community members for 1901–06; receipts for membership dues payments; Stadthagen bank statements on amounts in the community's accounts at that bank (1912–22); lists of persons having bequeathed property and financial assets to the community; files on registering bequests; and lists of persons having received material aid from the community. The collection also has registers of charitable contributions, financial transfer stubs, and documents of the charity committee.

The collection contains other German Jewish documents that may have been acquired by the Bromberg Community, or may be of other collection provenance: minutes of the Union of German-Jewish Communities, 1900–1903; bylaws of the Union of German Jews in Berlin, and reports on its activities, 1913–16; a circular letter to synagogue communities on the need for community efforts to create Jewish schools in which instruction would be based on an elementary school curriculum supplemented with Jewish disciplines; materials of the commission to publish a collection of documents on Jewish participation in the regional economy and on manifestations of antisemitism; an informational bulletin on relations with the Polish National Council; proclamations by the Permanent Committee for the Amelioration of the Conditions of the Jews in Russia condemning the pogroms of 1881; an Alliance Israélite Universelle fundraising appeal for aid to Jews expelled from Moscow in 1891; correspondence of the Alliance Israélite Universelle with the Central Committee of Russian Jews in Germany on measures to aid Russian Jewish victims of the expulsion from Moscow; instructions by the Central Committee of Russian Jews in Germany on procedures for transporting Russian Jews across the border and for their settlement in new locations; the Committee's third report (March 1892) and a listing of its local chapters; an appeal by the Union of Rabbis in Germany to the leaders of Jewish communities urging them to take part in an assembly (2–3 August 1886) in Breslau (Wrocław) aimed at drawing up a petition to the Reichstag, asking that body to reject the impending ban on Shechita (the ritual slaughter of livestock); an appeal by the board of the Jewish Community of Berlin to the Reichstag explaining the nature of the Shechita ritual and its origins and providing the conclusions of German scholars on that issue; the charter of the Central Association of G:rman Citizens of the Jewish Faith (Centralverein); a stenographic report of the 5th General Assembly of the Centralverein; and the program of the 6th General Assembly of the Union of German-Jewish Communities (June 1913).

The collection also has printed documents: charters of the Central Association of German Citizens of the Jewish Faith, of the Jewish community in Tornau; circulars of the Jewish Volksrat of Poznań; informational bulletins of the Central Archives of German Jewry in Berlin for 1908–11, and of the Union of German-Jewish Communities; a speech by Rabbi Walter (Bromberg, 30 October 1904) on the 50th anniversary of the Jewish Women's League; annual reports on the activities of synagogue communities of East and West Prussia, Westphalia, Saxony, Poznań, Pomerania, and of the board of the Union of Synagogue Communities of Breslau (Wrocław), Berlin, and Bromberg for 1901–15; the program of the 6th general assembly of the Union of Jewish Teachers in Germany, and a report on its activities for 1911–13; and a report by the teachers' organization of the Jewish community of Berlin (April 1914). The collection also has an inventory of the books in the Bromberg community library, and an eighteenth-century *mahzor* (holiday prayer book).

The documents are in German and Hebrew.

Microfilms are held by the United States Holocaust Memorial Museum Archives.

Tsentral'noe ob"edinenie nemetskikh grazhdan iudeiskogo verois-povedaniia (g. Berlin)

Centralverein deutscher Staatsbürger jüdischen Glaubens

Central Association of German Citizens of the Jewish Faith (Berlin)*

Fond 721k, 1869–1939. 4,370 storage units.

The Central Association of German Citizens of the Jewish Faith, established in 1893, was one of the first organizations to defend the rights of Jews in Germany. The Association represented the views of middle-class, liberal Jews, primarily adherents of Reform Judaism; it was opposed, on the one hand, to assimilation and mixed marriages, and on the other hand, to Zionism and Jewish nationalism. On the eve of World War I, the organization numbered 40,000 members; in 1926, it had 60,000 members, and consisted of 555 local chapters and 21 provincial federations. The organization had its own legal department, which engaged in lawsuits regarding defamations and other manifestations of antisemitism. The Central Association's publishing house, Philo-Verlag, published various books and journals on Jewish issues for both Jewish and non-Jewish readers. During the period 1895–1922, the official organ of the Central Association was the monthly *Im deutschen Reich*, and during 1922–38, the weekly *Central-Verein Zeitung*. Chairmanship of the Centralverein was held by M. Horowitz (1893–1917), Eugen Fuchs (1917–19), Julius Brodnitz (1920–35). The Central Association's director during the period 1908–33 was Ludwig Holländer. By order of the Nazi administration, the organization changed its name in 1936 to the Jewish Central Association. It was closed by the authorities 10 November 1938, and all of its subdivisions became part of the Reich Representation of Jews in Germany.

The collection's contents are catalogued in three inventories arranged by structure and document type.

Most of the materials in this collection originate from the 1920s and 1930s. The collection includes the charter of the Central Association

---

* A finding aid to the collection is available at http://www.sonderarchiv.de/fonds /fond0721.pdf.

and its local chapters; minutes of meetings of the Central Association's committee on drawing up a new charter (1926–28); minutes of the Central Association's board (1931) and of chapters (1932–38); reports by leaders of Central Association chapters on their activities; and reports on the state of the Jewish community in various German cities (1932–35).

The collection also has circulars and announcements by the Central Association: on organizing courses; on the Central Association's position on various parties in elections to a conference of Jewish community representatives; on collecting factual material serving as evidence on the boycott of Jewish businesses in Germany (1931); on the Essen burgermeister's reply to the Central Association's complaint regarding a boycott of Jewish livestock traders (1931); on preparations for a Jewish youth conference and the establishment of professional courses for young people without a trade (1931); on forging closer ties between Jewish organizations; on suing the Rudolph Karstadt firm, which had fired all of its Jewish employees (1933); and on procedures for the admittance of persons of "non-Aryan origin" into scientific, educational, and artistic institutions.

A large part of the collection (more than 1,000 files) documents the activities of the Central Association's local chapters. The collection contains correspondence with chapters and individual members on a wide range of topics, including plans to amend the organization's charter and create a commission on drafting a new charter (1931); on the election of Central Association board members (1928); on providing financial statements, planning annual budgets, and collecting membership dues; on providing material aid to the needy; on helping those fired on account of their "non-Aryan origin" get their jobs back; on organizing retraining courses for Jews; on the boycott of Jewish shops in German cities; on anti-Semitic articles in periodicals; and on procedures for expelling members from the Central Association. Also included is correspondence with publishing houses, booksellers, and the Jewish religious community of Berlin on acquiring literature for the latter's library; with the lawyers K. Bergman and H. Samson on providing Central Association members with the services of Jewish lawyers and notaries, and on the possibility of creating a Central Association Union of Lawyers; on drawing up standard answers to questions by Central Association members; and on the organization's mission and possible courses of action under the conditions of the Nazi regime.

Materials on the activities of the Central Association's youth divisions include reports on the activities of the youth education section for January–July 1936; educational curricula and journals of the Jewish youth leagues, "Ring" and "Herzlia"; announcements by the Union of German Jewish Youth "Ring" on events held by it; a list of members of the leadership of, and also of several local chapters of, the Union of German Jewish Youth "Ring" (1934); an announcement by the Union of German Jewish Youth "Ring" on the union's action plan for 1936; applications for admission to the Union of German Jewish Youth "Ring" (1934); and informational bulletins and letters from the Central Association and the Union of German Jewish Youth "Ring" to local chapters of these organizations on the admission of new members and the distribution of literature (1934–35).

The collection includes administrative and financial documents: lists of Central Association staff members and board members, guidelines (12 September 1934) with Central Association staff job descriptions, rules of internal procedure, and reports of financial audits of chapters.

The collection contains correspondence with various German Jewish organizations: the Union of Jewish War Veterans, The Union of Jewish Youth Associations in Germany, The Union of German Jewish Youth "Ring," Keren Hayesod, The German Jewish Aid Society (Hilfsverein), the German Grand Lodge of the Independent Order of B'nai B'rith, and other organizations. It contains correspondence with the newspapers *Jüdische Zeitung* (Bresslau), *Der Israelit* (Frankfurt am Main), *Die Jüdische Presse*, *Jüdisches Gemeindeblatt*, and others.

The collection includes the catalogue of books held by the Central Association library. Among the printed materials in the collection are these: Central Association informational bulletins for 1933–37; newspaper clippings devoted to the situation of Jews in the countries of Europe and America (1916, 1919), ritual murder accusations against Jews (1927–32), Jews' service in wars (1928–29), the activities of the Jewish Agency for Palestine (1929), and clashes between Arabs and Jews in 1929; clippings of antisemitic content from the Nazi newspaper *Der Stürmer* (1929); as well as clippings on the dissolution of Masonic lodges and the expulsion of Jews from social organizations and artistic and professional unions (1933–38), and on the adoption of the Nuremburg laws (1935).

The documents are in German.

Microfilms are held by the United States Holocaust Memorial Museum Archives.

Pravlenie sinagogal'noi obshchiny (g. Shtettina)

Vorstand der Synagogen-Gemeinde (Stettin)

Board of the Synagogue Community (Stettin)

Fond 726k, 1828–1938. 27 storage units.

Jews began settling in Stettin (modern-day Szczecin, Poland) no later than the first half of the thirteenth century. In modern times, however, there were no Jews in Stettin until the beginning of the nineteenth century, when the city changed hands from Sweden to Prussia. The Jewish religious community of Stettin was established in 1816; it remained the largest Jewish community (approximately 2,000 persons) in Pomerania right up until the start of the Second World War. During the Holocaust, the overwhelming majority of Jews were deported to Nazi death camps.

The collection's contents are described in two inventories arranged by document type.

The collection contains lists of Stettin Jewish community members who were community ("synagogue") tax payers; Stettin Jewish community members' resignations from the community and renunciations of the Jewish faith, as well as previous resignees' declarations of return to Judaism and applications for readmission to the community; instructions on admission to and resignation from the community; appeals by community leaders to stop the mass exodus of members from the Jewish community; announcements by the Stettin Court of First Instance on resignations from the community and renunciations of the Jewish faith; and lists of deceased members of the Stettin Jewish community, dates and causes of death, and places of burial (cemetery plot and grave).

The collection includes Stettin Jewish community leaders' correspondence with German charitable societies on the construction of hostels for the children of needy Jews, and on the transfer of funds for the deaf, blind, and sick, and for those disabled in the First World War.

The documents are in German and Hebrew.

Microfilms are held by the United States Holocaust Memorial Museum Archives.

Velikaia lozha Germanii evreiskogo ordena "Bnei-Brit" (UOBB) (g. Berlin)

Grossloge für Deutschland des Unabhängigen Ordens "Bne Brith" (UOBB) (Berlin)

German Grand Lodge of B'nai B'rith (Berlin)*

Fond 769k, 1844–1939. 2,412 storage units.

The Independent Order of B'nai B'rith (Sons of the Covenant) was established in New York in 1843 by a group of German-origin Jews headed by Henry Jones. B'nai B'rith was established to help raise the moral, spiritual, and social level of Jews, espousing philanthropy, charity, and fraternity. The order was free of any particular political or religious ideology. To administer its affairs, a charter was drawn up and, in 1851, the first grand lodge was established in New York.

In 1882, the organization's former secretary, Moritz Ellinger, was dispatched to Germany to establish the first German lodge in Berlin. The German Grand Lodge, district no. 8, with twelve affiliated lodges, was founded in 1885. The first president of the German Grand Lodge was J. Fenchel (1885–87), followed by presidents L. Maretzki (1888–98), B. Timendorfer (1898–1924) (who was subsequently its honorary president), and Rabbi Leo Baeck (1924–38). In 1885, the German Grand Lodge numbered 12 lodges and 1,150 members. By 1912, its numbers had increased to 79 lodges and 8,610 members. The German Grand Lodge sponsored various social welfare programs. It financed nursing courses and the Association of Jewish Nurses (1900–1930); it founded a Jewish orphanage and a school for retarded children in Berlin (1907–30), an employment agency (established 1910), and a cultural fund (1920) that supported educational institutions. The German Grand Lodge helped establish and finance the Union of Jewish Youth Associations in Germany in 1909, and it published the youth journal *Wegweiser für die Jugendliteratur* (1905–14), as well as numerous books and pamphlets for youth. Only men could be full members of the Grand Lodge; women's auxiliary lodges were established beginning in 1897.

* A finding aid to this collection is available at http://www.sonderarchiv.de/fonds /fond0769.pdf.

The German Grand Lodge's monthly organ *Bericht der Grossloge für Deutschland* was first published in 1891, and was soon renamed *Der Orden Bne Briss: Mitteilungen der Grossloge für Deutschland VIII.* On the eve of the Nazi assumption of power in 1933, Germany had 103 lodges of B'nai B'rith with 13,000 members. B'nai B'rith was banned by the Nazi authorities in April 1937, and its assets were confiscated.

The collection's contents are described in three inventories; the collection has a geographical index.

Deposited in the collection are the constitution of the Independent Order of B'nai B'rith; charters of the Grand Lodge and of affiliated lodges in Germany and the United States; the charters of the order's committees on youth organizations and Jewish women's organizations; the charters of affiliated lodges' courts of honor; draft charters of youth organizations; the charters of the women's charitable society Schwesternbund, of the Eintracht lodge's women's organization, and of the women's auxiliaries of lodges in East Prussia and elsewhere; the charter of the Association of Jewish Nurses; the charter of the B'nai B'rith employment bureau and of the Jewish labor exchange organizing committee; the charter of the local Eschwege lodge's home for the disabled; the charter of the Jaffe orphanage; the charter of the Jewish sanatorium for nervous disorders in Frankfurt-on-Main; the charters of the charitable societies Mädchen-Haus Pankow and the G. Tuch Society in Hamburg; and draft amendments to the charters of the Grand Lodge and its affiliated lodges.

The collection has documents of the 24th Congress of the German Grand Lodge, as well as materials on the activities of B'nai B'rith lodges in the United States, Palestine, Austria, Poland, Turkey, and Switzerland, and documents of the International Congress of B'nai B'rith held in Tel Aviv in 1934.

Deposited in the collection are reports on the activities of the Grand Lodge, of its general committee, the propaganda committee, and finance committee; as well as reports of the Union of Jewish Youth Associations.

A large part of the collection consists of documents of local affiliated lodges: minutes of meetings, correspondence, reports on personnel, and financial statements. The lodges with extensive documentation in the collection include East Prussia (in Allenstein/Osterode), Mamre, Montefiore (Berlin), Reichsloge, Berthold Auerbach (Berlin), Timendorfer, Akiba Eger, Westphalia, Lessing (Berlin), Manuel Josel, and Edward Lasker. There are reports on the activities of affiliated lodges' commissions on protecting mothers and children and of their women's auxiliaries.

The collection contains texts of speeches by Grand Lodge members and of reports read by members at Grand Lodge meetings; a report on the work of the Grand Lodge appeals court; reports by affiliated lodges on charitable activities; reports on the activities of the lodge members' employment bureau; reports of the committee to aid child victims of pogroms; reports on the activities of the children's holiday organizing committee; and reports on the work of, and financial statements of, the retirement home for B'nai B'rith members.

The collection contains reports by organizations that received financial support from B'nai B'rith: reports by the committee to aid Jewish veterans of the First World War; reports on the activities of the Association of Jewish Nurses; reports on the work of the Jaffa orphanage; and reports on the work of Jewish hospitals, the shelter for the blind in Jerusalem, nurseries, orphanages, and sanatoria. These include reports on the activities of the Society for the Advancement of the Interests of Jewish Deaf-Mutes, the Society for the Support of Jewish Farmers and Artisans in Syria and Palestine, and the Society for the Advancement of Agriculture among the Jewish Population of Germany; reports on the activities of the Mannheim Jewish community's charitable committee; reports on the work of Jewish hospitals in Marienbad and Kissingen; as well as reports on the activities of the Society for the Propagation of Trades and Agriculture among the Jewish Population of Prussia, the Superintendency of Jewish Nurseries and Kindergartens, the Society for the Propagation of Jewish Cuisine, the Society for the Promotion of Jewish History and Literature, the Jewish Reading Room, the Ezra League, and other organizations.

The collection also contains minutes of meetings of the Grand Lodge's presidium, general committee, executive committee, the propaganda committee, the editorial committee, the commission on Jewish youth organizations, and the arts commission; minutes of meetings of the finance committee and the audit commission; minutes on the founding of Jewish women's organizations and of their meetings, including minutes of meetings of the conference of the Union of Women's Auxiliaries of the Order (February 1920); minutes of meetings of the committee on nursing; and minutes of meetings of the Jewish labor exchanges organizing committee.

The collection also has circulars to affiliated lodges; circulars of the Union of Women's Auxiliaries of the Order to local women's auxiliaries; an Order lodge's instructions on organizing traveling art exhibitions; instructions for lodge presidents, vice presidents, and "mentors" on admitting new members; descriptions of rituals for admitting new members and for holding lodge memorial sessions; duties of those joining the order; and membership applications.

A large portion of the collection consists of correspondence with order members, with committees and subcommittees of the order, and with affiliated lodges on organizational matters, personnel, organizational activities, and financial accounting procedures; on ceremonially opening lodges, celebrating jubilees, establishing lodges, and assisting in the emigration of German Jews; on organizing reports on the history of B'nai B'rith, on the history of the Jewish people, and on literature and art; on drawing up lists of lecturers; on publishing activities; on organizing a committee on eugenics; and on creating Jewish sports clubs.

Much of the correspondence is with other German Jewish organizations: with the German Jewish Aid Society and the Union of German-Jewish Communities on the Grand Lodge's allocation of funds for teaching Jewish religious subjects, on distributing pamphlets on the activities of the Union of Communities, on drawing up questionnaires on the situation of Jews in Germany, on distributing B'nai B'rith literature, and on charitable activities; with the League to Combat Antisemitism on anti-defamation activities; with the Union of Jewish Youth Associations regarding disagreements with Zionist organizations; with the League of Jewish Women; with the Central Welfare Bureau of German Jewry, and the Jewish Association for the Defense of Women on methods of fighting prostitution among Jewish women; with the Association of Jewish Nurses regarding the training of personnel; with the Jewish Association for the Care of the Sick on setting up permanent clothing stations; with the League to Combat Antisemitism on recruiting doctors to work on the Grand Lodge's hospital train; with the Central Association of German Citizens of the Jewish Faith on creating Jewish professional consultation bureaus; with the Committee for the Care of Jewish Workers on procedures for granting financial aid to Jews in need, and on holding meetings of this committee; with the German Jewish Aid Society on organizing aid to child victims of anti-Jewish pogroms in tsarist Russia; and with German Jewish charitable societies regarding their financing.

Much of the correspondence is internal: correspondence with affiliated lodges on merging women's auxiliaries into the League of Jewish Women and on the merger of Jewish youth organizations; correspondence with members of the youth literature commission on reviews of children's books, on awarding prizes to authors, and on the activities of the commission; correspondence with affiliated lodges and members of the arts commission on organizing traveling art exhibitions and lectures on the history of painting, on awarding prizes, on providing material aid to artists in need, and on arranging concerts; correspondence with members of the bylaws and rituals commission on draft amendments to bylaws and lodge structure; correspondence with affiliated lodges on appeals submitted by their members; correspondence with affiliated lodges on creating lodge libraries and catalogues of books in lodge libraries; correspondence with members of affiliated lodges on setting up children's hostels, on celebrating the thirtieth anniversary of the Jewish women's organization Caritas, and on other matters; correspondence with affiliated lodges and members on recruiting Jewish women into B'nai B'rith activities and on establishing auxiliary lodges; correspondence with affiliated lodges on organizing lodge nursing courses, on the performance of rotations in Jewish hospitals by graduates of these courses, and on other matters; correspondence with affiliated lodges and their members on granting material aid to disabled veterans starting new jobs; correspondence with affiliated lodges regarding their members' and members' relatives' service in the First World War; correspondence with affiliated lodges on organizing lodge employment bureaus, on assisting lodge members and their relatives joining the workforce, and on providing work at industrial plants in Germany for Jewish refugees from Poland; correspondence with the editorial committee on preparing order jubilee collections for publication; and letters by members of the probationary committee regarding the issuance of letters of recommendation for order candidates.

The collection also contains lists of members of the Grand Lodge and affiliated lodges; lists of Jewish artists who provided their works for traveling exhibitions organized by the Grand Lodge; lists of presidents of the B'nai B'rith lodges in Germany; a list of Jewish agriculturalists; lists of doctors, hospital attendants, and service personnel of the Grand Lodge hospital train, including brief biographical information; lists of affiliated lodges and their members; statistical information on the personal composition of the affiliated lodges, Montefiore, Reichsloge, Spinoza, Heinrich Graetz, Henry Jones, Ferdinand Hamburg, and others; and a register of the personal composition of the Jewish lodges of Germany.

The collection also has cashbooks of the Grand Lodge and of the affiliated lodges Karl Friedrich (Karlsruhe), Maccabi (Konstanz), August Lamais (Mannheim), Munich, Gabriel Riesser (Trier), and others; financial statements of committees to aid relatives of members of Jewish lodges;

Grand Lodge financial statements pertaining to an audit of the budget; and financial statements of affiliated lodges.

There are also informational bulletins of the Grand Lodge; pamphlets and journals; articles from Jewish newspapers on the Yishuv in Palestine; reviews and bibliographic indexes of Jewish and German literature; issues of the Jewish youth magazine *Der Jugendbund* and the Masonic magazine *Die Bauhütte*; issues of the informational bulletin *Der Orden Bne Briss*, the women's magazine *Die Frau von Heute*, and other publications; a collection of depictions of the seals of Jewish lodges of America and Germany; newspaper clippings on the works of Goethe, Lessing, Zola, Wagner, and others; clippings on manifestations of antisemitism, on the activities of the committee to aid Jewish victims in Russia; and a portrait of Order of B'nai Brith founder Henry Jones.

The documents are in Hebrew, German, and English.

Microfilms are held by the United States Holocaust Memorial Museum Archives.

Ob"edinennyi arkhiv nemetskikh evreev. Kollektsiia Neimana (g. Berlin)

Gesamtarchiv der deutschen Juden

Central Archives of German Jewry, Neumann Collection (Berlin)*

Fond 1194k, 1811–1918. 382 storage units.

The Central Archives of German Jewry were founded in 1905 at the initiative of Ezechiel Zivier, with the support of the Union of German-Jewish Communities and of B'nai B'rith. Its aim was to collect and systematize documents on the history of the Jews in Germany. Its first director was Eugen Taübler, and the chairman of the academic council was M. Philippson. Taübler was succeeded as director by Jacob Jacobsohn in 1920. The archive held the original records and *pinkasim* of more than one hundred German-Jewish communities, including materials that dated back to the sixteenth century. It housed the archive of the Berlin Jewish community, the papers of the Union of German-Jewish Communities, the General Union of Rabbis in Germany, personal collections, and Jewish-related documents transferred from the Staatsarchiv in Poznań. The Central Archive collected handwritten copies and photographs of documents on Jewish history found in German municipal and state archives. It published six volumes of *Mitteilungen des Gesamtarchivs der deutschen Juden* between 1909 and 1926. When the Nazis came to power, they actively utilized the archive for genealogical research, and confiscated its collections in 1938.

Among other materials, the Central Archives included a collection of documents on Jewish history gathered by Salomon Neumann (1819–1908). Neumann, a physician and author on social medicine, composed statistical studies of German Jewry to refute the views of antisemitic authors. Neumann was one of the founders of the Berlin-based Hochschule für die Wissenschaft des Judenthums (1872). He maintained a collection of newspaper clippings on Jewish affairs which he bequeathed to the Central Archives of German Jewry.

The collection's contents are catalogued in four inventories. The inventories are arranged by document type.

---

* A finding aid to this collection is available at http://www.sonderarchiv.de/fonds/fond1194.htm.

Deposited here is a collection of German laws pertaining to the legal status of various social categories of Jews, and pertaining to the rights of Jews to engage in certain activities; charters of Jewish communities, organizations, and institutions in Germany; minutes of Reichstag sessions at which the legal position of Jews in Germany was discussed; minutes of meetings of the leaders of Jewish communities, organizations, and institutions; Jewish organizations' leaflets defending the rights of Jews in Germany and denouncing antisemitism; lists of members of Jewish communities and organizations.

Among the collection's legislative acts pertaining to Jews in Germany, are a print edition of Friedrich Wilhelm's Edict on the Jews of Prussia (1812); an 1815 law on the Jews; hand-copied laws concerning Jews from 1811, 1812, and 1834; *Gesetz-Sammlung* collections with laws concerning Jews in the kingdom of Hanover (1842–45) and in Prussia (1847); the Berlin informational bulletin *Amtsblatt* with 1848, 1855, and 1860 laws concerning Jews; and clippings from newspapers, in particular *National Zeitung* (1882), containing analysis of legislation concerning Jews.

The collection contains documents on the history of the Berlin Jewish community: materials on communal elections (1888–89, 1892–1901), on the Jewish community's infirmary (1832–98), and on philanthropic activities. It also contains public letters and notices issued by the General Union of Rabbis in Germany (1888–1901), and the resolution (10 May 1882) establishing the German Jewish Aid Society, as well as this organization's monthly reports for May, June, July, and September 1882.

A large part of the collection (more than 120 files) consists of newspaper clippings form 1845 to 1918 on a wide array of subjects, most of which were compiled by Salomon Neumann. The clippings deal with the legal position of Jews in Germany and other countries, on Jewish culture and literature, on issues pertaining to the reform of Judaism, on trials with Jewish defendants, on Jewish emigration from Russia, on the issue of the admission of Jews to institutes of secondary and higher education in various countries of Europe, and the like. The collection also contains an inventory of the Salomon Neumann collection of the Central Archive.

The collection contains extensive correspondence by Jewish organizations, public figures, and private individuals. Some of the letters (including letters by Salomon Neumann himself) are concerning the provision of aid to Jewish émigrés from Russia; correspondence of members of the Berlin Committee to Aid Pogrom Victims in Russia with various correspondents in St. Petersburg, Kiev, and Elizavetgrad, and with the Kiev,

Odessa, and Elizavetgrad committees on aid to pogrom victims, as well as with representatives of shipping companies in Berlin, Hamburg, and Antwerp on helping pogrom victims to emigrate (May–December 1881).

The topic of migration by East European Jews is covered in many documents. There are lists of Jewish émigré passengers aboard the Hamburg steamship company ships *Silesia*, *Lessing*, and others, en route from Hamburg to New York (in 1881); information on expenditures for the transport of groups of émigrés as well as of individual families; documents of the committees to aid Romanian and Russian Jews in Germany for 1872–1902; the participant list and minutes of a conference of aid committees in Brussels, 1–2 November 1872 (Adolphe Crémieux was a conference participant); appeals on behalf of Jewish victims of pogroms in southern Russia in 1881–82; charitable subscription forms on behalf of Rumanian Jews; reports and notifications by individuals on the wiring of charitable contributions (1881–82); financial reports by M. Kohn on charitable aid to Romanian Jews (1892–94); and a report by the Russo-Jewish Committee in London (A. Wolf, chairman) on prospects for Jewish emigration from Russia to various countries, and on possibilities for colonizing Palestine (1891).

Records of various Jewish social welfare institutions are included in this collection: a report on the work of the Jewish orphanage in Palestine for 1897; a detailed report by the board of directors on the establishment and functioning of the Ciocanul Jewish trade school in Bucharest (1902); announcements by the American Romanian Jew Emancipation Committee (the announcements were made in connection with speeches by the head of the Romanian Cabinet of Ministers, which included proposals for "electoral emancipation" for Jews, a discussion of their right to own land, and related issues); documents of the Central German Committee to Aid Jewish Victims in Russia; and minutes of that committee's constituent session (23 April 1882), in which representatives of the Israelitische Allianz (Vienna), the Alliance Israélite Universelle (Paris), the Special Committee in Cologne, and the Berlin Aid Committee took part.

The collection includes newspaper clippings

The documents are in German.

A man searches for a file from the executive committee of the Jewish community in Berlin.

United States Holocaust Memorial Museum (USHMM) courtesy Jüdisches Museum Berlin

Archive of the main library of the Jewish Community Center, Berlin, ca. 1938.

akg-images, Bildarchiv Abraham Pisarek

Archive of the main library of the Jewish Community Center, Berlin, ca. 1938.

akg-images, Bildarchiv Abraham Pisarek

Jews study at a long table in the reading room of the Jewish Community Center library, Berlin, ca. 1938.

USHMM courtesy of Bildarchiv Preussischer Kulturbesitz

Library of the Jewish Community Center, Berlin, ca. 1938.

Circulation desk at the library of the Jewish Community Center, Berlin, ca. 1938.

Books sorted in the offices
of the Central Cultural
Commission for Jews in the
Netherlands, May 1942-1943.

Nederlands Instituut voor
Oorlogsdocumentatie

"Farewell Letter to Our
Members" on the dissolution
of the Association to Combat
Antisemitism, Berlin,
July 7, 1933.

Russian State Military Achive
(RSMA)

Verein zur Abwehr des Antisemitismus e.V.

BERLIN W57, ELSSHOLZSTR. 21 / FERNRUF: B7 PALLAS 6775

Postscheck: Berlin 9506 / Bank: Deutsche Bank und Discontogesellschaft, Depos.-Kasse L2, Potsdamer Straße 35d, Berlin W57

Ein Abschiedswort an unsere Mitglieder

Verein zur Abwehr des Antisemitismus e.V.
i. A.: Dr. Horlacher.

In a warehouse in Ratibor, Upper Silesia, crates of materials confiscated by Einsatzstab Reichsleiter Rosenberg (ERR), ca. 1941–1943.

USHMM courtesy Yad Vashem Photo Archives

Discovered by ERR, a mound of prayer books and correspondence left by Jews in Amsterdam, ca. 1942–1943.

USHMM courtesy Yad Vashem Photo Archives

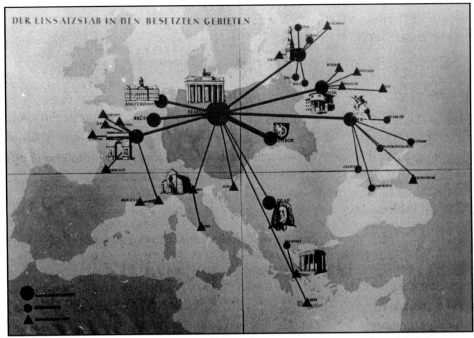

A map documenting the confiscation activities of Einsatzstab Reichsleiter
Rosenberg, from an album produced by the Offenbach Archival Depot. 1943

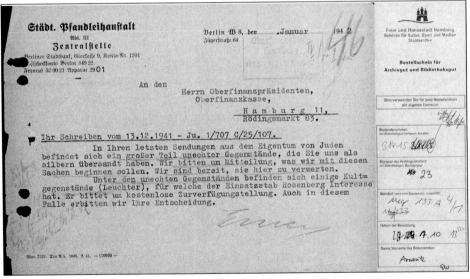

January 1942 letter appointing ERR responsibility for confiscating valuable
cultural assets from Jewish property in Hamburg.

The "Institut zur Erforschung der Judenfrage" (Institute for Research on the Jewish Question), founded in 1939 in Frankfurt am Main, was the first branch of the planned elite National Socialist university "Hohe Schule." Since 1940, the institute's staff had worked primarily for the ERR, which plundered Jewish archives, libraries and art collections in occupied Eastern and Western Europe. A large portion of the confiscated holdings came into the possession of the "Institute for Research on the Jewish Question," which dealt with the history of Judaism from a radical antisemitic perspective.

Nederlands Instituut voor Oorlogsdocumentatie

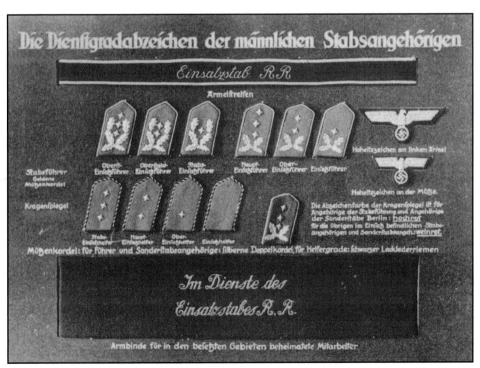

Service rank insignia of Einsatzstab Reichsleiter Rosenberg personnel. 1943.

USHMM courtesy Yad Vashem Photo Archives

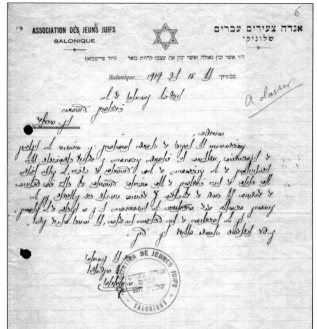

Letter from the Association of Young Jews in Salonika regarding the convening of a Greek Zionist Conference, May 1919.

RSMA

Membership card issued to Joseph Goldberg, of Zawiercie, Poland, by the He-Chalutz Pioneer Movement in Poland, 1925.

RSMA

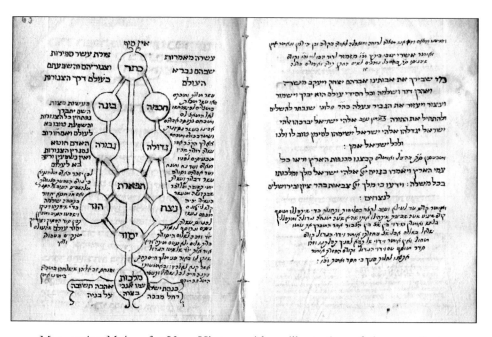

Birth records of the Jewish Community of Dubrovnik (Ragusa) for the years 1821–1823, in Italian.

RSMA

Manuscript *Mahzor* for Yom Kippur, with an illustration of the ten *sefirot*.

RSMA

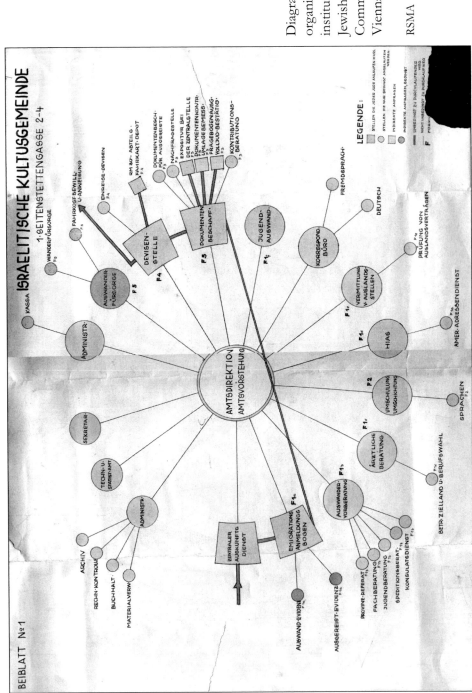

Diagram of organizations and institutions of the Jewish Religious Community of Vienna.

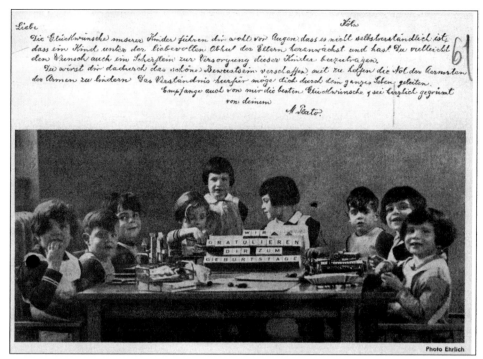

Liebe

Die Glückwünsche unserer Kinder führen dir wohl vor Augen, dass es nicht selbstverständlich ist, dass ein Kind unter der liebevollen Obhut der Eltern heranwächst und hast Du vielleicht den Wunsch auch ein Scherflein zur Versorgung dieser Kinder beizutragen.

Du wirst dir dadurch das schöne Bewusstsein verschaffen, mit zu helfen die Not der Ärmsten der Armen zu lindern. Das Verständnis hierfür möge dich durch dein ganzes Leben geleiten.

Empfange auch von mir die besten Glückwünsche y sei herzlich gegrüsst von deinem

A. Plato?

Fundraising postcard for the Jewish
orphanage in Cologne, Germany.

German-language brochure issued
by Keren Ha-Yesod, 1927.

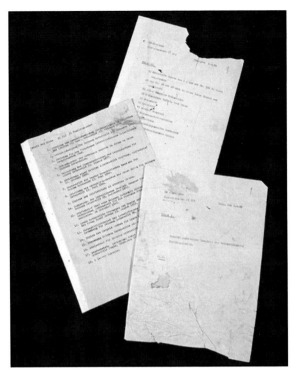

Schedule of Rothschild archives compiled by Sonderkommando IL.112 at the time of their seizure.

The Rothschild Archive, London

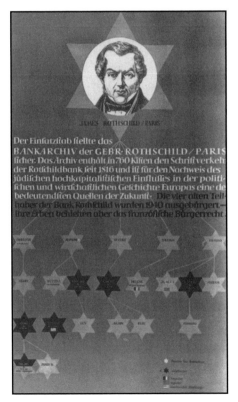

ERR diagram of confiscated Rothschild banking archives, described here as one of the most important sources for future political and economic histories of Jewish capitalism in Europe.

USHMM courtesy Yad Vashem Photo Archives

Exhibition of ERR-confiscated materials.

USHMM courtesy Yad Vashem Photo Archives

Rosenberg Inspects Collection in ERR Hq. Berlin.

Alfred Rosenberg inspects a collection at Einsatzstab Reichsleiter Rosenberg headquarters in Berlin. 1943.

USHMM courtesy Yad Vashem Photo Archives

Wrapped packages of looted Jewish books stacked in the cellar of the Institute for Research on the Jewish Question, Frankfurt am Main, July 6, 1945. Photo by Irving Katz.

USHMM courtesy National Archives and Records Administration

Two Soviet soldiers examining a partially burned Torah, Majdanek, 1944.

USHMM courtesy Yad Vashem Photo Archives

Exterior of the Russian State Military Archive.
RSMA

Archival Repository of the Russian State Military Archive.
RSMA

Reading Room of the Russian State Military Archive.
RSMA

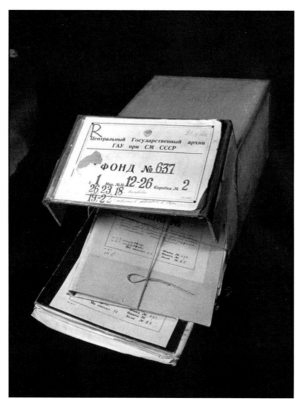

A box of Rothschild papers, showing the storage arrangement in the Russian State Military Archive.

The Rothschild Archive, London

A Rothschild document, after its return.

The Rothschild Archive, London

Soiuz evreiskoi molodezhi "Ring" (g. Berlin)

Bund Jüdischer Jugend "Ring"

Union of German Jewish Youth "Ring" (Berlin)*

Fond 1207k, 1913–1936. 12 storage units.

The Union of German Jewish Youth was established in 1933 upon the merger of several youth organizations, some of which belonged to the Central Association of German Citizens of the Jewish Faith. Its name was changed to "Ring" at the order of the Nazi authorities in 1936. "Ring" defined itself as an association of "young people, German by culture and place of birth, and Jewish by origin and creed." Adhering to anti-Zionist views, the union urged its members either to stay and live in Germany or emigrate — but not to Palestine. The union's use of uniforms and symbolism similar to those of the Hitlerjugend led to its being shut down by the Nazi authorities in 1937.

The collection's contents are catalogued in one inventory. The inventory is arranged by document type.

The collection includes the "Ring" union charter; circular letters of the union and its local chapters for 1933–36; lists of union members; the program of the 5th conference of the Association of Jewish Youth Societies in Germany, held in Düsseldorf; appeals by Jewish youth organizations on the holding of charity events; the Montefiore Jewish youth organization's plan of operation for 1925–26; correspondence with union members and local chapters on organizing lectures and submitting reports, on training local chapter leaders and admitting new members, and on financial issues; and correspondence with the Union of Jewish War Veterans, in Berlin, on cooperation (1934).

There are also documents of the local Mannheim chapter of the union, informational bulletins of the Union of German Jewish Youth and

* A finding aid to this collection is available at http://www.sonderarchiv.de/fonds/fond1207.pdf.

the Fortrupp union for 1935, clippings from German newspapers on the activities of Jewish youth organizations, and samples of Jewish youth organizations' flags, emblems, and badges.

The documents are in German.

Microfilms are held by the United States Holocaust Memorial Museum Archives.

Dochernie lozhi velikoi lozhi Germanii evreiskogo ordena "Bnei-Brit"

Affiliated Lodges of the German Grand Lodge of B'nai B'rith*

Fond 1219k, 1878–1937. 761 storage units.

See the historical note to Fond 769k on page 121.

The collection's contents are described in two inventories. In them, documents are catalogued by type.

The collection features an accumulation of documents of affiliated lodges of the German Grand Lodge of the Order of B'nai B'rith in 36 German cities, including East Prussia (in Alenstein/Osterode), Abraham Geiger (Berlin), Berthold Auerbach (Berlin), Gabirol (Berlin), Montefiore (Berlin), Spinoza (Berlin), Julius Fenchel (Berlin), Leopold Zunz (Braunschweig), Lessing (Berlin), Nehemia Nobel (Namburg), Leibniz (Hannover), Zion (Hannover), Friedrich (Heidelberg), Silesia (Berlin), Moritz Lazarus (Göttingen), Hillel (Hildesheim), Fraternitas (Dresden), Düsseldorf, Karl Friedrich (Karlsruhe), Rhineland (Cologne), Maccabi (Konstanz), Kant (Koenigsberg), Elias Grünbaum (Landau), Silesia (Liegnitz), Mendelssohn (Magdeburg), August Lamais (Mannheim), Munich, Humboldt (Neisse), Jakob Plaut (Nordhausen), Jakob Herz (Nuremberg), Amititia (Posen), Zaeringer (Pforzheim), Saar (Saarbrücken), Gabriel Riesser (Trier), Mosel (Trier), Frankfurt, Hardenberg (Frankfurt am Oder), Breisgau (Freiburg), Pomerania (Stargard), Allemania (Stettin), Stuttgart, Thuringia (Eisenach), Bergische Loge (Elberfeld), Menorah (Elbing), Glückauf (Essen), Julius Binn (Eschwege), Leipzig, Munich, and Jeremiah (Stoln).

The collection contains lodge charters, minutes of meetings, lodge members' personal files, applications for lodge membership, biographical information on lodge members, lodge circulars and reports on their activ-

* A finding aid to this collection is available at http://www.sonderarchiv.de/fonds/fond1219.pdf.

ities, lists, financial statements, and related materials. There is also correspondence between lodges, lodge leaders, and rank-and-file members.

The documents are in German.

Microfilms are held by the United States Holocaust Memorial Museum Archives.

Germanskaia sektsiia Mezhdunarodnogo soiuza rasistov (g. Berlin)

Bund "Völkischer Europäer," Abteilung Deutschland (Berlin)

Alliance of *völkisch* Europeans, German Division (Berlin)

Fond 1299k, 1933–1935. 31 storage units.

The International Alliance of *völkisch* (race-conscious) Europeans was founded on 30 May 1933; the German division of this alliance, on 4 June 1933. This organization had close ties with the Nazi Party. Its print organ was the newspaper *Der Reichswart*. The president of the German division of the International Alliance of *völkisch* Europeans was Johann von Leers.

The collection's contents are catalogued in one inventory. The inventory is arranged by document type.

Materials in the collection include charter documents and regulations of the Alliance of *völkisch* Europeans and the alliance's German division; correspondence with members of the alliance on its aims and goals, on admitting new members, and on organizational matters; correspondence with the German Ministry of Internal Affairs, the Taibner company, and various Nazi organizations, institutes, and museums on checking the Aryan origin of persons joining the alliance, on the possibility of determining racial affiliation by blood type, on publishing antisemitic literature, on antisemitic propaganda, and on the German-Polish youth camp in Liegnitz; and with local chapters of the German division of the alliance in Aachen, Breslau, Würzburg, Halle, Königsberg, and other German cities on establishing local chapters of the alliance, admitting new members, electing officers, and organizing racist propaganda; and lists of members of local chapters. The collection also contains the German division's correspondence with Nazi organizations and the Gestapo on antisemitic propaganda and on reading antisemitic reports; the Flemish-language pamphlet "Why Antisemitism?"; articles entitled "Stolen Jewish Documents" and "Preventive War"; and Baron Alfred Fabre-Luce's article, "My Impressions of Antisemitic Propaganda in Germany."

The documents are in German and Flemish.

Microfilms are held by the United States Holocaust Memorial Museum Archives.

Evreiskaia obshchina (g. Berlin)

Jüdische Gemeinde, Berlin

Jewish Community of Berlin*

Fond 1326k, 1725–1936. 178 storage units.

Jews settled in Berlin no later than the mid-thirteenth century. Following several expulsions and readmissions between the fourteenth and sixteenth centuries, seven Jewish families expelled from Vienna were permitted to settle in Berlin in 1670. A Jewish burial society was established in the city in 1676. In 1714, the Jews of Berlin were permitted to open a synagogue, and in 1723, a community charter was ratified. In 1730, the number of Jews in Berlin was restricted to 120 families. With Napoleon's conquest of Prussia (1812), the 3,000 Jews of Berlin became full citizens, but during the Restoration, restrictions were once again placed on their rights. It was only in 1860 that the more than 13,000 Jews of Berlin received full equality.

The modern Berlin Jewish community was established in 1847 in accordance with Prussian legislation on the status of Jews (1847) that required their membership in a local Jewish religious community. The revised 1895 charter of the community states that its purpose was "to support the conduct of prayer meetings, religious instruction for young people, and the arrangement of funerals and of all other institutions whose necessity is prescribed by our religion." The community was governed by a council of 21 members (increased to 41 in 1930) plus a seven-member executive committee. Orthodox Jews opened a rabbinical seminary in the city in 1873, and in 1889 they formed a bloc within the community council, called the Central Union. The Central Union's candidates prevailed against the liberal bloc in community council elections until 1895, when the latter, known as the Liberal Union, gained the majority on the council. The Berlin Zionist Union first put forward candidates in community elections in 1901. In 1905, their bloc took the name New Jewish Community Union, and, starting in 1920, it was renamed the Jewish People's Party. Liberals, Zionists, and Orthodox (whose bloc

* A partial finding aid to this collection is available at http://www.sonderarchiv.de/ fonds/fond1326.pdf.

was renamed the Conservative Party in 1920) represented the three most influential Jewish political tendencies in Berlin until the community's elimination in 1938.

The latter third of the nineteenth century, into the early twentieth century, saw an energetic migration of Jews to Berlin, and, by 1925, they numbered nearly 173,000. The first general elections to the community council were held in 1919. Beginning in 1925, the right to vote was extended to women. In 1930, the community maintained at its own expense 16 synagogues, five schools, a cemetery, a Jewish hospital, orphanages, retirement homes, a library, and other institutions. Among community chairmen in the interwar decades were G. Minden, J. Stern, and Heinrich Stahl.

When the Nazis came to power in Germany (1933), the Berlin Jewish community joined the newly established Reich Representation of Jews in Germany. The majority of Berlin Jews emigrated from Germany between 1933 and 1938, and nearly all those who remained fell victim to the Holocaust. The community was formally dissolved by the Nazis in 1943.

The collection's contents are described in one inventory. Documents in the collection are catalogued by structure and document type.

The collection contains documents from the eighteenth and nineteenth centuries: minutes of meetings of the Berlin Jewish community board on raising funds for material aid to community members in need (1839); *ketubot* (Jewish marriage contracts) of members of the Jewish community of Berlin (1871); a register of income and expenses related to the ceremony of ritual circumcision (1848–55); documents related to the census of the Jewish population of Berlin for 1744, 1749, and 1808; a list of children having undergone the bar mitzvah ritual in 1858; records of the purchase of synagogue seats; the text of a sermon delivered in the Berlin synagogue (April 17, 1875), and a record book of *yortzeits* in the Berlin community, listing the deceased between 1814 and 1850 according to their Hebrew date of death. It also contains a draft of a book on the history of notable figures of the Jewish community of Berlin (1670–1870), and drafts of studies of epitaphs at the Berlin Jewish cemetery.

The collection includes correspondence by the rabbis and scholars of Judaism, Zecharias Frankel and Eliezer (Leser) Landshuth, with the Society for the Reform of Judaism in Berlin, and with private individuals regarding trends in the development of Judaism, and also on the topic of collecting documents on Jewish history and tradition (1851–83); a letter to Zecharias Frankel from M. A. Stern and Eliezer Landshuth (10 August 1847) on exchanging literature; correspondence with the Jewish community of Hamburg in connection with polemics surrounding the development of

Reform Judaism; and correspondence by Professor Hermann Strack (1848–1922)

Many of the collection's documents are records of the twentieth-century community. These include birth registers of the Jewish communities of Berlin and Breslau (1913, 1918, and 1936); the Berlin Jewish community's cashbook for 1928–32; and reports on the work of the Berlin Jewish community library and museum (1912–19).

The collection also contains extensive correspondence of the Jewish community of Berlin with the Board of Deputies of British Jews; letters of the community council on renting seats in Berlin synagogues (1920); Berlin Jewish community members' correspondence on the study of Judaism and Jewish history, on admitting new members, and on collecting materials on Jewish history (1910–34); correspondence with the Chaver publishing house on publishing books on Jewish history (1923) and on organizing a community library exhibit devoted to Baruch Spinoza (1932–34); as well as correspondence of the Jewish community of Berlin library with the Sephardic community of Amsterdam (1931), the Spinoza Society of Frankfurt-on-Main (1932–33), the Breslau state library, libraries in Hanover and Halle (1932), and Hebrew Union College in Cincinnati (1932).

There are also letters to individuals who resided in Berlin: to Jeremiah Heinemann, to Simon Bernfeld, and to others; as well as books that belonged to the library of the Jewish community of Berlin.

The collection also contains German Jewish documents from outside Berlin: the declaration of Leopold Friedrich, Duke of Westphalia, permitting D. Frenkel and his household to live in the former's domain (1817); documents on the investigation of the "Damascus Affair" (1840–55); documents of the Frankfurt-based Society of Friends of Reform (1843 and later); and a list of members of the Augsburg Jewish community board (1871).

The collection also contains correspondence not related to the Jewish community of Berlin. These include letters by Asher Ginzberg (Ahad Ha'am), Yosef Klausner, Meir Dizengoff, Chaim Nahman Bialik, Simon Dubnow, Sch. Lazar (?), Shalom Albeck, Yehoshua Ch. Ravnitsky, and Shmuel Aba Horodetsky.

The collection also contains Hebrew manuscripts of varied provenance. Some are apparently from the collection of the Israelite Theological Institute (Fond 715k); others are from the collection of Rabbi Yosef Yitzchok Schneerson (Fond 706k).

Among the older manuscripts are a notebook recording texts of kabbalistic amulets; a collection of Hebrew poems, in Italian script, attributed to Leone Modena; a manuscript of *Sefer Shevet Yehuda* in Italian script; an eighteenth-century notebook of blessings and prayers for women, with explanations in Italian; an eighteenth-century manuscript of a commentary of the Zohar; and an eighteenth-century collection of Tekhines in Yiddish, *Adir Ba-marom shokhen be-gevurah.*

There are nineteenth-century handwritten copies of older manuscripts: of homilies attributed to Sayda Gaon; of extracts of the Munich manuscript of the Talmud, copied by Abraham Epstein; and other materials.

The collection includes nineteenth-century responsa and sermons from Germany, including a responsum by Rabbi Eliezer ben Mordechai of Leipzig.

The collections contains manuscripts and notes by nineteenth-century Wissenschaft des Judenthums scholars from Berlin and Vienna: manuscripts by Meir Friedmann (Meir Ish Shalom) of studies on the Bible (*Meir ayin el sefer yehoshua, Sefer meir le-ayin el sefer shmuel*), the Talmud, and midrashim; commentaries on *Bereshit Zuta* and *Bamidbar Rabba*; and a number of studies in manuscript prepared by Eliezer Landshuth — a study concerning the Jewish liturgy, a bibliographic index of halakhic and aggadic works by Ashkenazi rabbis, a list of Berlin rabbis and notables, and a list of works on Jewish history and tradition.

There are notebook fragments containing drafts of works by Prof. Wolfgang Wessely on the history of Jewish culture in the Biblical and post-Biblical periods; fragments of manuscripts by P. Halauer on the history of the Jews; and a work, by an unknown author, entitled "The Jewish Question and the Anti-Jewish Movement in Russia 1881–1882."

The collection contains a considerable amount of Chabad/Lubavitch materials. These include sermons, letters, and responsa by the third Lubavitcher Rebbe, Menachem Mendl Schneerson (1789–1866), some of which are dated 1863; *Barukh Ata,* an index to writings by Menachem Mendl Schneerson, dated 1924; *Kuntres tefilah 5640* (1879–80); and sermons and Torah commentaries by the fifth Lubavitcher Rebbe, Sholem Dov Ber Schneerson, including a sermon delivered on Simchat Torah, 1914.

Finally, the collection contains artwork: watercolor landscapes, abstract and symbolic paintings, children's pictures, and certificates; portraits of famous Jewish religious leaders and cultural figures; and photographs of Jews in Algeria, Tunisia, Morocco, and China.

The documents are in Hebrew, Yiddish, German, and Russian.

Microfilms are held by the United States Holocaust Memorial Museum Archives.

Fashistskie i profashistskie organizatsii Germanii

German Fascist and Pro-Fascist Organizations

Fond 1521k, 1919–1945. 61 storage units.

The collection's contents are described in one inventory. The documents are catalogued by document type, according to the organization to which they belonged.

The collection includes various documents of German Nazi, profascist, and nationalist organizations, including the Berlin-Charlottenburg Antisemitic Union and the German Union for Nationalist Propaganda Abroad. Among these are charter documents of organizations; correspondence between organizations and rank-and-file members; circulars, propagandistic literature, and Nazi periodicals; as well as membership cards, inventories, and personal files.

The documents are in German.

Glavnoe upravlenie imperskoi bezopasnosti Germanii (RSKhA) (g. Berlin)

Reichssicherheitshauptamt (RSHA) (Berlin)

Reich Security Main Office (RSHA) (Berlin)*

Fond 500k, 1933–1945. 3,005 storage units.

The Reich Security Main Office (RSHA) was created in September 1939 by the merger of the Security Police and the Security Service (Sicherheitsdienst or SD) of the Reichsführer-SS. The RSHA was headed by Reinhard Heydrich, and, after Heydrich's assassination in 1942, by Ernst Kaltenbrunner. The RSHA numbered approximately 70,000 employees, and its structure was altered repeatedly. As of October 1943, it included seven departments: I: organizational issues and the training of personnel; II: finance and economics; III: surveillance of internal political life; IV: the functions of the former Secret State Police Administration (Gestapo); V: criminal police (this department included the Criminal Technical Institute and the Criminal Biological Institute; the establishment of a central institute of forensic medicine was planned); VI: external reconnaissance; and VII: information, propaganda, and counter-propaganda. In 1944, after the elimination of the Abwehr, an eighth (military) department was created to lead reconnaissance-diversionary efforts. The departments were divided into groups, and the groups into sections. Leadership personnel of the RSHA included SS-Gruppenführer Pohl, SS-Brigadeführer Ohlendorf, SS-Gruppenführer Müller, SS-Gruppenführer Nebe, SS-Oberführer Panzinger, SS-Brigadeführer Schellenberg, SS-Oberführer Prof. Six, and SS-Obersturmbannführer Dittel. The RSHA was under the command of the Reichsführer-SS and chief of the German police Himmler. In 1943, Himmler became Reichsminister of the Interior and General Plenipotentiary for Reich Security.

In the spring of 1941, in the context of Operation Barbarossa, Heydrich formed the Einsatzgruppen, which were attached to Wehrmacht formations, to

---

* A finding aid to this collection is available at http://www.sonderarchiv.de/fonds /fond0500.pdf.

carry out the annihilation of Jews.

Section IV B 4 of the RSHA, under Adolf Eichmann, was responsible for the Jews. From late 1941, it directed the deportation of most of European Jewry to ghettos, slave labor, and extermination camps.

At the Nuremberg trial, the Gestapo, the SS, the storm detachments (SA) of the Nazi Party, and the Security Service (SD), by whose forces the RSHA had committed "crimes against humanity," were declared criminal organizations. Kaltenbrunner was executed by sentence of the Nuremburg tribunal.

The collection's contents are catalogued in six inventories. Inventories no. 1, 2, and 6 are arranged by structure and chronology, and catalogue documents of departments I, II, III, IV, V, VI, and VII of the RSHA. Inventories no. 3, 4, and 5 are arranged by document type. These inventories catalogue orders, edicts, directives, instructions, accounts, surveys, reports, dispatches, employee directories, surveillance files, and correspondence of the Reich Security Main Office and its subordinate entities regarding the issues indicated.

RSHA documents include orders, edicts, and other regulations on the structure, interaction, internal procedure, and recordkeeping of the SD, the Gestapo, and the police in the RSHA system.

The collection's materials include extensive documentation from the prewar period on the Jews: orders, edicts, circulars, reports, dispatches, accounts, surveys, references, statistical information, letters, articles, pamphlets, bulletins, and newspaper clippings on the situation of Jews in Germany and other countries; on the activities of Jewish organizations; on repressive measures against Jews in Germany, in particular, on the restriction of the rights of Jews in economic, political, and social life, including with regard to property rights; on stripping Jews of German citizenship and confiscating their property; on restrictions on the Jewish press; on closing, dissolving, and banning Jewish political, social, religious, and cultural-educational organizations, individual newspapers and other media, schools, and libraries; on actions against the Jewish population (arrests, pogroms, bans on assembly, and internment in concentration camps); on entities engaged in deporting Jews; and on the forced deportation of Jews, financed by funds and property confiscated from the victims.

There are documents of a review and analytical nature on the history of the Jewish people, its role in international life, and on plans to establish a Jewish state in Palestine. These include a Gestapo report on the conduct of and preparations for the World Jewish Congress (WJC) in

Geneva (1934–37); newspaper clippings on the situation of Jews in Germany (1934); overviews of the activities of various Jewish organizations in Germany (1934–36); overviews of the activities of the World Zionist Organization (WZO), including maps of the jurisdictions of its regional bodies (1936); the report "Jewish Political Organizations of Germany as of 15 February 1936" (the report contains information on the following Jewish organizations: the Reich Union of Jewish Veterans, the Union of German Jewish Youth, the Association of Liberal Judaism, Keren Kayemeth LeIsrael, Keren Hayesod, the Jewish Girls' Association for Labour in Palestine, and the Jewish Women's League).

The collection contains edicts and decrees on the Jews: an edict by Hitler's Nazi Party deputy, Hess, forbidding party members from associating with Jews; Gestapo reports on the activities of Jews in Germany; decrees that Jews be resettled to a separate city quarter in their respective municipalities, that Aryan domestic servants be forbidden to work in Jewish homes, that Jewish merchants be instructed to offer their goods to Aryans by telephone, in writing, or through middlemen, that strict surveillance be kept on the children of Jews who had left Germany, and that they be stripped of their German citizenship (1935–38); foreign newspapers and journal articles on the persecution of Jews in Germany (1935–38); explanations by the German Minister of Justice regarding Nazi race laws pertaining to Jews (1936–38), including laws on stripping them of their citizenship, on firing all employees of non-Aryan origin, on introducing a quota for Jews in German schools and institutions of higher learning, on defining the concept of "Jew," and on rules for resettling Jews to a specially designated city quarter; a Darmstadt Gestapo telegram on measures against Jews in Heusenstamm (1937); decrees, laws, edicts, and notes on removing Jews from Germany's public life (1938–39); a file on the confiscation of Jewish orphanages and charitable institutions (1939); a law on concluding apartment rental contracts with Jews; and a Ministry of Communications circular forbidding Jews from using sleeping cars and restaurant cars (1938). The collection also contains documents requiring any child with a Jewish father and a non-Jewish mother to take the mother's last name; the banning of Jewish political organizations; a dispatch from the Breslau Gestapo on confiscating the property of a local B'nai B'rith lodge (1937); a file on the abolition of the Central Association of German Citizens of the Jewish Faith (1937–38); and a file on drawing up a plan to abolish the Zionist organizations of Germany (1938).

The collection contains extensive documents on Jewish emigration from Germany in the 1930s: reports of the Hansa Transport Bureau and its correspondence with the Reich Resettlement Bureau on resettling German Jews (1937–38); correspondence of the Hansa Bureau with the Gestapo and with private individuals on resettling Jews in Ecuador and Brazil; German Jewish Aid Society correspondence with the Gestapo on speeding up Jewish emigration from Germany; and Aid Society correspondence with HICEM, the JCA, and the JDC, all of which were prepared to finance this project. Also contained are documents on financial aid to Jews in Germany; financial statements of entities in charge of Jewish emigration; the minutes of interrogations of Jews on their preparations for resettlement (1934–37); Gestapo accounts and reports on the establishment of trade schools to prepare Jews for resettlement, and the curricula of these schools (1935–39); and lists of Jewish retraining camps (1937–38). The collection also contains reports and newspaper clippings on plans to resettle Jews in Mexico (1938), Italy (1932), Paraguay (1938), Poland (1938), Canada (1938), Madagascar (1938), Rhodesia (1928), and Australia (1938).

The collection contains reports, overviews, and notes on various Jewish organizations, including the Jewish People's Council Against Fascism and Anti-semitism in London, Israelitische Allianz, the Reich Representation of Jews in Germany, the Committee to Defend the Interests of Austrian Jews, the Organization of Legitimist Jewish War Veterans, the International Union of Revisionist Zionists, the Association of Jewish Medical Students, the Jewish Women's League, the Union of Jewish War Veterans, the youth league Hechaver, and the Jewish Colonization Association. The collection also contains statistical data on Jews in the cities of Germany.

The collection also includes documents of Vienna-based Jewish organizations, such as (in chronological order) a report by the Jewish religious community of Vienna (1930), that contains data on the number of Jews living in Vienna, on the income of that organization, and on the issue of Jewish migration from the provinces to Vienna; a report on Jewish emigration from Vienna to the United States, Britain, and Palestine, and on contacts and collaboration of the Vienna community with the American Jewish Joint Distribution Committee, the Ezra Society, the Jewish Colonization Association, the Zionist Federation of Germany, Hechalutz, Agudath Israel, Keren Hayesod, the Central Association of German Citizens of the Jewish Faith, and the Alliance of Non-Aryan Christians; the charter of the Jewish State Party in Austria, and information on branches of the Jewish State Party in Czechoslovakia; the charter of the Jewish People's Party (Vienna); materials of the Judäa Union of Jewish Students in Vienna and of other Jewish organizations in Vienna (1933–38); dispatches of the Jewish Telegraphic Agency (JTA); newspaper clippings and other materials on the Berne trial regarding *The Protocols of the Elders of Zion* (1934–35); documents on the activities of the B'nai B'rith, and confiscated documents of this organization (1933–38); a report by the leader of the Jewish religious community of Vienna on the activities of the community in November–December 1938; and a memo by the Jewish religious community of Vienna on the Second World Conference of Polish Jews (1938–39).

The collection contains Gestapo bureau correspondence on the activities of Jewish organizations (1940–43); alphabetized lists of German Jews residing in Paris in 1939–41. The collection also includes reports by Einsatzgruppe, police and Security Service squads, and informational bulletins on their activities in the mass annihilation of Jews and the creation of ghettos (the report of Einsatzgruppe A, attached to the Army Group North, on the annihilation of 229,052 Jews in the territory of Lithuania, Latvia, Estonia, Belorussia, the Ukraine, and the northwestern regions of Russia during the period October 1941–January 1942).

The documents are in German.

Microfilms are held by the United States Holocaust Memorial Museum Archives.

Upravlenie gosudarstvennoi tainoi politsii (Gestapo) (g. Berlin)

Geheimes Staatspolizeiamt (Berlin)

Office of the Secret State Police (Gestapo) (Berlin)

Fond 501k, 1933–1945. 930 storage units.

The German Secret State Police (Gestapo) originated in the political department of the police headquarters in Berlin during the Weimar Republic. With the Nazi assumption of power in 1933, this agency, renamed the Gestapo, came under the control of Hermann Göring and Rudolf Diels, and later, of Heinrich Himmler and Reinhard Heydrich. It was given broad powers of arrest and wiretapping, and engaged in torture and executions. Section II 1 of the Gestapo was charged with fighting the "enemies" of the regime, including the Jews. After Kristallnacht (November 9–10, 1938), the Gestapo became the main instrument of the Nazi regime's anti-Jewish policies.

In 1939, the Gestapo was fused with other security arms (the Sipo and SD) to form the Reichssicherheitshauptamt (RSHA). The Gestapo took part in the enslavement of "inferior races," "pacifying" and subduing the occupied territories, and persecuting the Jews; it carried out a major role in the "Final Solution." It supervised deportations from the ghettos to extermination camps, and pressured German-allied countries to deport their Jews.

A significant portion of the collection's contents was transferred to the German Democratic Republic in the 1950s–70s. (These materials are noted in the inventories and are not included among the collection's files.)

The collection's contents are catalogued in three inventories.

Documents in the collection contain information on communist, social-democratic, anti-fascist, religious, and Jewish organizations in Germany; reports on "unreliable" persons; information on Masonic lodges; police surveillance files (for example, on the conduct of the 1936 Olympic Games in Berlin); agents' dispatches by agents on the activities of émigré organizations outside Germany; and clippings from German and foreign newspapers, journals, and other printed publications concerning the situation in Germany.

The documents on Jewish affairs relate to the period before the Second World War.

The collection includes documents and surveillance related to the Zionist movement in Germany: correspondence of the Reich and Prussian Minister of the Interior and of the Prussian Gestapo Office with the Zionist Federation of Germany; reports by the Jewish Telegraphic Agency (JTA) on the twenty-fifth congress of the Zionist Federation of Germany (1936) and other materials of the conference; reports by Gestapo agents and correspondence with them, regarding the twenty-fifth conference of the Zionist Union of Germany; a message from the Berlin Zionist Union to the Berlin Gestapo on the departure for Jerusalem of union leaders Dr. G. Landauer and K. Blumenfeld with a pledge to report to the Gestapo on the situation in Palestine and on the development of the Zionist movement in Palestine (28 January 1936); results of elections of the Zionist Federation of Germany leadership (chairman: S. Moses; secretariat: I. Eisner, H. Friedenthal, G. Joseftam, R. Katzenstein, A. Lehmann, G. Lubinski, A. Michaelis, J. Prinz, E. Rosenberg, M. Traub, S. Chertok, and K. Tuchler); a list of other top officers of the Zionist Union of Germany, as well as of Keren Kayemeth LeIsrael.

The collection contains a bibliography of Jewish literature that was drawn up for the Gestapo, and that includes among the listed publications books on the Jewish question, on the history of the Jews and Judaism, and on the situation of Jews in Germany, Hungary, Britain, and other countries.

The collection contains internal Gestapo correspondence and intelligence: a file on the work of Gestapo agents Beneber and Münzer in collecting materials on a London antisemitic conference on boycotting Jews; correspondence with Gestapo offices in Kassel, Elbing, and Münster on Jewish organizations, and overviews of the activities of Jewish organizations; a Gestapo agent's report on the nineteenth World Zionist Congress in Lucerne (Switzerland), and attachments to the report (minutes of speeches, including that of Nachum Sokolow on the situation of Jews in Germany, and statistical tables of Congress participants by country); a file on surveillance of meetings, conferences, and conventions of Jewish organizations; minutes of a meeting of the board of the Reich Representation of Jews in Germany from 15 June 1937, and lists of members of this organization's board; lists of members of various Jewish societies; and correspondence with the Gestapo office in Elbing on the discovery of the corpse of Sh. Vishnik, a.k.a. "Black Paul," and a description of the murdered man.

There also are lists of German Jews having emigrated to Italy; these documents contain intelligence on those Jews prior to their departure, on their tax debts, their economic and political activities in Germany and Italy, and related matters. There is also a list of persons of Jewish origin en route through Germany (a "blacklist").

The collection also has documents on the situation of Jews in the USSR; these include reports and communiqués from the German Embassy in the USSR on Jewish organizations in the USSR, particularly on the activities of Agro-Joint, and a surveillance file on the activities of the Society to Promote the Agricultural Resettlement of Jews in the Soviet Union (OZET). There is Gestapo correspondence on expelling Jewish Soviet citizens from Germany, including lists of Jewish Soviet citizens expelled or subject to expulsion from Germany.

The documents are in German, English, Polish, Spanish, French, and Italian.

Microfilms are held by the United States Holocaust Memorial Museum Archives.

Tsentral'noe stroitel'noe upravlenie voisk SS i politsii (g. Aushvits)

Waffen-SS und Polizei. Zentralbauleitung in Auschwitz

Waffen-SS and Police, Central Construction Office in Auschwitz

Fond 502k, 1940–1945. 7,391 storage units.

The Construction Office of the Waffen-SS and Police at Auschwitz (Oświęcim), subsequently renamed the Central Construction Office of the Waffen SS and Police, was created in 1940 with the commencement of construction of the concentration camp. Here, in October 1941, construction began on a prisoner of war camp. In 1943, the Auschwitz concentration camp was divided into three independent camps: Auschwitz I (the main camp), Auschwitz II (Birkenau), and Auschwitz III, subsequently renamed the Monowitz concentration camp.

The Central Construction Office of the Waffen-SS and Police at Auschwitz was in charge of constructing installations within the concentration camp and around it; construction was carried out by means of camp prisoner manpower. The Construction Office was under the command of the Silesia Construction Inspectorate and Office Group II of the SS Economics and Administrative Main Office (WVHA) in Berlin. The head of the Central Construction Office of the Waffen-SS and Police at Auschwitz was SS-Sturmbannführer Karl Bischoff; he was succeeded in this post in 1943 by SS-Obersturmführer Werner Jothann, who, working in this office, had risen from rank-and-file SS man to office chief. A significant portion of the installations in the concentration camp were constructed under contracts concluded by the Central Construction Office of the Waffen-SS and Police at Auschwitz with proxy firms, which took an active part in the construction and equipping of camp installations and the use of practically gratis prisoner labor. Among these firms were Anhalt (Berlin), Friedrich Boos (Köln-Bickendorf), Karl Brandt (Halle), Deutsche Bau AG (Breslau), Industrie-Bau AG (Bielitz), Huta (Kattowitz), and others. The firm Topf und Söhne (Erfurt) took a notable part in constructing and outfitting the camp's crematoria and barracks. All of these firms used the labor of internees and prisoners of war, as well as of persons captured from and brought back from the occupied territories of the Soviet Union and other countries of Europe, to produce armaments, ammunition, and equipment for the Wehrmacht.

The collection's contents entered the RGVA among materials brought by the Soviet Army from the territory of Poland in 1945; some of the materials came from the Main Directorate of the KGB in 1957 and from the Leningrad Synthetic Rubber Research Institute and the Moscow Institute for Synthetic Rubber in 1965.

The collection's contents are catalogued in five inventories. The inventories are arranged by document type.

The collection contains orders, edicts, directives, reports, correspondence, memoranda, plans, explanatory notes, estimates, blueprints, computations, drafts, diagrams, photographs of installations, bookkeeping documentation, staff inventories, lists of employees, personnel files of security guards, memoranda, index cards of camp prisoners and workers, death notices, and lists of prisoners.

Documents of the Central Construction Office of the Waffen-SS and Police at Auschwitz include orders, edicts, and directives of offices of the SS Economics and Administrative Main Office on organizing the construction and operation of individual concentration camp installations; estimates, blueprints, and computations regarding the construction of installations, including crematoria, prisoner barracks, disinfecting and delousing chambers and stations, storage facilities for corpses, and industrial, agricultural, and other installations; contracts, financial computations, and correspondence with German firms taking part in the construction of the camp; documents transferring finished buildings to the local SS office; service records and index cards of camp prisoners and workers; death notices; and documentary materials of the IG Farbindustrie factory at Auschwitz (the structure of the factory, lists of workers and employees, blueprints of workshops, maps of the area of the factory, and photos of installations).

The collection contains Central Construction Office correspondence with the camp commandant's office, the Silesia Construction Inspectorate, and the Main Office on providing prisoners for work; as well as reports and memoranda on the necessity of constructing facilities for corpses, on a new, third crematorium going into operation, on the total 4,756-persons-per-day processing capacity of all five crematoria, and on the conduct of "special" measures entitled "Holland," "Heinrich," "Hungary," and "Jewish action." Among the collection's documents is a large quantity of death notices, index cards, and work records of Jews.

The documents are in German.

Microfilms are held by the United States Holocaust Memorial Museum Archives.

Upravlenie gosudarstvennoi tainoi politsii (Gestapo) (g. Shtettin)

Geheime Staatspolizeistelle (Gestapo) (Stettin)

Office of the Secret State Police (Gestapo) (Stettin)

Fond 503k, 1933–1945. 982 storage units.

The Gestapo office in Stettin was under the command of the Berlin Gestapo office. The Stettin office conducted surveillance on all organizations active in the region, and on individual persons suspected of political unreliability; it also engaged in counterintelligence. The structure of the Gestapo office as of 31 December 1939 included three sections, which in turn were organized into departments. The first section dealt with organizational issues; the second, with domestic surveillance of "enemies" of the Nazi regime; and the third, with intelligence and counterintelligence, including surveillance of foreigners. The jurisdiction of the Stettin Gestapo office included the border commissariats of Stettin, Swinemünde, and Stralsund, the border police post in Sassnitz, and the "foreign service" of Greifswald. Primary functions of the Stettin Gestapo included surveillance of Jews and Jewish organizations, conducting regional operations to register and expel the Jewish population, and pursuing other discriminatory measures with regard to Jews. The third section in particular dealt with the expulsion from Germany of Jewish foreign nationals and enforced the ban on foreigners of Jewish origin passing through Germany. The activities of the Gestapo ceased upon the defeat of Nazi Germany in 1945.

The collection's contents are described in three inventories. Inventories no. 1 and 2 are systematized by structure; they catalogue documentary materials of the first section (organizational issues), the second section (domestic political surveillance), and the third section (intelligence and counterintelligence). The files catalogued in inventory no. 3 are systematized thematically: Stettin Gestapo circulars and internal documents; surveillance of the Communist Party of Germany and of anti-fascists; surveillance of persons suspected of espionage, and of companies, the mail, and the press; and surveillance of Jewish and religious organizations. The inventories include introductions and section indexes. There is a geographical index to the collection's files.

The collection contains orders, edicts, circulars, reports, dispatches, correspondence, financial documents, and information regarding surveillance of the Church, Jews, Freemasons, communists, homosexuals, and national minorities, as well as "wanted" lists, investigation files, files on investigations of unreliable persons, lists, journals, newspapers, articles on the Gestapo, and other materials.

The documents on Jewish affairs relate to the period before the Second World War.

Documents on the surveillance of Jews and Jewish organizations, including religious ones, constitute 73 storage units. These include circulars of the Berlin Gestapo office on creating an office Central Bureau for collecting information on Jews and Freemasons and on creating a card file of Jews in Germany; orders and edicts of the Ministry of the Interior, the Ministry of Foreign Affairs, and the Berlin and Stettin Gestapo offices on forbidding Jewish citizens of Poland to reside in Germany, on interning Jewish citizens of the United States, and on expelling Jews from Germany; radiograms from the Gestapo main office to all police departments on taking measures against Jewish stores; copies of decrees of the Minister of Economics allowing Jews to open restaurants and cafes; edicts of the Stettin Gestapo office on procedures for issuing passports (including foreign-travel passports) to Jews; an instruction booklet for participants in the campaign to expel Jews; and questionnaires, for persons of Jewish origin, on capital and real estate in their possession.

The collection contains various lists of Jews, Jewish organizations, and Jewish-owned property: a list of Jewish organizations in Pomerania, lists of Jews arrested for the purpose of deportation to Poland, records of Jews having emigrated from Germany (including to Shanghai), and a file cataloguing Jewish land holdings in Germany.

There are surveillance files of Jewish organizations (sports, youth, and women's organizations); on surveillance of members of the Reich Union of Jewish War Veterans and members of the Union of Jewish Youth; and on the confiscation of the Jewish-owned journal *Die Grüne Post*; investigative files on Jews being stripped of German citizenship; files on establishing trusteeship of the property of arrested Jews; dispatches by Stettin police agents on anti-Jewish pogroms and the boycott of Jewish shops; and reports by the Gestapo of Stralsund, Köslin, and Swinemünde on German individuals' contacts with Jewish firms and on Jews working in German firms.

The documents are in German.

Microfilms are held by the United States Holocaust Memorial Museum Archives.

Nachal'nik politsii bezopasnosti i SD na okkupirovannoi territorii sovetskoi pribaltiki (g. Riga)

Befehlshaber der Sicherheitspolizei und des SD Ostland (Riga)

Chief of the Security Police and SD in the Occupied Soviet Baltic Territories (Riga)

Fond 504k, 1941–1944. 46 storage units.

The Security Police and SD in the occupied Baltic territories were, in operational terms, under the command of the Reich Security Main Office in Berlin; in organizational terms, this regional structure was under the Reichskommissariat Ostland, based in Riga. The documents of the collection entered the RGVA among captured materials taken to the USSR by the Red Army; some of the materials came from the KGB Investigative Department at the USSR Council of Ministers in 1955 and, in 1970, from the USSR Council of Ministers Main Archive.

The collection's contents are catalogued in two inventories. The inventories are, for the most part, arranged chronologically.

The collection contains dispatches, German translations of documents, minutes, circulars, orders, reports, reviews, secret publications, accounts, correspondence, special bulletins, transcripts of testimony, and assorted other materials, such as copies of documents (from the German Democratic Republic) and maps. There is information on the participation of Jews in the partisan movement in the Baltics, and notes by the head of the Main Office of the Security Police and SD in Berlin on a meeting on conscripting Jews for labor duty in case of war and on creating special camps for this purpose. Participants in the meeting were representatives of the German High Command and of the Main Office of the Police and SS, and Gruppenführer Eicke, the Inspector of Concentration Camps.

The documents are in German.

Microfilms are held by the United States Holocaust Memorial Museum Archives.

Kollektsiia dokumentov, sobrannykh imperskim arkhivom (g. Potsdam)

Archivalien des ehemaligen Heeresarchivs (Potsdam)

Records of the Former Military Archive (Potsdam)*

Fond 1275k, 1838–1945. 1,730 storage units.

The Heeresarchiv in Potsdam was established in 1919 with the goal of collecting, preserving, and using documents of the German military, as well as documents on the history of Germany. From 1931 to 1935, it was headed by Generalmajor Hans von Haeften, and from 1936 to 1945 by Ernst Zipfel. The Reichsarchiv Protection Authority was responsible for surveying archives in Nazi-occupied territories, and evacuating select records to the Reich.

Documents in the collection came to the RGVA from the state archives of the Khmelnitsky, Zhitomir, Stalingrad, Semfiropol, and other oblasts of the former USSR, from the USSR Central State Archive of the October Revolution, the Belorussian SSR Central State Archive of the October Revolution, the USSR Central State Military History Archive, and the USSR Ministry of Foreign Affairs, and also from among documents brought by the Red Army from the territory of Germany in 1945.

The collection's contents are catalogued in five inventories. The inventories are arranged thematically; inventory no. 3 is organized by subject.

This collection's materials were consolidated from various sources.

The collection includes select materials on Jewish affairs: minutes of meetings and assemblies of the Central Association of German Citizens of the Jewish Faith; correspondence of that association's president with the German Ministry of Foreign Affairs on protecting the rights of the Jewish

---

* A finding aid to this collection is available at http://www.sonderarchiv.de/fonds /fond1275.pdf.

population of Romania and Poland and on providing work to Jews in Germany (1918); minutes of meetings of the German Jewish Committee on Aid to Poland (1916); an article (undated, author unknown) on "Hermann Cohen's Interpretation of Kant: An Apologia for the Jews"; and antisemitic leaflets of a branch of the National Socialist German Teachers Union.

The documents are in German, English, French, Spanish, Russian, Ukrainian, and Czech.

Microfilms are held by the United States Holocaust Memorial Museum Archives.

Politseiskie i administrativnye uchrezhdeniia Germanii i vremenno okkupirovannykh eiu territorii

Deutsche Polizeieinrichtungen in den okkupierten Gebieten

German Police and Administrative Offices in the Temporarily Occupied Territories*

Fond 1323k, 1806–1945. 681 storage units.

All police entities in Germany, from the Reich Security Main Security Office (RSHA) down, were under the command of the Reichsführer-SS and chief of the German police Heinrich Himmler, who in 1943 became Reichsminister of the Interior and General Plenipotentiary for Reich Security. Police offices in occupied territories conducted a policy of mass terror and annihilated Jews. Police offices and the RSHA ceased activities in 1945 with the defeat of Nazi Germany.

The collection's contents are described in three inventories, which are arranged by structure. Within the structural divisions, files are catalogued for the most part by document type.

The collection is a consolidated archival collection. It consists of heterogeneous documentary materials of police offices in Germany and the German-occupied territories of Poland, Czechoslovakia, Austria, and the Soviet Union. The collection also includes documents of German police services in the occupied territory of the Soviet Union, including the Ukraine and Belorussia.

The collection contains minutes of official meetings; bulletins, reports, overviews, dispatches, and summaries; correspondence, personnel files, and personnel lists of police offices and police entities; minutes of interrogations, investigative files, and "wanted" lists; and leaflets. Docu-

---

* A finding aid to this collection is available at http://www.sonderarchiv.de/fonds /fond1323.pdf.

ments of German police and administrative offices in German-occupied territories also include orders and edicts of Heinrich Himmler and other high-ranking SS and police officials on establishing police offices and services (including in the occupied territory of the Soviet Union) and appointing staff.

Documents in the collection include orders by Security Police and SD chiefs in the Ukraine, Belorussia, the Caucasus, and the Baltics for 1941–43; overviews of the military and economic situation in the occupied territories of the Ukraine, the Caucasus, and Belorussia; correspondence of Security Police and SD officers in the Caucasus and Belorussia for 1942; and dispatches of the heads of Secret Field Police (GFP) formations.

The collection contains reports by gendarmeries and police regiments on arrests and executions of Jews carried out on Ukrainian and Belorussian territory in 1942. These documents include dispatches of the 133rd and 244th Police Regiments on operations to annihilate Jews in the occupied territory of the Ukraine in 1941–43; of Group "Ost" on the annihilation of Jews in the area of the Eichenhain installation in the Vinnitsa region in 1942; and of heads of Einsatzkommandos and senior officers of the 24th Police Regiment of the Distrikt Galizien on the execution of the Jewish population, and also on the conduct of an operation to deport 4,769 Jews from Kolomyja to the Bełżec death camp.

The documents are in German.

Microfilms are held by the United States Holocaust Memorial Museum Archives.

Imperskoe ministerstvo po delam okkupirovannykh vostochnykh oblastei (g. Berlin)

Reichsministerium für die besetzen Ostgebiete (Berlin)

Reich Ministry for the Occupied Eastern Territories (Berlin)

Fond 1358k, 1941–1945. 1,068 storage units.

The Reich Ministry for the Occupied Eastern Territories, created on 17 July 1941, carried out the civil administration of the occupied territory of the USSR. The ministry was headed by Alfred Rosenberg, and was organized as follows: the central office, for recordkeeping and organizational-economic issues; main department I, for policy; main department II, for governance and administration; main group III W, for political-economic cooperation; main group III E, for food and agriculture; main group III FH, for forestry and woodworking industries; and main department A, labor.

Subject to the ministry were the Reichskommissariat Ostland in Riga, headed by Gauleiter Hinrich Lohse; the Estonian Generalkommissariat in Reval (Tallinn), headed by SA-Gruppenführer Karl Sigmund Litzmann; the Latvian Generalkommissariat in Riga, led by Oberbürgermeister Otto-Heinrich Drechsler; the Lithuanian Generalkommissariat in Kowno (Kovno, Kaunas), led by Dr. Adrian von Renteln; the Belorussian Generalkommissariat in Minsk, led by Gauleiter Wilhelm Kube; the Reichskommissariat Ukraine in Kiev (previously in Rovno), headed by Gauleiter Erich Koch; and the Generalkommissariat of Volhynia in Lutsk, led by SA-Obergruppenführer Heinrich Schöne.

Each Generalkommissariat also had a local administration, made up of local collaborators who helped the Germans carry out their extermination policy against the Jews.

The documents of the collection entered the RGVA among materials brought by the Soviet Army from the territory of Germany, Czechoslovakia, and Poland in 1945–46, and from the Special Department of the Ministry of Internal Affairs of the USSR in 1953.

The collection's contents are catalogued in four inventories. The inventories are arranged by document type.

Among the collection's documents are orders, edicts, directives, dispatches, reports, briefings, job descriptions, accounts, overviews, memoranda, summaries, bulletins, employee directories, certificates of commendation, questionnaires, official documentation of employees' business trips, and ministry correspondence with the Reich Security Main Office and with Reichskommissariats in the occupied eastern territories.

Documents in the collection reflect the policy of the Nazi occupation authorities with regard to the Jewish population residing in those occupied territories. The ministry's administrative and summary documentation contains information on mass arrests and robberies of Jews, the establishment of ghettos, and "actions" involving the annihilation of Jews. The collection's documents include a monthly report (dated 10 November 1941) by the Wehrmacht Ostland commander's commandant of Belorussia on plans for the total annihilation of Jews and on "actions" already taken, and statistical information on Jews residing in Poland, Romania, and Hungary.

The documents are in German.

Microfilms are held by the United States Holocaust Memorial Museum Archives.

Imperskoe ministerstvo prosveshcheniia i propagandy Germanii (Berlin)

Reichsministerium für Volksaufklärung und Propaganda (Berlin)

Reich Ministry for Public Enlightenment and Propaganda (Berlin)

Fond 1363k, 1933–1945. 646 storage units.

The Reich Ministry for Public Enlightenment and Propaganda was created after the Nazis came to power in 1933. It presided over radio, the press, and cultural institutions, and controlled the sphere of art. Every department of the ministry engaged in antisemitic propaganda. Works by Jewish authors were banned and destroyed. Antisemitic ideas were espoused in radio broadcasts and in leaflets and pamphlets distributed by the ministry, headed by Joseph Goebbels. Between 1933 and 1937, his closest associate was Walther Funk, Deputy Minister of Propaganda and the Reich government official in charge of the press. Funk was one of the ideologues of German antisemitic policy, and he took part in organizing anti-Jewish pogroms. The ministry ceased to exist in 1945 with the defeat of Nazi Germany.

The collection's documents came to the USSR Central State Archive (now the RGVA) during 1953–69, from the First Special Department of the USSR Ministry of Internal Affairs, the Historical-Diplomatic Administration of the USSR Ministry of Foreign Affairs, and the International Department of the Central Committee of the Communist Party of the Soviet Union. The collection was systematized by the staff of the Historical-Diplomatic Administration of the USSR Ministry of Foreign Affairs and of the former USSR Central State Archive during the period 1946–81.

The collection's contents are described in seven inventories. The inventories are arranged by document type and contain circulars, instructions, and directives of the Ministry for Public Enlightenment and Propaganda; minutes of conferences held by Joseph Goebbels; reports, questionnaires, announcements, staff personnel files, personnel lists, correspondence, texts and overviews of radio broadcasts, articles (including articles by Goebbels), informational bulletins on the "Jewish question," pamphlets, and lists of German-language newspapers published in the occupied eastern territories. There is a geographical index to the collection's files.

The collection contains informational bulletins, journals, and articles on the Jewish question, entitled "Jewish Problems and Aspirations after the War," "The Jewish Brigade," "Jewish Terror in Palestine," "The Jewish Committee of National Liberation," "Jews in Chile," "Jews in the Soviet Union," "Jewish Contributions to Universities in the United States," "The Solution of the Jewish Question from the Point of View of Jews," and the like; and newspaper clippings on the persecution of Jews in Germany. There are also documents on hiring personnel for the Nazi Institute for the Study of the Jewish Question.

The collection's documents are in German.

Microfilms are held by the United States Holocaust Memorial Museum Archives.

Dokumenty kontsentratsionnykh lagerei i lagerei voennoplennykh v Germanii

Documents of Concentration Camps and Prisoner of War Camps in Germany

Fond 1367k, 1933–1945. 289 storage units.

The collection's contents are described in two inventories. The inventories are arranged structurally and by document type.

The collection contains documents of concentration camps and POW camps (arranged for the most part in alphabetical order by camp name. regulations, instructions, daily reports on the prisoner population, lists, summaries, journals, personnel files, card files, questionnaires, registers, and correspondence.

The collection includes fragmentary compilations of documents of the Sachsenhausen, Buchenwald, Wewelsburg, Gross Rosen, Dachau, Lublin (Majdanek), Natzweiler, Neuengamme (Hamburg), Treblinka, and Esterwegen concentration camps; of POW camps III-A in Luckenwalde, I-A in Stablak, IX-C in Bad Sulza, No. 352 in Minsk, No. 122 in Compiegne (France), the Polish officers' POW camp in Murnau, the Hammelburg officers' camp, Stalag XIII (for interned civilians) in Wulzburg (Bavaria); the Berlin-Falkensee camp for Italian and other foreign workers; and others.

Among the collection's documents are lists of Jews transferred from the Auschwitz concentration camp to the Sachsenhausen concentration camp (1944); lists of prisoners of the Sachsenhausen concentration camp, among whom were Jews (1938–44); daily reports of the Sachsenhausen concentration camp on changes in the prisoner population, with lists in which the names of Jewish inmates appear (1938); and rosters of prisoners, among whom Jews are indicated, who left personal items in the Sachsenhausen concentration camp's storage facility (1941–43).

The documents are in German.

Microfilms are held by the United States Holocaust Memorial Museum Archives.

Operativnyi shtab Reikhsleitera Rosenberga po delam okkupirovan-nykh oblastei (Berlin-Sharlottenburg)

Einsatzstab Reichsleiter Rosenberg für die besetzten Gebiete (ERR) (Berlin-Charlottenburg)

The Reichsleiter Rosenberg Task Force for the Occupied Territories (ERR) (Berlin-Charlottenburg)

Fond 1401, 1918–1945. 77 storage units.

The Reichsleiter Rosenberg Task Force for the Occupied Territories (ERR) was established on Hitler's orders (5 July and 17 September 1940). Its mission was to plunder art, libraries, and archives owned by Jews and others who were declared enemies of the Reich. In a subsequent order, in 1942, the ERR's mandate was broadened to include the seizure of all materials of use to the ideological tasks of the Nazi regime. During the first year of its existence, the ERR was active in France, Belgium, and the Netherlands. In Paris, it seized art from private collections owned by Jews. One of the ERR's priority activities was to provide books and archival records to the Hohe Schule, the planned university-level research and training facility for the Nazi elite, whose central library was in Berlin, and for the Institute for the Study of the Jewish Question, in Frankfurt am Main.

The ERR established special headquarters and subordinate task forces in German-occupied territories; these constituted the ERR's executive organs. Following the German attack on the Soviet Union, in June 1941, the ERR's focus of activity shifted to the occupied Soviet territories, particularly to the plunder of books and archives in Minsk, Kiev, and Vilna. In the summer of 1943, it established a special depository for books from the occupied eastern territories, the Öst-bücherei, in Ratibor (Polish: Racibórz), Silesia. The ERR ceased operation with the fall of the Nazi regime.

The collection includes a photocopy of Göring's directive establishing headquarters in German-occupied territories for the confiscation of valuables from Jewish and Masonic organizations, Rosenberg's orders establishing the Task Force and laying out its objectives, as well as memoranda and correspondence of the ERR special headquarters in the Ukraine and Croatia.

The collection further includes logs of searches carried out in Zagreb and Ragusa (Dubrovnik) among Jews and members of Masonic lodges; lists of Masonic lodges in Yugoslavia and lists of Jewish writers; inventories of Jewish *belles lettres*, and scientific and political literature; and a card file of Zagreb and Ragusa Jewish organizations and Masonic lodge members whose valuable books were confiscated.

The documents are in German.

Microfilms are held by the United States Holocaust Memorial Museum Archives.

Nemetsko-fashistskie administrativnye i sudebnye organy na vremenno okkupirovannykh territoriiakh

Nazi German Administrative and Judicial Agencies in the Temporarily Occupied Territories

Fond 1447k, 1935–1945. 444 storage units.

The collection's contents entered the RGVA among materials brought by the Soviet Army from the territory of Germany, Czechoslovakia, and Poland in 1945–46, and from the First Special Department of the USSR Ministry of Internal Affairs in 1953.

The collection is described in one inventory, arranged structurally.

The collection includes a broad range of documentary materials of German administrative and judicial agencies in the occupied territories of the Soviet Union, as well as edicts and orders of the occupation authorities on the structure of administrative services and degrees of jurisdiction, on economic and food issues, on the use of manpower, on establishing local institutions, on operating railroads, and on setting price controls. It also includes minutes of court sessions and investigative files.

The collection contains edicts of the Reichskommissariat Ukraine, the Generalkommissariats in Dnepropetrovsk, Rovno, Kiev, Nikolaev, Zhitomir, and Volhynia-Podolia, and of the German Governor-General of Galicia for 1942–44; as well as circulars and edicts of the German district commissariat in Grodno, the Reichskommissariat (Ostland) for the Baltic region, and the office of the General Government on occupied territories of Poland. Among the documentation preserved in the collection is a circular letter from the Governor-General of the eastern territories (Krakow) to district and regional officials on evacuating Poles and Jews from the eastern territories of Germany and housing them in the lands of the General Government, and reports on executions of Jews in Grodno.

The materials also deal with economic and administrative issues, and include dispatches by the administration of Minsk-Mazowiecki (Poland) on foreigners living in the city, and correspon- dence on their status. There is also a circular from the Warsaw district head closing Jewish photography studios in the city. Also noteworthy are a list of Jewish foreigners registered in the city of Reisdorf.

The collection also contains edicts, directives, and announcements by the head of General Government on the Jewish problem, including on receiving, daily, two trainloads of Jews being resettled from Germany to occupied Poland, and on procedures for this resettlement, on establishing the office of Commissar of the Jewish ghetto in Warsaw, and on creating a Jewish ghetto in Lvov and special isolation zones for Jews in a number of regions of Poland and Galicia (in Lvov, Bobrka, Novyi Yarichev, Grudek, Rudki, Yavorov, Zlochev, Peremyshlany, Brody, Rava Russkaya, Lyubachev, Busk, Sokal', Brzeżany [a ghetto], Bukachevtsy, Podhajce, Rohatyn, Tarnopol [a ghetto], Skałat, Trembovla, Zborov, Zbarazh, Chertkov, Buchach, Borshchev, Kopyczyńce, Tłuste, Stanislav, Stry, Drogobych, Borislav, and Sambor).

The documents are in German.

Microfilms are held by the United States Holocaust Memorial Museum Archives.

Imperskoe ministerstvo ekonomiki (g. Berlin)

Reichswirtschaftministerium (Berlin)

Reich Ministry of Economics (Berlin)

Fond 1458k, 1919–1945. 13,502 storage units.

Prior to 1917, guidance of the German economy fell under the jurisdiction of the Reich Office of the Interior; it was subsequently transferred to the jurisdiction of the Reich Economics Office, which in 1919 was converted into a ministry. In 1934, the ministry subsumed the Prussian Ministry of Economics. Besides purely economic, legal, and financial issues, the ministry was responsible for restricting the civil and property rights of Jews, and expelling them from Germany and German-occupied territories. The German Ministry of Economics was headed by Dr. Kurt Schmitt (1933–35), Hjalmer G. Schacht (1935–37), Herman Göring (1937–38), and subsequently by Walther Funk (1938–45). In 1942, by arrangement with Himmler, Funk made Reichsbank vaults available for storing valuables taken from the Jewish population and brought from prisons and camps. The Reich Ministry of Economics ceased activities in 1945 with the defeat of Nazi Germany.

The collection's documents came to the USSR Central State Special Archive (now the RGVA) in 1959–62 from the USSR Central Archive of Foreign Trade and the Historical-Diplomatic Administration of the USSR Ministry of Foreign Affairs. The collection was systematized by the staff of the USSR Central Archive of Foreign Trade and of the former USSR Central State Special Archive during the period 1950–60.

The collection's contents are catalogued in 54 inventories, all of which are arranged by structure. The inventories are loose-leaf and typewritten, and include inventory section indexes; there is a cartographic index to the collection's files and an index of inventory titles.

The collection contains thematically organized files consisting of circulars, orders, decrees, and correspondence devoted to restricting the rights of Jews in Germany and German-occupied territories (including the Soviet Union, the Baltic republics, and Belorussia) with regard to personal and property insurance, the issuing of credit and bank loans, payment for work, and sick pay. There are, moreover, individual circulars, orders, directives, decrees appended to legislative acts, stenographic reports of speeches, and minutes of secret meetings of senior Reich officials Hermann Göring, Walther Funk, and Labor Minister Franz Seldte on excluding Jews from the German economy and commerce, on confiscating Jewish-owned plots of land and property in German territory and in German-occupied countries, including the Soviet Union, and on expelling Jews from Germany; and analytic surveys and papers on German legislation with regard to Jews.

Most of the documents are in German.

Microfilms are held by the United States Holocaust Memorial Museum Archives.

INDIVIDUALS

Miuller fon Gauzen Liudvig, predsedatel' antisemitskoi organizatsii "Obshchestvo po bor'be s vliianiem evreev" i Komiteta po izucheniiu masonstva

Ludwig Müller von Hausen

Fond 577k, 1800–1938. 1,044 storage units.

Ludwig Müller von Hausen (1851–1929) was a German army captain who became a prominent Völkisch and anti-Semitic publicist. Von Hausen was leader of the Society against Jewish Arrogance (Verband gegen Überhebung des Judenthums), and editor of its journal *Auf Vorposten* (1912–25). In 1920, he published the first German-language edition of the *Protocols of the Elders of Zion* under the pseudonym Gottfried von Beek, which was reprinted several times prior to Alfred Rosenberg's 1923 edition. Von Hausen was an active exponent of the notion of a vast Judeo-Masonic conspiracy. He was active in the ultra-conservative National Union of German Officers.

The collection's contents are catalogued in two inventories arranged by document type. There are geographical and subject indexes to the inventories.

The collection contains the personal documents of Ludwig Müller von Hausen, reflecting his passage through military and civil service, participation in the activities of German monarchist and nationalist organizations, and maintenance of business contacts.

The materials of the Society against Jewish Arrogance and of the Committee for the Study of the Freemasons include bylaws and circular letters of these organizations; personal files of members (these constitute the majority of the collection's contents); and documents on financial activity, including statements of membership dues paid.

The collection contains correspondence with the All-German Union, the German Fatherland Party, offices of various fascist organizations, the Vienna Antisemites' League, the German People's Freedom Party, other nationalist organizations, and private individuals. Topics include exchanging information and printed publications, and taking joint measures — including with regard to the economic boycott of Jews. Correspondents included Russian émigré monarchist figures, such as Ataman Semenov, Erin Freiberg, Alexander Nechvolodov (a monarchist historian), Col. Bessonov, and Count L. Saltykov. Also reflected in this collection is Gen. Erich Ludendorff, with whom correspondence was conducted in connection with his lawsuit against the Central Association of German Citizens of the Jewish Faith, which he accused of defaming him.

There are documents on the arraignment of von Hausen himself and of his cohorts (F. Köstler, P. Kruger, et al.) for distributing antisemitic leaflets and publishing libelous material about Jews.

The collection also contains a large quantity of printed materials: articles and treatises on the Jewish question, on Jewish participation in the economic life of Germany, on the influence of Judaism on the Lutheran Reformation, on the attitude of Reformation figures toward Jews and Judaism, on comparing Judaism and Christianity, on Jewish participation in secret societies and German Masonic orders, and on the situation of Jews in Europe, America, Russia, and other countries in the first two decades of the twentieth century. The collection also includes documents of branches of B'nai B'rith and of Zionist organizations (collected by the Society against Jewish Arrogance for the purpose of studying their activities), and materials of the publishing house *Auf Vorposten*.

The documents are in German.

Natan, Paul', prezident Tsentral'noi evreiskoi federatsii Germanii

Paul Nathan

Fond 628k, 1874–1923. 23 storage units.

Paul Nathan (1857–1927) was a German Jewish public figure close to Theodor Barth and Ludwig Bamberger who published the political weekly *Die Nation* until 1907. A representative of the Liberal Party's left-democratic wing, he joined the Socialist Party after the First World War. He first became active in Jewish affairs as a leader of the League to Combat Antisemitism, and of the Committee for Defense against Anti-Semitic Attacks. In the 1890s, he published a number of polemical works against antisemitism, including "Crime among the Jews of Germany" (1896) and "Jewish Soldiers" (1896).

Nathan was one of the founders of the German Jewish Aid Society in 1901, and until 1914 served as its first vice chairman and treasurer. He traveled in this capacity to Russia and used German Jewish Aid Society funds to support Jewish liberal and radical parties in Russia. In 1915, he joined the newly founded German Association for the Interests of East European Jews. Nathan was a member of the executive council of the Central Association of German Citizens of the Jewish Faith, and one of the most highly regarded figures in German Jewry. An opponent of Zionism, he favored solving the Jewish question by strengthening liberal and socialist forms of governance in the countries of Europe, and supported the acculturation and social integration of Jews.

The collection's contents are catalogued in two inventories. The inventories are arranged by theme.

The collection includes personal documents: diplomas from the University of Heidelberg and from the Friedrich Wilhelm University philosophy department, a Berlin police certificate of Nathan's political reliability, and photographs of Nathan and his relatives.

The collection contains documents connected with Nathan's public activity: correspondence with members of the New York-based American Rumanian Jewish Emancipation Committee, on Jews being granted Romanian citizenship; with the lawyers Schwarzfeld and Herrenstein on the situation of Jews in Romania; with John Gregory and Israel Zangwill on their visit to Angola; with cultural figures on collecting signatures to protest the imprisonment of those who took part in the Revolution of 1905 in Russia; with the German Jewish Aid Society on the situation of Jews in Palestine and on providing aid to Jewish victims of pogroms in Russia; and with the Technion (Haifa) board of trustees members Kalonymus-Volf Wisotzky (Moscow), James Simon, and Jacob Schiff (New York) on organizing the academic curriculum.

Documents collected by Nathan include a draft charter and the charter of the German Jewish Aid Society; the text of a statement of protest by German public figures against the indictment of Mendel Beilis, and letters from the Jewish communities of Dresden and Munich as well as newspaper clippings on this issue; and minutes of meetings of the board of trustees of the Technion in Haifa and of the pedagogical council of the Simonsche Stiftung Trade School for 1912, and reports on the work of the Technion and the school.

There are also draft notes and printed texts of Nathan's articles, including his article, "The Jewish Question in Ancient Morocco," and his pamphlet *England und Wir* (1912).

The documents are in English, German, Russian, and French.

V

GREECE

ORGANIZATIONS

Evreiskaia obshchina (g. Afiny)

Jewish Community of Athens

Fond 1427k, 1609–1941. 117 storage units.

The earliest reliable information on Jewish settlement in Athens dates to the second century of the Common Era. Having been expelled from the city during the Greek Rebellion (1821–29), Jews began once again to settle in Athens in 1834. The Jewish religious community of Athens was officially established in 1889. Its first president was Charles de Rothschild. In 1891, a Jewish cemetery was opened, and, in 1906, a two-story synagogue/school building. The first Rabbi of Athens was Rabbi Ch. Kastel (d. 1922), who was succeeded by Rabbis I. de Javez and Elias Barzilai. Athens was seized by the Nazis in April 1941. In May 1941, Jewish community leaders were arrested, their documents seized, and the community itself ceased to exist.

The collection's contents are not systematized, although many files have been grouped together by theme.

The collection includes community registration documents; bylaws of the Jewish community of Athens; bylaws of the community religious court (Bet Din), minutes of its sessions, court decisions, marriage contracts and divorces filed at the Bet Din, and related documents; financial documentation of the Jewish community of Athens; as well as documentation on instruction at Jewish religious community schools and on the teaching of Judaism at Jewish secular schools.

The collection contains registers of members of the Athens Jewish community (personal information, places of residence, social position, and photographs of community members); as well as references, attestations, and certificates issued to members by the chief rabbinate or Jewish community leaders.

Included are numerous documents on the religious life of the community, on the conduct of synagogue services, and on synagogue officials and vacancies. There are schedules of services and daily prayers, documentation on service attendance by Jewish community members, and announcements on the conduct of special services devoted to extraordinary events (Greek national holidays, youth services on the birthday of the Greek king or queen, and mourning services — for example, for Jewish settlers killed in Palestine in 1936).

The collection contains official communal correspondence: correspondence of the chief rabbinate and Athens community leaders with Greek central and municipal authorities; correspondence of community leaders and the chief rabbinate with Jewish international organizations (Keren Kayemeth LeIsrael, Keren Hayesod); correspondence with banks, businesses, and enterprises regarding economic issues; correspondence with leaders of Jewish communities in other Greek cities and abroad; correspondence of Athens Jewish community leaders with private individuals on personal matters, on searches for relatives and respondents; and documentation on the transport of Jewish refugees from Western and Eastern Europe to Palestine via Greece.

The documents are in Hebrew, Ladino, Greek, and French.

Microfilms are held by the United States Holocaust Memorial Museum Archives.

Evreiskaia obshchina (g. Saloniki)

Jewish Community of Salonika

Fond 1428k, 1844–1941. 297 storage units.

A Jewish community existed in Salonika as early as the first century B.C.E. In 1680, Jews from various cities of Greece, Germany, Spain, Italy, Portugal, and Provence established in the city a single community headed by a council of three rabbis and seven notables. Starting in 1886, the Jewish community of Salonika was headed by a chief rabbi or *hakham bashi*, who represented the community's interests before the Turkish authorities. During the period 1886–1907, this office was held by Yaakov Kuvo; during 1908–19, by Yaakov Meir. The *hakham bashi* headed both the local rabbinical council, which dealt with halakhic, religious, and educational issues, and the 70-member general assembly, which oversaw, for the most part, charitable programs. All regular tax-paying members of the community voted in elections for the general assembly, whose members in turn chose an executive council of fifteen persons. On the eve of the First World War, when the Jewish population of Salonika numbered 90,000 — that is, over half the population of the city — the community maintained more than thirty synagogues, about fifty cheders, and ten yeshivas. The community also ran the Baron M. Hirsch Jewish Hospital, retirement homes, homeless shelters, the "Bikur Cholim" society to aid the sick, and several other charitable institutions. The city's 1917 fire left almost 50,000 Jews homeless. This, along with several other circumstances, caused the Jewish population of Salonika to decrease after the First World War, the city having been seized by Greece in 1912, during the First Balkan War. The twentieth century saw several representatives of the Modiano and Allatini families serve as presidents of the general assembly. The last president of the community was Y. Kazez, who held this office during the period 1921–41; and the last chief rabbi was Zvi Hirsch Koretz. The Nazis seized Salonika on 9 April 1941, and, on 15 April 1941, the entire leadership of the Jewish community was arrested.

The collection's contents are not systematized, although many files have been grouped together by theme.

The collection contains registration documents of the Jewish community of Salonika, including bylaws of the community and the religious court (Bet Din); court documentation: minutes of sessions of Bet Din and its decisions, and marriage contracts and divorces filed with the Bet Din;

records of the Salonika chief rabbinate; and the record book (*pinkas*) of the Jewish community of Salonika, and birth registers of the Jewish community of Salonika, including community member marriage contracts. The registers contain numerous photographs of members of the Jewish community. Also included are biographical material; a writ of protection issued by the Salonika prefect; Jewish community members' applications for permission to relocate to Palestine; and financial documents of the Jewish community of Salonika.

The collection's contents include numerous documents on the religious life of the community, on the conduct of synagogue services, and on synagogue officials and vacancies. There is documentation on service attendance by Jewish community members, sermons by Greek rabbis, and passages from religious treatises.

The collection houses materials of the Salonika Jewish community's education commission and documentation on instruction at Jewish religious schools, on the teaching of Judaism at Jewish secular schools, and on related matters.

The collection also contains correspondence of Jewish community leaders and the rabbinate of Salonika with Greek government institutions and with Jewish organizations and communities in Greece and beyond (primarily in Macedonia); with the Greek Ministry of Finance on tax issues; with commercial organizations in Greece and other European countries on organizational, charitable, and financial matters; and items of correspondence of leaders of the Jewish community and the Jewish religious court of Salonika with leaders of Jewish communities of cities in Greece and abroad on legal procedure, issues of Jewish law, and financial and personal matters.

The collection features the voluminous correspondence of the chief rabbi and community council with international Jewish religious and Zionist organizations — the World Federation of Sephardic Communities, Mizrachi, Shivat Zion, Keren Kayemeth LeIsrael, Keren Hayesod, B'nai B'rith, B'nai Zion, Alliance Israélite Universelle, and others. There is correspondence between the leaders of the Jewish community of Salonika and those of other cities and countries, on delivering provisions necessary for public needs and for the celebration of Jewish religious holidays, on searches for relatives, and on other issues.

There are platform and charter documents of Zionist organizations and documents of Zionist congresses in which representatives of the Jewish community of Salonika took part. The collection also includes documents on receiving refugees and on organizing the evacuation of Jewish refugees from Western and Eastern European countries occupied by the Nazis; this includes lists of refugees. There are documents on the collection of donations to aid Jewish settlers in Palestine and meet the needs of international Zionist organizations; documents on the life of Jewish settlers in Palestine, including information on émigrés from Salonika; materials of the central bureau of Keren Kayemeth LeIsrael and of its branches in Greece, including financial documentation; and documents on the activities of the Orient Grand Lodge of B'nai B'rith.

Also included are materials properly belonging to other collection originators: records of the Jewish community of Athens (Fond 1427k) and of Jewish charitable organizations of various cities of Greece. There are manuscript compendia and books on Jewish religious law and scholarship that were collected by the Jewish community of Vienna (see Fonds 707k and 717k) including a manuscript of part of *The Book of Zohar*. The collection also has printed materials.

The documents are in Ladino, Hebrew, Greek, French, Turkish, and Arabic.

Microfilms are held by the United States Holocaust Memorial Museum Archives.

Sionistskoe palestinskoe biuro (g. Saloniki)

Palestine Bureau (Salonika)

Fond 1435k, 1918–1940. 56 storage units.

On 10 June 1918, the Zionist Federation of Greece was established as a union of the Zionist organizations of fourteen Greek cities; it was headquartered in Salonika. The Federation's Palestine Bureau focused on information and coordination, and propagandized for Jewish colonization in Palestine. The federation raised funds on behalf of Jewish settlement in Palestine and conducted campaigns to support Zionist projects.

The collection's contents are catalogued in one inventory, which is arranged alphabetically.

The collection includes reports, news bulletins and appeals of the Palestine Bureau: general reports on the activities of the Salonika-based Palestine Bureau for 1924–26; reports to leaders of the Zionist Federation of Greece on the state of Jewish settlements in Palestine and on work completed (1919); an appeal by leaders of Salonika's Zionist organizations to the Jewish communities of Greece on the start of a fundraising campaign on behalf of Jewish settler victims of Arab pogroms in Palestine (summer 1930); fundraising bulletins on behalf of Jewish victims of pogroms in Palestine and on resettling Salonika Jews in Palestine (1921–39); a register of funds that the Jewish community of Salonika donated to meet the needs of Jewish settlers in Palestine (1935); a register of salary payments to employees and of other expenditures of the Palestine Bureau; and other financial documents.

The collection also contains the Palestine Bureau's extensive correspondence: with the chief rabbis and Jewish community councils of Salonika and other Greek cities; with the Association of Young Jews, the Mizrachi and Salonika-Palestine societies, the Zionist Federation of Greece, *La Renessencia Judia* (The Jewish Renaissance), the Carasso-Benveniste shipping company, Keren Kayemeth LeIsrael, Keren Hayesod, the organization Drorim Maccabi, Alliance Israélite Universelle, the Achdut network of educational institutions, Zeirei Zion, the Zionist society Hatikvah, the World Zionist Organization's department of education and culture (in London), the Zionist Federation of France, the Salonika Jewish religious court, the Workers' Zionist Socialist Party of Greece, the Max Nordau Zionist organization, the Jewish sports club *Hakoah*, the union of radical Zionists Artzeinu, the Shivat Zion society, the World Federation of Sephardic Communities, Kupat Ashrai Eretz Israel, the Zionist Information Bureau for Tourists in Palestine (Jerusalem), the organization Halutzei Ha-mizrach, Betar, the Union of Revisionist Zionists, the Zionist organization Mevakshei Zion, the Amelei Zion society, the Zionist youth organization Hatehiya (Dimotika), the Zionist society Tel Aviv, Irgun Olei Yavan (an organization of Greek Jewish repatriates in Palestine), the Histadrut Olei Salonika society, the Geula society (Dráma), the Association of Young Jews (Kastoria), the Volos branch of the Poale Zion party, the Agudat Herzl society (Sérrai), the Ohavei Zion society (Larissa), the Jewish community of Kerkyra (Corfu); and with private individuals.

The correspondence concerns selecting candidates for immigration to Palestine, organizing and sending tour groups to Palestine on familiarization trips, and describing conditions of life and work for Halutzim on kibbutzim (1930–36). There is correspondence with the Armenian party Dashnaksutiun; B. Taranto's correspondence with Palestine Bureau leaders concerning the Mikveh Israel school in Palestine and sending young Jews from Dráma, Veria, Préveza, and other Greek communities to study in Palestine (1933); correspondence by Salonika settlers living in Palestine with the Salonika Palestine Bureau containing reports on the social and economic life of these settlers in Palestine and on solving problems connected with getting settled, proposals for business cooperation, and requests to help relatives obtain visas and depart for Palestine (1933); letters of the director of the Bezalel School of Art and Design (Jerusalem) to leaders of the Zionist Federation of Greece on the progress of joint projects in Palestine (1919); and letters from the London bureau of the WZO concerning the conduct in Greece of Shekel Day, a fundraising event to benefit Jewish settlers in Palestine (March and June 1919), and expressing gratitude for the high quality of events held (June 1919).

The collection also has a letter from D. Alkalai, president of the Zion society of Belgrade, to leaders of the Zion society of Salonika regarding a Romanian Jewish group's trip to Palestine (1919); letters from the Irgun Olei Danzig society (Tel Aviv) requesting assistance with transporting representatives of the Jewish community of Danzig to Palestine (1939); a letter from members of the Association of Young Jews (Salonika) to the

Committee of the Zionist Federation of Greece expressing interest in taking part in the Conference of Greek Zionists (1919); a letter from Jewish Community of Salonika committee and from community members I. Alvo, S. Benvenisti, Sh. Fetz, and others to the chairman of the Zionist Federation requesting to take part in a Zionist conference; a letter from leaders of the Central Zionist Bureau in Warsaw to leaders of the Palestine Bureau in Salonika on working with Halutzim and organizing summer youth camps for Polish Jews in Palestine (1926); a letter from International Migration Bureau director D. L. Reitner (Athens) on the possibility of taking in, in Salonika, 25 orphans expelled from Palestine due to problems with documents; and a letter from the Palestine Bureau's immigration department to the general manager of the newspaper *Avante*, demanding that the newspaper publish a retraction of its article "Cases of Zionist Criminals" (published 9 June 1937), and the article "The Situation of Jewish Fishermen from Salonika in Eretz Israel," drawn up by way of refutation.

The collection also contains applications filed with the Palestine Bureau for permission for Jews to emigrate from Greece to Palestine (1933), (these include applicants' basic biographical data); personal files of candidates for emigration, including applications for permission to emigrate for permanent residence in Palestine, applicant photos, proof of having found work in Palestine, certificates of applicant membership in a Zionist organization (usually the Tel Aviv societies Irgun Olei Yavan or Geula), applicant autobiographies, recommendations from Zionist organizations, and medical certificates (1933–39); lists of persons emigrating arranged by profession, age, and marital status; photographs of candidates for emigration to Palestine (437 in all); the chairman of the Palestine Bureau's correspondence with the British Consul General on the issuing of emigration certificates, visas, and Palestine entry permits for Greek Jews; immigration certificates for entry into Palestine issued by the British consulate in Salonika; work contracts and agreements to terms of employment in the port of Haifa signed by Salonika Jews; a declaration by Halutzim and their parents accepting terms for three years of work on a kibbutz in Palestine; a list of persons recommended for repatriation with guaranteed job placement drawn up in Tel Aviv by the organization of Salonika Jews Histadrut Olei Salonika (1932); Greek Jewish émigrés' contracts for employment in Palestine; Jewish Agency for Palestine circulars and explanations on entry rules, on prospects for job placement in Palestine, kibbutz work, and more.

The collection also includes a resolution by the Jewish Congress of Greece (convened 10 March 1919 in Salonika) on formally recognizing the right of Jews to national autonomy in every country in which they reside, on prospects for establishing a Jewish state in Palestine and Jewish representation at the League of Nations, and on formally recognizing Jewish civil and religious rights (1919); letters from leaders of the Zionist Federation of Greece to Greek Jewish communities on Jewish education and on raising the coming generation in the spirit of Jewish tradition; the program of the Fifth Conference of the Zionist Federation of Greece (Salonika 1927); a financial statement and draft budget of the Zionist Federation of Greece for the 1927–28 fiscal year; a circular (27 November 1925) issued by the Jewish National Fund's commissariat on Greece to all Zionist societies and groups in Greece on procedures for designating conference delegates; and copies of the Salonika Palestine Bureau's bulletin *Halutzim*.

The collection also contains a request by the Salonika chief rabbi to leaders of the Salonika Zionist Federation for aid to Russian, Polish, and Palestinian Jews, and for the establishment of a commission to aid them (April 1919), as well as materials on the emigration of Polish Jews to Palestine (1920–25)

Some materials seem to originate from Fond 1428k ("The Jewish Community of Salonika"): a memorandum from the chief rabbi of Salonika to the Greek authorities on the sale of meat in kosher stores and on the system of kosher food; letters from employees of Jewish community institutions and synagogues to the chief rabbinate; letters of gratitude from Salonika Chief Rabbi Zvi Hirsch Koretz to members of the city's Jewish community who had donated funds to aid homeless members of the Jewish community from the Teneke Mahale quarter; lists of donors, and money transfer receipts; applications for divorce; minutes of sessions of the Salonika chief rabbinate's religious court (Bet Din); marriage contracts; and Bet Din summonses.

The documents are in Hebrew, Ladino, Greek, English, French, German, and Yiddish.

Microfilms are held by the United States Holocaust Memorial Museum Archives.

Aktsionernoe obshchestvo "Salonika-Palestina" (g. Saloniki)

Salonika-Palestine Corporation

Fond 1437k, 1924–1941. 13 storage units.

The Salonika-Palestine Corporation was the financial banking agent associated with the Salonika Palestine Bureau and served the purpose of supporting, financially and otherwise, the work of the Palestine Bureau. It assisted in selecting candidates for emigration and helped finance their move to Palestine, created employment for them and for temporary migrants (including Halutzim headed to Palestine for three years of temporary employment), and financed kibbutzim and Jewish industrial projects in Palestine. It also aided in the purchase of lands for the establishment of agricultural and urban settlements in Palestine.

The collection is catalogued in one inventory arranged by structure.

The collection contains Salonika-Palestine Corporation correspondence with branches of the Anglo-Palestine Bank in Jaffo (Palestine); with Greek, Palestinian, English, Italian, Lebanese, American, and other banks; and with private individuals on banking operations and on establishing and dissolving firms and companies with shares in the corporation; with representatives of industrial firms in Europe and Palestine regarding the production and sale of various goods; with the leaders of Jewish religious communities of Greece, Palestine, and other countries regarding banking operations and other actions of a financial and economic nature; as well as checks, loan certificates, accounts, and other financial documents. There is also personal correspondence.

The documents are in English, Greek, Ladino, Hebrew, French, Arabic, and German.

Microfilms are held by the United States Holocaust Memorial Museum Archives.

VI

ROMANIA

GOVERNMENT AGENCIES

Ministerstvo vnutrennykh del Rumynii (g. Bukharest)

Ministerul de Interne (Bucureşti)
Ministry of Internal Affairs of Romania (Bucharest)

Fond 1376k, 1903–1942. 72 storage units.

According to the constitution of the Kingdom of Romania, adopted in 1866 and revised in 1884, executive power was held by the Cabinet of Ministers, which included the Ministry of Internal Affairs. The Ministry of Internal Affairs was vested with the function, among others, of registering charters and issuing permits for the conduct of activities of various public organizations in Romania.

The collection is described in one inventory. Materials are catalogued chronologically. The file was transferred to the archive from the archival administration of the USSR Ministry of Foreign Affairs.

The collection contains applications received by the Bucharest prefecture from cultural, youth, religious, and other societies for licenses to engage in activities stipulated in the societies' charters. There are charter and other documents on Jewish religious, cultural, philanthropic, and other organizations active on Romanian territory: the Intaitarea society to help poor students with clothes and books; the Asistenţă society; the Inflorea cultural society; the Socialbilitatea cultural society; the Botezul Copiilor Soraci society (the "Society to Aid in the Circumcision of Sons of the Law

of Moses from Poor Families"); the Libertatea society; and the Avoidas Is-
roel society.

The documents are in Romanian, French, and German.

VII

YUGOSLAVIA

ORGANIZATIONS

*Velikie lozhi evreiskogo ordena "Bnei-Brit" v Iugoslavii i Gretsii
i ikh dochernie lozhi*

**The Grand Lodges of B'nai B'rith in Yugoslavia and Greece
and their Affiliated Lodges (consolidated collection)**

Fond 1225k, 1875–1941. 60 storage units.

In the late nineteenth and early twentieth centuries, the jurisdiction of district 11 of the Independent Order of B'nai B'rith included the entire Eastern Mediterranean region. A lodge was established in Belgrade in 1911, with Adolf Resovski as president. The Zagreb lodge, founded in 1927, was Zionist in orientation, as was the Sarajevo lodge, founded in 1933. In 1935, Yugoslav lodges succeeded in breaking away from B'nai B'rith district 11 and forming district 18 for the Yugoslav Kingdom. Its grand master was Dr. Bukiç Pijade. The lodges' members consisted of the social elite of Yugoslav Jewish communities. They sponsored lectures, discussions of current Jewish issues, and donated money to local, national, and foreign Jewish institutions. In August 1940, a decree of the Ministry of Interior dissolved all B'nai B'rith lodges in Yugoslavia.

In 1956, thirty-five files for the period 1913–41 catalogued in inventory no. 1 were transferred to Yugoslavia. Inventory no. 2 has a geographical index and a brief summary of the collection's contents.

The collection includes documents reflecting the activities of the Grand Lodge of B'nai B'rith in Yugoslavia and its affiliated lodges "Serbia," "Sarajevo," and "Zagreb." These include circulars from leaders of the Grand Lodge to affiliated lodges; a register of proceedings of the "Serbia" lodge, and a list of its board members; brief biographical information on the leaders of B'nai B'rith in Yugoslavia; letters of recommendation and application forms of candidates for membership in the "Serbia" lodge; a manuscript on the traditions, history, and customs of B'nai Brith (1895); historical information on the activities of the Belgrade lodges "Serbia" and "Ivan Drašković"; texts of the charter, with draft amendments and addenda to the charter, of the "Serbia" lodge; documents of the Zagreb lodge (the lodge's charter, letters between lodge members, lodge meeting agendas, bylaws and instructions on internal procedure, and rules of conduct and interaction among lodge members); minutes of meetings of the Sarajevo lodge regarding B'nai B'rith president Alfred Cohen's stepping down and the election of Henry Monsky to succeed him; minutes and agendas of meetings of the "Solomon Alkalaj" lodge in Novi Sad (1934–35); and a list of members and leaders of the "Menorah" lodge in Osiek and the "Matnat Yad" lodge in Subotica.

The collection also includes documents on the participation of B'nai B'rith figures (for example, "Serbia" lodge head Friedrich Pops) in the political life of Yugoslavia, and on the attitude of the B'nai B'rith toward political events within the country (for example, its reaction to the assassination of King Alexander of Yugoslavia in Paris in 1934, and its support for national unity); correspondence with Yugoslav authorities, ministries, and departments on political, financial, international, and other issues; and letters of Aron Alkalaj of the Belgrade lodge.

The collection also contains various reports. Among them are excerpts from a report (6 March 1938) by the secretary of the Yugoslavia Grand Lodge on its activities in 1937, on the struggle against anti-Semitic speeches of the "Falcon" movement and other radical groups, and on the maintenance of lodge discipline; a report by Leon Steindler, "On the Causes and Nature of Antisemitism"; a report by Aron Alkalaj and A. Shatner on their participation in the work of the B'nai B'rith London lodge; and letters from the headquarters of the British and Irish Grand Lodge of B'nai B'rith to Aron Alkalaj on the conduct of holiday events (1939).

There are documents on fundraising on behalf of the Jewish refugees who poured into Yugoslavia from Germany, Austria, Romania, Hungary, Poland, and other countries during and after 1938–39. There are also "Serbia" lodge member M. Iosip's European travel notes, which describe the situation of Jews, particularly refugees from Germany, in Austria, Great Britain, Hungary, Holland, France, and Switzerland.

The collection also contains documents of B'nai B'rith lodges in

Greece: a 25 April 1925 report by the charity commission of the "Philon" lodge (Athens); applications for admission to the B'nai B'rith lodge in Salonika; and account books of the "Acropolis," "Grand East of Greece," "Byzantium," and other lodges; correspondence of the B'nai B'rith lodge in Athens with affiliated lodges regarding financial accounting and joint participation in charity events; a letter from N. Kaiserman, chairman of the B'nai B'rith "Carmel" lodge (Haifa), to the chairman of the "Philon" lodge (Athens) requesting aid in raising funds to establish a Jewish orphanage in Haifa; and a resolution of protest adopted at a meeting of the Zionist Federation of Greece (mid-1930s) against the actions of the British authorities with regard to Jews in Palestine.

The collection also contains materials of other (non-B'nai B'rith) provenance, apparently from the Jewish community of Belgrade: the texts of speeches delivered at a conference of the Union of Jewish Religious Communities of Yugoslavia; correspondence on the election of David Albala as head of the Sephardic Jewish community of Belgrade, on the Amsterdam Conference of the World Federation of Sephardic Communities, and on the grave situation of the Jews of Germany, Austria, Poland, Romania, and Hungary (1939); materials on the construction of the Belgrade synagogue, the religious center of the Ashkenazi community of Serbia; a list of cultural, charitable, and Jewish religious educational institutions and their chairpersons in Yugoslavia; lists of Belgrade Jewish community electors for 1931, with addresses and surnames; minutes of a meeting of the Executive Committee of the Union of Jewish Religious Communities of Yugoslavia; documents of the Yugoslavia-Palestine Economic Committee (Yugolevant), including a report, drawn up 13 September 1935, on the state of trade between Yugoslavia and Palestine; the charter of the Yugoslav Committee for the Development of Economic Ties with Palestine, ratified by the Yugoslav Ministry of Trade and Industry; materials on Yugoslavia's participation in the Levant Fair in Tel Aviv in 1936; designs for the Yugoslav pavilion at this fair; and the above committee's correspondence with the Yugoslav Ministries of Finance and Foreign Trade on Yugoslavia's collaboration with Jewish economic entities in Palestine.

The collection also contains printed material: a book of lyrical poems by I. Sonneschein (1920s); *Sefer melekhet yad* (Hebrew text with German translation by I. Alkalay, with translator's introduction, notes, and indexes, 1906); English-language pamphlets with ready answers for anti-Semitic myths (the blood libel, participation in the Bolshevik revolution, Jewish control of world financial markets, etc.); a pamphlet of L.

Abramovich's lecture "The Great Tragedy of Jewry," delivered 9 May 1933 at the "Podbratim" lodge in Belgrade, with the author's dedicatory inscription to Chief Rabbi Isaac Alcalay; articles on the international Evian Conference, on the World Jewish Congress's appeal to participants of this conference (1938) to fight for the granting of entry visas to Jewish refugees, and on supporting the resolutions of the Evian Conference; issues of the journal of the Hanoar Union of Jewish Youth Organizations of Yugoslavia for 1935; typewritten printouts of newspaper publications on Jewish emigration, the role of Jewish capital, and antisemitism (1937–40).

The documents are in German, Serbo-Croatian, Greek, and English.

Microfilms are held by the United States Holocaust Memorial Museum Archives.

Evreiskaia sinagogal'no-prosvetitel'naia obshchina (g. Belgrad)

Crkveno-školska evrejska opština (Beograd)

Jewish Synagogue and School Community of Belgrade

Fond 1429k, 1815–1941. 351 storage units.

Jews from Italy and Hungary began settling in Belgrade in the thirteenth and four-teenth centuries, as did, in the first half of the sixteenth century, Jews expelled from the Iberian peninsula. The legal status of the Jewish community of Belgrade was formalized by an official charter in 1866. Its first president was Jahiel Ruso, and its rabbi during the period 1886–94 was the famous Berlin scholar Simon Bernfeld. Ashkenazi Jews, whose religious autonomy was recognized by the Ser-bian government, established their own community in 1892.

In 1939, of the 10,388 Jews of Belgrade, 8,500 were Sephardim; 1,888 were Ashkenazi. Jewish membership in a religious community was required by law. According to its 1926 charter, the Sephardic community's primary mission consisted of "meeting the religious, educational, social, and cultural needs of com-munity members." The community was led by a council of eleven members who were elected every four years. The council had financial, cultural-educational, so-cial-charitable, and religious committees. In the 1920s and 1930s, Rafailo Finci, Solomon Alkalaj, S. Bemayo, Jakov Celebenovic, Bukić Pijade, and David Albala served as community presidents. The chief rabbi was Isaac Alcalay (1881–1971). The Sephardic community's budget, amounting in 1929 to 2.5 million dinars, was funded by community taxes, payments for synagogue seats, fees for the conduct of divorce and funeral ceremonies, fines, and the sale of kosher meat and matzah. The small Ashkenazi community was led during 1910–41 by Friedrich Pops; its Chief Rabbi was Ignjat Schlang. Both communities were liquidated after the Nazi occupation in April 1941.

The collection's contents are catalogued in one inventory arranged by document type.

The collection contains bylaws, minutes of meetings, and lists of members of the Jewish community of Belgrade; correspondence with Jew-ish charitable societies and with various individuals on the construction of buildings, on establishing Jewish schools, shelters, and a choir, on raising funds for the community fund, and on providing material aid to community members in need; birth registers and marriage contracts (1866–1940); a resolution on the payment of pensions to community employees; contracts with various firms and private individuals regarding the purchase of physical plant equipment and the leasing of buildings; lists of persons having made donations to the community; cash flow documents; stubs and receipts for the payment and receipt of funds from the community cashier's office (1911–40); and correspondence with Yugoslav authorities regarding construction permits for synagogue buildings, prayer houses, and other community institutions, and regarding the payment of taxes and Jewish emigration from Yugoslavia.

The documents are in Serbo-Croatian, Ladino, and Hebrew.

Microfilms are held by the United States Holocaust Memorial Museum Archives.

Komitet pomoshchi evreiskim bezhentsam (g. Zagreb)

Odbor za pomoć židovskim izbeglicam (Zagreb)

Committee for Aid to Jewish Refugees (Zagreb)

Fond 1430k, 1933–1941. 1,163 storage units.

In 1933, the Jewish community of Zagreb set up a local committee to aid Jews from Germany; it was sponsored by the JDC, HICEM, and the Jewish communities of Yugoslavia. The committee was headed by Zagreb Jewish community council vice president Makso Pscherhof. In 1933, 4,400 Jewish refugees from Germany settled in Zagreb; in 1934, 4,200. In all — from 1933 to 1941 — 55,000 Jewish refugees passed through Yugoslavia. The Zagreb Committee was the main HICEM committee in Yugoslavia.

The collection's contents are described in one inventory, which is arranged by structure and chronology.

Deposited in the collection are documents connected with the activities of the Zagreb HICEM Committee regarding the reception, settling, and transport to third countries of Jewish refugees from Germany and Austria. It includes correspondence with HICEM committees in Austria, the United States, Britain, Germany, Italy, and other countries, and with the Union of Jewish Religious Communities of Yugoslavia, the German Jewish Aid Society, the Jewish religious community of Brody, the JDC, the National Committee to Aid Refugees from Germany/Victims of Antisemitism (Paris), HIAS, the Swiss Zionist Union (Basel), the Palestine Bureau (Berlin), the Jewish community of Antwerp, Keren Hayesod, and the High Commission for Refugees from Germany. The correspondence touches upon issues of providing material aid to Jewish refugees from Germany and Austria, their job placement, filing documents for exit to third countries, and fundraising. There is also correspondence with Jewish émigrés and refugees on filing entry documents and on seeking refugees' family members. There are refugee questionnaires, "blacklists" of swindlers posing as refugees for the purpose of receiving material aid, and bulletins of the HICEM central committee on organizational issues and on the activities of the committee.

The documents are in Serbo-Croatian, German, French, Hebrew, Yiddish, English, Italian, and Hungarian.

Microfilms are held by the United States Holocaust Memorial Museum Archives.

Evreiskaia obshchina (g. Raguza)

Comunita Israelitica (Ragusa)

Jewish Community of Ragusa (Dubrovnik)

Fond 1439k, 1709–1940. 12 storage units.

The first mention of Jewish merchants from Durazzo, Albania settling in Ragusa (Dubrovnik) dates from 1368. With the expulsion of Jews from Spain in 1492, Dubrovnik became an important transit center for Sephardic exiles bound for the Balkans, some of whom settled in the city. In 1546, a Jewish ghetto was created, the inhabitants of which were subject to a special tax. 1755 saw the introduction of a ban on residence outside the walls of the ghetto. These restrictions were lifted by Napoleon in 1808. Dubrovnik was transferred to Austria by decision of the Congress of Vienna in 1815. The Jews of Dubrovnik were emancipated in 1873. After the First World War, Dubrovnik became part of Yugoslavia. Data from the year 1939 records 250 Jews living in Dubrovnik. In June 1943, the Jews of Dubrovnik were sent to the Italian camp at Rab (northern Dalmatia) along with other Yugoslavian Jewish residents of territory occupied by Italian forces.

The collection's contents are described in one inventory, arranged by structure.

The collection's documents include marriage registers of the Jewish community of Ragusa (Dubrovnik), indicating dates of wedding ceremonies performed and personal information of those entering into marriage (and of their parents); death registers, with dates, causes of death, and other personal information indicated; and birth registers, with dates of birth and parents' personal information indicated.

This collection contains financial accounting documentation as well as registers of dues and fees toward the needs of the Jewish community. There is also an account book of the Jewish community of Dubrovnik.

The documents are in Italian, Serbo-Croatian, Hebrew, Albanian, and German.

Evreiskaia obshchina (g. Zagreb)

Israelitićka bogoštovna općina (Zagreb)

Jewish Community of Zagreb

Fond 1441k, 1923–1941. 6 storage units.

Jews from Hungary settled in Zagreb in the mid-fourteenth century. An Ashkenazi community was in existence until the expulsion of Jews from the city in the mid-fifteenth century. Jews once again received the right to live in Zagreb in the 1780s. In 1806, twenty Ashkenazi families from Central Europe established a new Jewish community in the city. Religious reform carried out by the Zagreb synagogue in 1841 forced a small group of Orthodox to separate from the main community and establish their own prayer house. In 1867, a large Reform (Neologue) synagogue was opened in Zagreb. In 1939, Jews living in Zagreb numbered 9,467. Of these, 8,712 were Ashkenazi Reform, 625 were Sephardim, and 130 were Ashkenazi Orthodox.

The Jewish religious community of Zagreb was governed by a 45-member council headed by a president, vice president, secretary, and treasurer. Among its presidents were Josip Siebenschein, who held this office during the periods 1873–83 and 1891–1906, and his son Robert Siebenschein (1912–20). The first Zionist victory in a community presidential election occurred in 1920. The Zionist leader Hugo Kon was president of the community from that year until 1935. The position of chief rabbi from 1887 to 1923 was held by Hosea Jacobi (Hermann Jacoby), who was succeeded by Gavro Schwarz.

Starting in the second half of the nineteenth century, the Zagreb Jewish community sponsored a four-year elementary school, at which secular as well as Jewish subjects were taught in Serbo-Croatian. In the interwar period, the community's annual budget, which went mainly to social and philanthropic projects, averaged 2.5 million dinars.

The collection's contents are catalogued in one inventory.

The collection's documents consist primarily of correspondence: internal community correspondence (on public events, the execution of intracommunity administrative duties, educational issues, religious issues, the distribution of Zagreb synagogue positions, and so on); correspondence with Jewish and Zionist organizations, including the Union of Jewish Religious Communities of Yugoslavia, the Ashkenazi community of Belgrade, the Sephardic community of Sarajevo, the Hochschule for Jewish Studies in Berlin, the Dr. Bernard Singer Jewish charitable organization (Subotica), the Jewish religious community of Croatia, the Palestine Bureau in Yugoslavia, the Union of Rabbis of Yugoslavia, the Jelena Prister Jewish society to aid Jewish refugees, the Zionist Federation of Yugoslavia, the association of Jewish retirement homes and orphanages in Novi Sad, the Zagreb Union of Zionist Women, Keren Hayesod, and Keren Kayemeth LeIsrael. There is also correspondence with the HICEM office in Paris on support for Jews emigrating to Palestine.

The collection also contains correspondence with Yugoslav authorities (the Ministry of Religious Confessions) and Zagreb city authorities on various issues. Included are petitions, requests, complaints, applications for Yugoslav citizenship and Zagreb residence permits, and for the extension of Yugoslav visas for certain foreign Jewish figures.

The documents are in Serbo-Croatian, German, Hebrew, Czech, and Hungarian.

Microfilms are held by the United States Holocaust Memorial Museum Archives.

VIII

MIXED COLLECTIONS
(FROM MORE THAN ONE COUNTRY)

ORGANIZATIONS AND GOVERNMENT AGENCIES

Dokumenty politicheskogo, ekonomicheskogo i voennogo kharaktera uchrezhdenii i organizatsii Frantsii, Bel'gii, i dr. stran (kollektsiia)

Political, Economic, and Military Documents of Government Offices and other Organizations in France, Belgium, and other Countries (consolidated collection)

Fond 116k, 1901–1940. 1,990 storage units.

The bulk of the collection's documents entered the archive among other captured materials in 1955; 469 storage units came to the archive from the Belorussian SSR Central State Archive of the October Revolution (now the National Archive of the Republic of Belarus).

The collection constitutes an accumulation of documents of various institutions and organizations, often of undetermined collection provenance, compiled at the Central State Special Archive. These are documents of a political, economic, and military nature of various institutions and organizations in France, Belgium, and other countries. The collection includes materials on history, philosophy, politics, and economics, as well as information on the armed forces, police, intelligence activities, political parties and organizations in various countries.

The collection's contents are described in ten inventories, in which materials are catalogued by subject.

Deposited in the collection are varied records and documents of Jewish organizations. There are the texts of official announcements of the Committee of Jewish Delegations to the Paris Peace Conference in 1919, protesting anti-Jewish pogroms in the Ukraine and other Eastern European countries; and a communiqué on the Kiev pogrom of 14–18 October 1919.

The collection also includes documents from the period 1918–23 on the situation of Jews in Romania (possibly documents of L. Kubowitzki); a communiqué on anti-Jewish excesses in Romania, as well as an amendment to a Versailles Conference bulletin of 8 October 1919 dealing with the situation of Jews in Romania; statistical data on the ethnic composition of the population in various regions of Romania, including information on the number of Jews according to the 1930 Romanian census and on the ethnic composition of those who were born and who died in Romania in 1936 and 1937; and statistics on Jewish emigration from Romania for 1936 and 1937.

The collection includes reports of the executive committee of the central board of the vocational training society ORT for 1935–36.

Many documents deal with the problem of Jewish refugees and emigration in the 1930s: a report by a representative of the Jewish Colonization Association on prospects for Jewish colonization in Paraguay, presented to the JCA general directorate on 24 May 1934; the text of an appeal by the Committee for the Defense of the Rights of Jews in Central and Eastern Europe to participants of the international Evian Conference (1938); a report by the central directorate of the OZE presented to the intergovernmental Evian conference on the refugee problem (30 June 1938); a report by the Committee to Aid Jewish Refugees covering the period 20 July 1936–30 June 1938; and minutes of May 1939 meetings of the coordinating commissions of the Committee to Aid Jewish Refugees.

The collection contains materials of Zionist organizations: news bulletins of the international women's Zionist organization, Hadassah, (1931–33); reports and documents of the Palestine Bureau in France (1932–34); materials of the French section of Hechalutz, on arranging instruction and temporary job placement in France for the organization's members (May–August 1935); and memoranda to the French government on the mission and nature of the activities of the French section of Hechalutz. It also contains letters to Boris Pregel, vice president of the Franco-Palestinian Chamber of Commerce (1938–39).

The collection also contains materials on British-Zionist relations, and on the Yishuv in Palestine: minutes of a session, and the text of a speech by Chaim Weizmann, at a conference (28 December 1920) on the political situation in Palestine; a memorandum (5 June 1939) on legal aspects of a declaration by the British Mandate authorities in Palestine; an addendum to a letter from Weizmann to the High Commissioner of the Permanent Mandate Commission (31 May 1939); circulars of the British passport service to foreign sections on restrictions on the import and export of goods to Palestine; on annulling invalid and false passports, in particular the passports of Jews stripped of Palestinian citizenship, including for illegal receipt of Palestinian passports; and on restrictions on the right for organizers of illegal Jewish immigration to enter Palestine (1937–40); handwritten notes (undated) on the problems of urban and agricultural water supply in Mandate Palestine; the text portion of a film strip on the Palestinian Yishuv (1939); and informational bulletins on the Mikveh Israel Agricultural School (1932), on Bet Ha-kan, the first agricultural colony of Bulgarian Sephardim in Palestine (1934), on Kibbutz Degania (1935), and on the Givat Brenner colony (1935).

The collection contains documents on the condition of Jews in Nazi Germany: documents of the international conference (30 November–1 December 1935, Paris) on Nazi legislation of the Third Reich; a systematic selection of documents on the legal position of Jews in Germany in 1933–35: fragments of discriminatory legislation, of public speeches by German government figures and leaders of the Nazi party, and of publications in the Nazi press on the need to force Jews out of the systems of higher education, medicine, and the law, on the unacceptability of "educational camps" for returning Jewish émigrés, on the boycott of Jewish shops, and on alleged ritual murders; protests by American, French, and British church leaders (1933); a draft appeal on nonrecognition of the discriminatory laws passed by the Reichstag in Nuremburg on 15 September 1935; a report by representatives of the Jewish community of Danzig at a HICEM-sponsored conference of Jewish émigré aid organizations (22 August 1939); a memorandum delivered at the same conference by a community of Turkish Jews living in Germany (about 150 families) on problems connected with recognition of their Turkish citizenship and on being granted the possibility of repatriation to Turkey; an English translation of an anonymous letter to the newspaper *Das Neue Tage-Buch* from 18 November 1938 (the author of the letter had been imprisoned for six weeks in the Buchenwald concentration camp; the system of the camp's functioning and conditions in which prisoners were held are described for the period from mid-June to the end of August 1938); and excerpts from publications in the Jewish press during the years 1933–35 condemning Nazi Germany's discriminatory policy toward Jews.

The collection has materials on the legal status of Jews in France before and during World War II: a letter from the Committee for the Defense of the Rights of Jews in Central and Eastern Europe to French prime minister Edouard Daladier, to the ministers of the Interior, Justice, and Finance, and to the prefect of the police on the unjustified tightening of procedures (by decree of 2 May 1938) for granting temporary residence in France to foreigners and, particularly, to Jewish refugees from Germany, Austria, Poland, and Romania, and on needlessly harsh measures (arrests and deportations) against the refugees; and a copy of a query (14 August 1941) from the French State Secretariat for Public Education's directorate of technical education to the Commissioner for Jewish Affairs on removing Jews from educational institutions' public administrative councils.

There are articles (for the most part typewritten) from 1938–39 on the situation of Jews in Czechoslovakia.

The collection holds the texts of various speeches, articles and printed materials from the time of the Second World War: a Paris speech given by General Władisław Sikorski at the opening of the National Council of the Polish Republic in Paris (23 May 1940) entitled "Pro-Hitler and Anti-Semitic Policy as Factors in the Defeat of Poland"; an article on the persecution of Jews in German-occupied Polish territory (no earlier than March 1940); detailed reports on the situation of Jews in Łódź and concerning the Lublin "Reservation"; issue no. 5 (20 February 1940) of the informational bulletin *Dekada Polska* of the Paris-based Center for Information and Documentation of the Polish Republic, presenting materials on the persecution of Jews in the German-occupied territories of Poland; and the 1940 articles "The Situation of the Jews in Łódź," "The Situation of the Jews in Poland," and "The Situation of the Jews in the Protectorate of Bohemia-Moravia."

The collection contains some materials on the Dreyfus Affair: articles by Alfred Dreyfus's son, Pierre, published in the London *Daily Telegraph* from 24 August to early September 1936, letters from various correspondents and readers in response to Pierre's articles, and reminiscences of the trial of Alfred Dreyfus. There is also a selection of articles from Swiss and French newspapers (including Russian-language émigré newspapers) for the period 28 October–10 November 1934 on the public trial in Berne against Theodor Fischer, leader of the Swiss section of the National Socialist Party, and members of the National Front, who were sued by the Union of Jewish Communities of Switzerland for publishing *The Protocols of the Elders of Zion.*

The collection contains clippings from Belgian, French, German, Swiss, British, Dutch, and American newspapers and other periodical and informational publications with articles on Jewish issues (April 1938).

The documents are in French, Romanian, Polish, German, English, Russian, Hebrew, and Yiddish.

Kollektsiia materialov po istorii i kul'ture evreev v Evrope

Collection of Documents on the History and Culture of European Jewry*

Fond 1325k, 1764–1944. 392 storage units.

The collection's contents are described in one inventory arranged geographically and thematically. It consists of documents from Austria (67 files), Belgium (1), Britain (1), Czechoslovakia (1), France (3), Germany (87), Latvia (1), Poland (3) Yugoslavia (1), various countries of Europe, Asia and Africa (40), Zionist organizations (8), Jewish emigration (4), Jewish political organizations (8), societies against antisemitism (4), studies of Jewish religion, philosophy and culture (23), and miscellaneous materials.

Among the materials of Austrian Jewish organizations, it holds the charters of the Jewish Choral Society of Graz, the Judäa Union of Jewish Students in Austria, and the Austrian Grand Lodge of B'nai B'rith; and the platform of the New Zionist Organization (Vienna, 1938). Other documents from these organizations are also contained in the collection: minutes of meetings of the Jewish Choral Society of Graz (1926–38), with the membership register and membership cards of this organization; correspondence of the Jewish Choral Society of Graz with the Graz police department on organizational issues, and the organization's cashbooks (1925–38); statistical reports on the activities of the Austrian Grand Lodge of B'nai B'rith (1935–38) and lists of its members; correspondence of the Jewish Academic Union of Technicians in Vienna with the executive committee of the Judäa Union of Jewish Students in Austria on sending representatives to congresses of the World Union of Jewish Students, on holding conferences of Zionist students in London, and on organizing technical courses for Jewish students (1919–26).

The collection contains extensive correspondence by the Union of Austrian Jews, with the Fatherland's Front of Austria, the Zionist Club, the Vienna police department, the New Zionist Organization (the Revisionist Zionists), the editorial offices of periodicals, members of the organizing

---

* A partial finding aid to this collection is available at http://www.sonderarchiv.de /fonds/fond1325.pdf.

committee of the New Zionist Organization congress (1935), the "Mifkada Eliona" in Tel Aviv on cooperation (1937), and with the Graz Zionist organization and the Palestine Bureau agency on insuring the property of Jewish immigrants to Palestine (1932–37). Also included is the cashbook of the New Zionist Organization (1937–38).

The collection also contains documents, mainly correspondence, of various other Austrian Jewish organizations. There is correspondence by Austrian Hechalutz groups with other Zionist organizations and Jewish communities on the resettlement of Austrian Jews in Palestine, on charitable activities in Palestine during 1919–37, and correspondence with regard to publishing an appeal to combine the efforts of all Jewish organizations in Austria (1934–35). The collection likewise contains the cashbooks of the Austrian Hechalutz movement (1937–38). There is correspondence of the Union of Jewish Youth Hashomer Hatzair with the Jewish Sports Club "Hakoah" in Graz (1936–37). There are reports on the activities of Agudath Israel in Austria (1932–38) and the cashbook of the Vienna Chevra Kadisha (1929–38).

Among the materials of German Jewish organizations, the collection contains charters of the Union of German-Jewish Communities (Berlin), of the Union of Rabbis in Germany (1896), the Jewish community of Braunschweig (1835), the Jewish community of Dresden, the Union of Jewish Communities of Bavaria (1937), and charitable institutions of the Jewish community of Frankfurt-on-Main (1845–46).

The collection contains correspondence of the local Allenstein chapter of the Union of Jewish War Veterans (1931–32), of the Union of Jewish Communities of Prussia (Berlin) with the German Ministry of Internal Affairs (1918–36), of the Jewish People's Party with the Association of Liberal Judaism, of the Hochschule for Jewish Studies (1920–30), and of the Society of Friends of the Library of the Hebrew University in Jerusalem with the editors of the newspaper *Jüdische Wochenblatt* on organizational issues.

There are minutes of meetings of the board of the Jewish community of Prichsenstadt (1887–1938); various German Jewish community membership cards; circulars of the German Jewish Aid Society (Berlin); a report on textbooks for the systematic study of Jewish tradition in Jewish schools of Saxony (7 April 1929); lists of students of the Berlin Rabbinical Seminary for Orthodox Judaism (1934–36) and of members of the local chapter of the Association of Liberal Judaism in Heidelberg; the cashbook of the Jewish community of Worms (1897–99); documents on the creation of the A. M. Levy Charitable Foundation (1863–1901); documents of the education section of the Reich Representation of Jews in Germany; and documents on the financial and charitable activities of the Union of Jewish Communities of Bavaria (1934–37).

Also deposited in the collection are charters and minutes of meetings of the Jewish community of Antwerp (1925–40).

The collection also contains manuscript materials from the collection of the Jewish Theological Seminary of Breslau (Wrocław). These include a composition (Prague, 1575) interpreting difficult words in the *Zohar*; a treatise by Saul Berlin, *Besamim Rosh* (late eighteenth century), with a flyleaf inscription: "A gift to the library of Rabbi Dr. Geiger from the head and members of the local Jewish community of Berlin, March 1875."; and a work by Yehuda Bariel devoted to polemicizing with Christians based on interpretation of the Bible (1808 manuscript, recopied from a 1702 manuscript). There is a notebook with manuscript copies and excerpts from the following works: "Sefer lehaye 'olam"; "Sefer nikkud"; "Sefer ha-itbir"; David Kimchi's commentary on the Book of Genesis, *Midrash Rabbah*, and *Midrash Tanhuma*; excerpts (1757) from Jacob ben Asher's treatise *Turim*; a notebook with the works "Haye Moshe" and "Mot Aharon" (author unknown); a copy of the Paris manuscript of a commentary on the Book of Job discovered by I. Bayer; a manuscript of *Sefer evronot*, dedicated to astronomy and the Jewish religious calendar; a manuscript of responsa (author unknown); a manuscript of Yomtov Lipman Heller's *Megilat 'eiva*; a Purimspiel script *Ahaseurus-shpil*; excerpts from the anti-Christian treatise *Toledot yeshu*; the manuscript "Maamar mahut ha-rabbanim" (which lays out, section by section, the duties of rabbis and the ritual laws of Judaism pertaining thereto); notes by an unidentified author on the *Book of Pseudo-Saadia*; analytical notes (author unknown, from Worms) on a rabbinical commentary on the Pentateuch entitled "Te'amim shel humash"; a manuscript (author unknown, from Worms) with a commentary on the *Midrash Rabbah* devoted to episodes pertaining to Adam and Eve; a manuscript book from the collection of W. Kossmann with the text of sermons on the *parshiyot*; and a manuscript from the collection of W. Kossmann with the text of commentaries and sermons (author unknown) on the Haftorahs.

The collection also contains manuscripts of works of nineteenth-century Jewish scholarship: manuscripts of Chanoch Albeck's works on halakhic midrashim, Talmudic treatises, and Jewish mystical teachings; a manuscript of a nineteenth-century work on the order of prayers according to the Ashkenazi rite; a German manuscript translation by Dr. S. Hauder (Vienna) of individual passages from the Judeo-Arabic treatise *Mu'allaqa of Imru'al-Qays*, with a philological and lexicological commentary on this medieval work; L. Hausdorf's work "The Kriat Shema Blessings" (Leipzig, 1877); a composition (author unknown) on the uses of the various names of God in the Hebrew Bible (nineteenth century); notes (author unknown) on *Sefer Yetsirah*; a work by W. Wessely comparing the Hebrew and Greek texts of the Hebrew Bible and discussing Judeo-Christian parallel terms such as *church (ecclesia)* and *Knesset Israel* as well as peculiarities of interpreting the terms "kingdom of heaven," "kingdom of God," "holy spirit," and "spirit of God" (dated 26 March 1841); Abraham Epstein's work on tombstones of the Jewish cemetery in Worms; excerpts by Epstein on Jewish sources on the history of Jews in Worms and Germany (1899); outlines and preparatory materials (1880s–90s, by Abraham Epstein?) on the history of the Jewish community of Speyer in the twelfth to sixteenth centuries.

There are also nineteenth- and early twentieth-century collections of sermons, religious thought, and polemics: Rabbi Friedmann's commentary on individual chapters of the Book of Genesis; the manuscript (by an unknown author) of "Talmud: The Wolf's Grasp of the Jews (Wölferfaß der Jüden)," containing excerpts in German translation from various Talmudic tractates, Midrashim, the Zohar, and other classics of Jewish religious literature; as well as a notebook of sermons by M. Elzter (1891–92).

The collection also contains documents on the social history of German and Austrian Jewry: trade licenses issued to the Jewish community of Heidelberg and resolutions of the Westphalian authorities governing its status (1764–1831).

The collection also has drafts and printed texts of articles: Schneidemann's "The Solution to the Jewish Problem," W. Koch's "The Social Question in Revisionism," W. Koch's "Why Am I in Betar?" and "Possibilities for Further Development of the Ideas of Betar," and an essay by Dr. I. Gleiser on Jewish history; informational bulletins of the Women's Zionist Organization of Austria (1935); accounts of the activities of the Graz Chevra Kadisha society for 1924–39; a report on the financial, educational, and organizational activities of the Keren Hayishuv (1932); informational bulletins on the activities of the School for Jewish Youth (Berlin, 1923) and of the Jewish Agency Palestine Bureau (1938); the pamphlet *Was ist Hechalutz?* (Berlin, 1933); and a pamphlet containing a report on the activities of the Lehranstalt for the Study of Judaism (Berlin).

The documents are in German and Hebrew.

Microfilms are held by the United States Holocaust Memorial Museum Archives.

INDIVIDUALS

Dokumental'nye materialy razlichnykh lits (kollektsiia)

Documentary Materials of Various Individuals (consolidated collection)

Fond 1329k, 1839–1945. 505 storage units.

The collection's contents are catalogued in two inventories, which are arranged by document type in order of the collection originators' surnames.

The collection constitutes an accumulation of various individuals' documents united only by authorship or by the documents' belonging to a particular individual. This collection of documents was compiled by archival staff from unsystematized files.

The collection includes notes (author unknown) on the situation of Jews in Austria; correspondence of S. Barber with Jewish émigrés from Czechoslovakia on helping them obtain residency rights in countries of Western Europe (1938–39); correspondence of the journalist Rudolf Breitscheid with H. Mann, M. Braun, and F. Wolram, and with publishers and other addressees, on creating a German people's front to fight the Nazi regime and on renewing Breitscheid's contributorship to the newspaper *Pariser Tageszeitung* (1938–39); correspondence of A. Roth with Jewish organizations about obtaining a Cuban immigration visa, and with relatives and acquaintances on personal matters (1934–40); and letters from relatives of Shattner in Romania and Palestine on personal matters (1939–40).

The collection also includes manuscripts of various articles by E. Berlin, K. Eberlein, I. Goldstein, and others (1909–36); Iu. Kozharskii's play (undated) "Titus, or the Destruction of Jerusalem"; Rabbi Meyer Landsberg's manuscript "The Spirit of the Babylonian Talmud" (1853); R. Löwe's memoir of J. Ziegler and others (1889–90); I. A. Vidal's article "Liberty, Equality, Fraternity, and Progress as Interpreted in the *Protocols of Zion*" (1933); a monograph entitled "The Jewish Spirit in the German Mind" (1933); and a review of Alexander Stein's book *Adolf Hitler: Schüler der "Weisen von Zion"* (1936).

The documents are in German, English, Russian, Greek, and Romanian.

Sochineniia, vyrezki iz gazet, razroznennye materialy ne ustanovlennykh organizatsii, uchrezhdenii i lits po voprosam politiki, ekonomiki, filosofii, istorii (kollektsiia)

**Writings, Newspaper Clippings, and Various Materials
of Unidentified Organizations, Institutions, and Individuals
on Matters of Politics, Economics, Philosophy, and History
(consolidated collection)**

Fond 1346k, 1527–1944. 546 storage units.

This is a collection of documents compiled by archival staff from unsystematized archival materials.

The collection's contents are catalogued in three inventories. Inventories no. 2 and no. 3 are arranged geographically, that is, by country name; inventory no. 1 is arranged by theme.

The collection represents an accumulation of documents of various persons, unidentified organizations, and institutions, and miscellaneous documents of varied content.

The collection contains anti-Semitic articles by an author writing under the pseudonym Hermann the German: "The Nationalization of British Mines," "Prospects for Bolshevism in England," "The Locarno Agreement," and others (1925–26); works by unknown authors directed against Freemasons and Jews (1912–30); "What Is Freemasonry?" "Freemasonry: A Jewish Organization," and "Jews: Freemasonry's Destroyers" (1927); an article (author unknown) entitled "Jewish Mastery of the World, with the Help of Freemasonry"; a work (author unknown) entitled "A Comparison of Jewish and Masonic Symbolism and Rituals"; articles (author unknown) directed against the Jews of Germany and Freemasons; German translations of anti-Jewish articles by a Romanian commentator (1944); and an issue of the informational bulletin of the Independent Order of B'nai B'rith for 1928.

The documents are in German, English, Hungarian, Romanian, Russian, Greek, Polish, Latin, French, Flemish, and Estonian.

AUSTRIA

INDIVIDUALS

Shtern Al'fred – professor filosofii briussel'skogo nauchno-issle-dovatel'skogo instituta, avstriiskii emigrant

Alfred Stern*

Fond 660k, 1920–1940. 8 storage units.

The collection's contents are described in one inventory.

The collection contains printed materials, materials of an autobiographical nature, and correspondence concerning, for the most part, the academic and publishing activities of Alfred Stern. The letters reflect the collector's ties with Jewish organizations such as the German Jewish Business Consortium in Brussels, the Jewish Readers' Society (in which A. Stern served as lecturer), and the Seminar on Jewish Literature and History in Brussels.

The documents are in German, French, and English.

---

* Transferred to Austria in 2009.

Shmerler Abram, advokat

Abraham Schmerler, Attorney*

Fond 664k, 1923–1934. 106 storage units.

The collection's contents are catalogued in one inventory. The inventory is arranged by theme and includes the following sections: law practice, documents on payment for Abraham Schmerler's legal services, lists of clients, files on civil suits against his own clients, literature on legislation, files on applications for Austrian citizenship, files on civil suits, other documents, and files on Schmerler's activities in the Jewish religious community of Vienna.

The collection reflects Schmerler's activities as a member of the Jewish religious community of Vienna and as a Jewish public figure. These include correspondence on renting a site for a synagogue, on providing food aid to Jewish community members in need, on job placement for unemployed members of the Jewish community, and on taking part in the activities of the Austria-Palestine Chamber of Commerce.

The documents are in German.

---

* Transferred to Austria in 2009.

BELGIUM

ORGANIZATIONS

Bel'giiskii komitet Vsemirnogo evreiskogo ob"edineniia "Al'ians izraelit iuniversel'"
(g. Antverpen)

Alliance Israélite Universelle, Belgian Committee (Antwerp)*

Fond 156k, 1913–1940. 5 storage units.

The Alliance Israélite Universelle was founded in 1860 in Paris. The Alliance's goal was to "work for the emancipation and moral progress of Jews." The governing organ of the Alliance was its central committee, located in Paris. Local Alliance committees were established in French cities and abroad; one of these was the Belgian Committee in Antwerp.

Materials in the collection include minutes of committee meetings for 1921 and 1927–39, and committee financial statements for 1931–39; lists of committee members; committee correspondence with the Alliance central committee in Paris and with Jewish agencies regarding organizational and financial issues; and a register of membership dues payments, and lists of dues-paying members, for 1924–40.

The documents are in French, Flemish, and Hebrew.

Microfilms are held by the United States Holocaust Memorial Museum Archives.

---

* Transferred to Belgium in 2002, and currently located at the Consistoire Central Israélite de Belgique, Brussels. Microfilms are available at RGVA.

Dokumenty sionistskikh i drugikh evreiskikh organizatsii Bel'gii (kollektsiia)

Documents of Zionist and Other Jewish Organizations in Belgium (consolidated collection)*

Fond 160, 1869–1940. 50 storage units.

The collection is an accumulation of documentary materials of various Belgian Jewish organizations, communities, consistories, and parties. The collection's contents are catalogued in two inventories.

This collection contains statutes and charters of the Central Jewish Consistory of Belgium, the Hebrew University study circle in Brussels, the Jewish Center of Brussels, the Belgium-Palestine Committee, the Jewish National Home, and other organizations.

Included are numerous minutes of meetings of, and reports on the activities of the Council of Jewish Associations (Brussels), the Brussels Zionist Union, the Assistance Committee for Jewish Refugees (Brussels), the "Ezra" Philanthropic Society for Aid to Emigrants, the Interfederal Association of Zionist Youth in Europe, The Federation of Zionist Youth in Belgium, The Association of Jewish Students (Brussels), and others. Of particular interest is the Council of Jewish Associations' 1940 survey on the situation of Jews in Belgium.

The collection also has the correspondence of Jewish communities, associations, and consistories from Brussels, Antwerp, and Geneva, concerning the provision of material aid to their members, the results of regional rabbinical council elections, the construction of synagogues, the organizing of religious courses, and related matters. There are lists of members of Jewish organizations, charitable subscription forms, financial documents (reports, cashbooks), and printed publications (informational bulletins, pamphlets, newspaper clippings, and journals).

The documents are in French, German, Flemish, English, and Hebrew.

* Transferred to Belgium in 2002, and currently located at the Consistoire Central Israélite de Belgique, Brussels. Microfilms are available at RGVA.

Redaktsiia zhurnala "Khatikva," organ federatsii tsionistov Bel'gii, g. Briusel' 1920–1936

Editorial Office of *Hatikva*, Organ of the Zionist Federation of Belgium*

Fond 145k, 1920–1940. 4 storage units.

[No RGVA descriptive information is available on this collection.]
Microfilms are held by the United States Holocaust Memorial Museum Archives.

---

* Transferred to Belgium in 2002, and currently located at the Consistoire Central Israélite de Belgique, Brussels. Microfilms are available at RGVA.

ORGANIZATIONS

Frantsuzskaia sektsiia Mezhdunarodnoi ligi bor'by protiv rasizma i anti-semitizma
(g. Parizh)

Section française de la Ligue Internationale contre le racisme et l'an-tisémitisme (Paris)

French Section, International League against Racism and Anti-semitism (Paris)*

Fond 43k, 1881–1940. 1,684 storage units.

The International League against Antisemitism (LICA) was founded in 1928 in Paris by Bernard Lecache and Pierre Paraf. This organization was popular, especially among young Jews, both natives of France and émigrés from Eastern Europe. In 1934, its members numbered eight to ten thousand — 32,000 in 1938. Lecache (1895–1968) was the president of LICA, and edited the League's journal, *Le Droit de Vivre* (1932–39; circulation 30,000 copies).

LICA was the organization that took the most radical positions with regard to French and German antisemitism. Its representatives engaged in street clashes with antisemitic groups and boycotted firms that did business with Nazi Germany. LICA decisively rejected the "policy of silence" practiced by the Consistory and other leading Jewish organizations with regard to antisemitism.

In 1936, the organization unofficially changed its name, becoming the International League against Racism and Antisemitism, although informally the

---

* Transferred to France in 2000, and currently located at the Centre de documentation juive contemporaine, Paris. Microfilms are available at RGVA.

former name was still used. From that point on, the league claimed that it was no longer a Jewish organization, and began speaking out against all forms of racism. During 1936–39, it worked closely with the French Popular Front and supported the Socialist prime minister Leon Blum. Besides individual members, the league included 60 institutional members: political parties, unions, and organizations that participated in its activities.

The collection's contents are described in three inventories. The inventories include a geographical index and indexes to inventory sections.

Documents of the collection include bylaws of the International League against Racism and Antisemitism, of its sections and committees. It also includes bylaws of other Jewish organizations, apparently of other collection provenance: the Union of Jewish Communities of France, the World Union of Jewish Combatants, the Jewish Brotherhood, the World Committee against War and Fascism, HICEM, the International Bureau to Provide Refuge and Aid to Political Emigrés, the Friends of Progress society, the Brotherly Duty society, Agudat Akhim, and Keren Kayemeth LeIsrael — as well as information on their creation and action plans.

The collection contains circular letters of the league central committee; minutes of meetings of the league central committee for 1935–39; accounts, reports, and information on league activities; and documents on the preparation for and conduct of the second through the ninth league congresses and international conferences.

Included in the collection are numerous items of correspondence of league governing bodies with league federations (primarily in the Seine Department) and sections; with government institutions, departments, and ministries; with public organizations; and with members of the league and its central committee. The correspondence covers a whole range of issues pertaining to activities of the league: its holding of congresses, conferences, and meetings; aid to Jews (the provision of refuge, material support, and help obtaining visas); the admission of new members; and the payment of membership dues. Several documents reflect the league's activities with regard to organizing a French boycott of goods produced in Nazi Germany and a protest campaign against the holding of the 1936 Olympic Games in Germany.

Documents reflecting the activities of league committees and commissions make up a significant portion of the collection. These include circulars, minutes of meetings, work reports, and correspondence. Files opened on individuals of Jewish origin, so as to provide them with all man-

ner of aid, are singled out in a separate group. This group of files is systematized alphabetically and chronologically. Also deposited in the collection are lists of members of the league and of its sections; applications and
questionnaires of those joining the league; financial documents (cashbooks,
financial statements, subscription forms, and income statements); reports,
articles, overviews, and information on repressive measures against Jews,
on anti-Semitic propaganda, and on the situation of Jews in France and
other countries; as well as bulletins, placards, leaflets, copies of newspapers
and journals, and pamphlets reflecting the activities of Jewish organizations
and the situation of Jews in various countries of Europe and Africa.

The documents are in French.

Microfilms are held by the United States Holocaust Memorial Museum Archives.

Frantsuzskii komitet Vsemirnogo ob"edineniia bor'by protiv rasizma i antisemitizma
  (g. Parizh)

Comité français du Rassemblement mondial contre le racisme et l'antisémitisme (Paris)

French Committee of the World Union against Racism and Antisemitism (Paris)*

Fond 97k, 1936–1939. 147 storage units.

See the historical description of Fond 43k on page 231.

The collection's contents are catalogued in two inventories, which are arranged by structure.

Documents in the collection include a draft resolution and reports on the founding of the World Union against Racism and Antisemitism; regulations for the conduct of the World and French committees of the union, and their circular letters. Separate groups of documents comprise materials on preparations for and the holding of World Union congresses and conferences; these include informational works, delegate mandates, minutes of sessions, reports, and resolutions. The collection contains minutes of meetings of the French committee and secretariat for 1937–39 and reports on the work of the union's French committee.

Included are numerous items of French committee correspondence with societies and organizations on union activities, on holding congresses and conferences, on intensifying anti-fascist propaganda, on collaboration, membership dues payments, and other issues. Financial documentation of the committee includes account books and income statements for 1938–39. There are lists of parties, unions, organizations, and societies affiliated with the World Union and belonging to the French, Belgian, and US na-

---

* Transferred to France in 2000, and currently located at the Centre de documentation juive contemporaine, Paris.

tional committees; and lists of members of the international executive committee and the French committee's executive office. The collection contains union informational bulletins, copies of the newspaper *Le Droit de Vivre*, and other printed materials.

The documents are in French and English.

Microfilms are held by the United States Holocaust Memorial Museum Archives.

Mezhdunarodnoe ispolnitel'noe biuro Mezhdunarodnoi federatsii lig bor'by protiv rasizma i antisemitizma (g. Parizh)

Bureau exécutif international de la fédération internationale des ligues contre le racisme et l'antisémitisme (Paris)

International Executive Office, International Federation of Leagues against Racism and Antisemitism (Paris)*

Fond 98k, 1931–1940. 223 storage units.

See the historical description of Fond 43k on page 231.

The collection's contents are catalogued in two inventories, which are arranged by structure.

Documents in the collection include the charter of the International Federation; documents on preparations for and the conduct of International Federation congresses and conferences, including the First International Conference in September 1934; correspondence regarding preparations for conferences; as well as lists of delegates, minutes of meetings, agendas, accounts of proceedings, reports, resolutions, appeals, and the like. The collection contains circulars of the International Federation executive office and minutes of its meetings for 1935–39, and reports on its activities.

The collection also features the International Federation's voluminous correspondence with national committees and with other societies and organizations: the Union of Jewish Communities of France, the World Union against Racism and Antisemitism, the American Jewish Congress, the Association against Racism, the Canadian Jewish Congress, the Anti-Nazi League, the World Union for Peace, the World Jewish Congress, and the Jewish community of Istanbul. The correspondence concerns collaboration in organizing a boycott of goods produced in Nazi Germany and

---

* Transferred to France in 2000, and currently located at the Centre de documentation juive contemporaine, Paris. Microfilms are available at RGVA.

protests against holding the 1936 Olympic Games in Nazi Germany, and so on.

The International Federation's financial documentation contains projections and income statements. A separate group of documents comprises reports, information, and overviews of the situation of Jews in various countries and the struggle for their rights.

The documents are in French, German, and English.

Microfilms are held by the United States Holocaust Memorial Museum Archives.

Mezhdunarodnyi ispolnitel'nyi komitet Vsemirnogo ob"edineniia bor'by protiv rasizma i antisemitizma (g. Parizh)

Comité exécutif international du Rassemblement mondial contre le racisme et l'antisemitisme (Paris)

International Executive Committee of the World Union against Racism and Antisemitism (Paris)*

Fond 99k, 1935–1940. 141 storage units.

See the historical description of Fond 43k on page 231.

The collection's contents are catalogued in two inventories, which consist of the following sections: materials on the founding, structure, and activities of the World Union; materials on union contacts with various organizations; financial documents of the union; and printed materials (bulletins, leaflets, and the like).

The collection contains draft bylaws of the World Union against Racism and Antisemitism, union platforms and overviews of its activities, procedural policies of the Union's international executive committee (and its circulars), and lists of organizations belonging to the World Union.

Particularly noteworthy is the group of documents on preparations for and the conduct of the First and Second International Congresses of the World Union; this group includes lists of delegates, their mandates, minutes of meetings, reports, as well as resolutions and appeals adopted by the congresses. The collection also contains minutes of meetings of the union's international executive committee for 1936–39; lists of members of the committee and of chairmen of the union's national committees; correspondence of the committee with national committees, with various societies and organizations—the American Committee for Democracy and Freedom,

---

*   Transferred to France in 2000, and currently located at the Centre de documentation juive contemporaine, Paris. Microfilms are available at RGVA.

the Council for American Democracy, the Vigilance Committee of Anti-Fascist Intellectuals, the International Legal Association, MOPR (The International Society for Aid to Revolutionaries), the French branch of the Workers' International (SFIO), the General Confederation of Labor (VKT), and the French Socialist Party. Also contained in the collection is correspondence with writers, scholars, and political and government figures (P. Cotte, J. Ducleau, P. Perrin, F. de Tessan, et al.) on collaboration with the World Union, on its activities, on arranging congresses and taking part in them, on joining the union, and on like matters. Financial documentation includes cashbooks for 1937–39 and income statements for 1938.

The collection also includes informational bulletins of the World Union; leaflets (for example, protesting Germany's occupation of Czechoslovakia); an appeal to fight racism and antisemitism and join the union; an address to the League of Nations demanding that the rights of Jews living in Romania be defended; copies of newspapers and journals; surveys of the press regarding persecutions of Jews in various countries; and other printed materials.

The documents are in French, English, and Spanish.

Microfilms are held by the United States Holocaust Memorial Museum Archives.

Tsentral'nyi komitet Vsemirnogo evreiskogo ob''edineniia

Alliance Israélite Universelle, Central Committee (Paris)*

Fond 100k, 1860–1940. 458 storage units.

The Alliance Israélite Universelle was founded in 1860 in Paris to aid Jews throughout the world. Among the aims of the organization, the most significant were "To work for the emancipation and moral progress of Jews everywhere, to give aid to all those who suffer because of their Jewish identity, and to encourage publications which might help bring about the emancipation of Jews and further their moral development." Considering education to be the primary means of "moral improvement," the Alliance, beginning in 1862, initiated the creation of a network of Jewish schools, for the most part in the countries of the Near East and the Balkans. On the eve of the Second World War, more than 150 such schools (the majority in Turkey) were in operation; instruction was conducted in French. The governing body of the Alliance was the central committee, headquartered in Paris. Local and regional committees of the Alliance were created in other French cities and abroad. Chairmen Adolphe Crémieux (1863–66, 1868–80) and Narcisse Leven (1898–1915) had a significant influence on Alliance activity.

For a detailed description of collection holdings, see:
http://www.aiu.org/biblio/Archives/invenrusse.html

*   This collection was transferred to France in 2000, and is currently located in the library and archives of the Alliance Israélite Universelle, Paris.

Federatsiia departamenta Seny frantsuzskoi sektsii Mezhdunarodnoi ligi bor'by protiv rasizma i antisemitizma (g. Parizh)

Fédération du département de la Seine de la section française de la Ligue internationale contre le racisme et l'antisémitisme (Paris)

Federation of the Seine Department of the French Section, International League against Racism and Antisemitism (Paris)*

Fond 103k, 1926–1940. 143 storage units.

See the historical description of Fond 43k on page 231.

The collection's contents are catalogued in two inventories, which are arranged by structure.

Among the collection's documents are the charter of the International League against Racism and Antisemitism, draft charters of the territorial Federation of the Seine Department and the league's Women's Federation Committee, and circular letters of the league central committee and the federation of the Seigne department committee. A separate set of documents comprises materials on preparations for and the conduct of Seine federation congresses for 1929–31, 1933, 1935, and 1937. These include lists of delegates, their mandates, agendas and minutes of congress sessions, accounts of the federation's work, reports, and resolutions adopted by federation congresses. The collection also includes minutes of meetings of the Seine federation committee and bureau for 1929, 1932, and 1934–40; of meetings of the federation's conflict commission for 1935 and 1937–38; and of meetings of Seine federation sections.

A significant portion of the collection is made up of correspondence with the league central committee and with federation departments and individual members on organizing federation work; on holding con-

---

* Transferred to France in 2000, and currently located at the Centre de documentation juive contemporaine, Paris.

gresses, conferences, and meetings; on subscribing to the newspaper *Le Droit de Vivre*; on providing aid to federation members; as well as on paying and forwarding membership dues and other organizational matters. There are also financial documents of the federation (a cashbook, financial statements, subscription forms to raise funds for financial aid for the editorial office of the newspaper *Le Droit de Vivre*, and expense accounts of federation departments). Also deposited in the collection are lists of members of the league central committee and of federation departments, and informational bulletins of the league.

The documents are in French.

Evreiskii pedagogicheskii institut (g. Parizh)

École normale israélite orientale (Paris)

Alliance Israélite Universelle Teacher Training School (Paris)*

Fond 104, 1892–1939. 49 storage units.

The Alliance Israélite Universelle Teacher Training School in Paris was founded in 1867. Upon completing the four-year course of study and passing examinations, its students — the top graduates of Alliance schools from North Africa and the Near East — received a French primary school teaching certificate. The academic curriculum included the study of French language and literature, Jewish religion and Hebrew, world history and geography, pedagogy, mathematics and science, music, the arts, and gymnastics. Its instructors included the pedagogues I. Carré and Ferdinand Buisson.

The collection's contents are described in two inventories. The documents are catalogued by type.

The collection's documents include charters of the Alliance Israélite Universelle Teacher Training School, the school's academic curricula, its annual budget estimates and balances, personnel records of its faculty members with yearly salary indicated, and lists of members of the Teacher Training School's board. A significant portion of the collection is made up of the school's correspondence with department prefectures about receiving bequests willed to the school by various individuals.

Another portion of the collection comprises director A. H. Navon's correspondence on work and personal matters. The collection also includes materials of the Conference of Sephardic Communities (London, May 1935), minutes of meetings of the World Federation of Sephardic Communities executive committee, minutes of a session of the election commission of the Sephardic Religious Association of Paris, and other materials.

The documents are in French, English, and Hebrew.

* Transferred to France in 2000, and currently located at the Centre de documentation juive contemporaine, Paris.

Dokumenty sionistskikh i drugikh evreiskikh organizatsii Frantsii (kollektsiia)

Documents of Zionist and Other Jewish Organizations in France (consolidated collection)*

Fond 161, 1866–1940. 60 storage units.

The collection constitutes an accumulation of documents and printed publications of Jewish organizations in France, often of undetermined collection provenance.

The collection's contents are described in two inventories.

The collection contains surveys, references, reports, compendia of documents, and the texts of articles on the history, culture, and religion of the Jewish people; on the situation of Jews in various countries, particularly in Germany, Poland, and pre-revolutionary Russia; on the establishment of a Jewish state and its future legal status; and on providing material aid to Jewish émigrés and refugees.

These materials include a variety of reports: a report by the director of the International Labor Bureau on labor conditions in Palestine in 1928; a report, "Problems of Arab-Jewish Reconciliation," by Boris Gurevich, vice president of the Committee for the Defense of the Rights of Jews in Central and Eastern Europe; reports by the Central Yiddish School Organization (TsISHO) in Poland on the founding and functioning of its schools; reports on anti-Semitic propaganda in Alsace-Lorraine; and reports on the situation of Jews in Latvia. The collection includes reports on the activities of Jewish émigré aid committees for 1939, reports on the work of HICEM in Vilna for January–March 1940, and reports of the Technion (Haifa) for 1935–37.

There also are documents of various Jewish organizations: the Swiss Union of Jewish Communities, the Zionist Pro-Palestine Group in France, the Keren Kayemeth LeIsrael in France, the Association of Ger-

---

* Transferred to France in 2000, and currently located at the Centre de documentation juive contemporaine, Paris. Microfilms are available at RGVA.

man-Jewish émigrés in France, the Jewish Religious Community of Vienna, the Committee to Aid Jewish Refugees (in Brussels), the Jewish community of Prague, the Jewish religious community of Danzig, the French branch of the Women's International Zionist Organization (WIZO), the French branch of the Union of Jewish Youth, the Federation of Austrian Émigrés, the American Jewish Joint Distribution Committee, the Technion (Haifa), the International Labor Bureau, the International Council for the Rights of Jewish Minorities, the Committee for the Defense of the Rights of Jews in Central and Eastern Europe, and HICEM. These include correspondence, lists of committees and commissions, as well as financial documentation, particularly cashbooks and income statements, including a financial statement of the JDC for 1938.

Also included are materials on preparing and holding world Jewish congresses and conferences, and informational bulletins, copies of newspapers, and newspaper clippings.

The documents are in French, German, English, Russian, and Hebrew.

Evreiskaia konsistoriia (g. Bordo)

Consistoire Israélite de Gironde (Bordeaux)

Jewish Consistory of Gironde (Bordeaux)*

Fond 139, 1550–1940. 72 storage units.

The first reliable information on the Jewish community of Bordeaux dates to the ninth century. In 1790, the Sephardic Jews of Bordeaux and Bayonne received the rights of French citizens. In March 1812, aiming more effectively to control the Jewish minority and hasten the process of its integration into France, Napoleon decreed the creation of the consistorial structure of French Jewish community life. The legal status of Jewish consistories was reformulated by law in 1862 and 1872. These laws provided for the existence of a Central Consistory (based in Paris) and consistories in the departments. The consistories remained the official representative bodies of the Jews of France until the legislative separation of church from state in 1905. In 1905, the Central Consistory established the Union of Jewish Religious Associations of France, which most of the department associations joined. The Jewish Religious Association of the Gironde department commenced functioning on 1 December 1906. That association's goal was to support the Jewish religion and the observance of Jewish rituals according to the Sephardic rite and local traditions. The association was led by a council called a consistory. The consistory was made up of the chief rabbi and ten or eleven elected members. Eligible for election to consistory membership were male French citizens of at least twenty-five years of age. The Consistory of the Gironde department was located in Bordeaux.

The collection is described in three inventories. The documents catalogued in the first two inventories are organized into two parts: materials directly related to the activities of the collection's originator, and supplementary materials. The documents catalogued in inventory no. 3 have not been subjected to any sort of systematization.

---

* Transferred to France in 2000, and located at the Consistoire israélite de la Gironde in Bordeaux. Portions are available on microfilm at RGVA

Inventories Nos. 1 and 2 catalogue circulars of French government institutions; bylaws of the Jewish Religious Association of Gironde; minutes of sessions of the Consistory of the Gironde department for 1913–40; correspondence of the Consistory with Jewish religious, educational, and charitable organizations and with private individuals; speeches by Consistory Chief Rabbi L. Cohen; information on the activities of various Jewish organizations, with charters, reports, and minutes thereof; copies of newspapers and journals; circulars of the French Ministries of Justice and War and of the Central Jewish Consistory on legal and organizational matters; edicts of the French Ministry of the Interior and the prefecture of the Gironde department appointing Bordeaux regional notables for 1809–29; and a draft budget and financial statement of the Consistory for 1936.

A significant portion consists of correspondence of the Consistory of Gironde with the Central Jewish Consistory in Paris and its chief rabbi; with the consistories of other departments of France; and with a number of Jewish organizations, including the Association for the Development of Primary and Professional Education, the Committee of Jewish Primary Schools, the Committee to Aid Refugees, the Achdut society of Jewish immigrants, and several others. Also included is correspondence with members of the Jewish Religious Association of Gironde and those of other Jewish communities. The letters encompass a range of issues pertaining to various aspects of Jewish Consistory activity: economic (membership dues payment and the provision of material aid), organizational (admitting new members, electing assembly delegates, observing religious holidays, and holding events), legal-charitable (defending the interests and rights of the Jewish population and providing housing to Jewish immigrants), and other.

Most of the documents catalogued in inventory no. 3 relate to the Jewish community and Consistory during the period of 1550–1871. These include Henry II's, Henry III's, and Louis XVI's charters to the Jews of Spanish and Portuguese descent who had settled in Bordeaux, the texts of royal edicts, decrees of the State Council of France, decrees of Napoleon, and a number of other historic documents.

The documents are in French, Spanish, and Hebrew.

Ob"edinennyi arkhivnyi fond: Sionistskie i drugie evreiskie organizatsii Frantsii

Zionist and Other Jewish Organizations of France, Consolidated Archival Collection*

Fond 186, 1891–1940. 476 storage units.

The organizations represented in the collection were established in France in the nineteenth and twentieth centuries. Many of them had international standing.

The collection's contents are catalogued in three inventories arranged by structure.

Inventory no. 1 catalogues documents of the international bureau of Zionist Youth of Western Europe, the Society for Jewish Emigration and Colonization (Emcol), the Committee for the Defense of the Rights of Jews in Central and Eastern Europe, the Federation of Zionist Youth of France, and the Jewish Committee for the Defense of the Rights of Children from Germany and Central Europe.

Inventory no. 2 catalogues documents of the Jewish Colonization Association (JCA), the Federation of Jewish Societies of France, the central committee of ORT, OZE (Jewish public health association), the Society of Jewish Volunteers in the Service of France 1914–18, the Association of Polish-Jewish Veterans of the War in France, the Central Association of Sephardic Jews, the Committee to Aid Refugees (CAR), and Jewish youth and religious organizations. The collection also contains documents of a number of other Jewish organizations active in France and beyond. JCA documents (about 340 files) constitute the main body of the collection.

The collection includes reports on the history of the Jews and their religion; surveys on the situation of Jews in various countries in the period between the wars, particularly in Nazi Germany; as well as materials on

---

*   Transferred to France in 2000, and currently located in the library and archives of the Alliance Israélite universelle, Paris. Microfilms are available at RGVA.

Jewish emigration and on the activities of Jewish organizations. Among the materials are charters of a number of associations and organizations, such as the JCA, the Center for the Study of the Rights of Jewish Émigrés in France, the Association of Polish Jews in France, the Central Association of Sephardic Jews, B'nai Israel, and others. There is also information on the founding and activities of Emcol, OZE, the World Organization of Hashomer Hatzair, and ORT.

Further, there are circulars of the Federation of Zionist Youth in France for 1938–39; minutes of sessions of the international bureau of Zionist Youth of Western Europe, of the bureau of the Committee for the Defense of the Rights of Jews in Central and Eastern Europe for 1934–36, the administrative council of the JCA for 1897, 1898, 1926–34, and 1938–40, the Association of Polish Jewish Veterans of the War in France, and the Central Association of Sephardic Jews; accounts of the activities of the Federation of Zionist Youth in France, the central executive committee of ORT (1938), and the administrative council of the JCA for 1896, 1897, 1905, 1907, and 1910; and reports by JCA council members on their trips to JCA-sponsored Jewish agricultural colonies in various countries.

The collection also features correspondence among the above-listed Jewish entities on organizational, financial, and personnel issues; on the activities of Jewish youth and children's organizations of Europe in the interwar decades; and on job placement for Jewish émigrés and their provision with material assistance. There are lists of Jewish organizations and lists of their members; questionnaires of Jewish émigrés from Hungary; financial documents of the JCA, the Federation of Jewish Communities of France, ORT, and other entities; informational bulletins, pamphlets, and leaflets; and copies of newspapers.

The documents are in English, German, Russian, French, Yiddish, and Hebrew.

Microfilms are held by the United States Holocaust Memorial Museum Archives.

GOVERNMENT AGENCIES

Glavnoe upravlenie natsional'noi bezopasnosti Frantsii (g. Parizh)

Direction générale de la Sûreté Nationale (Paris)

Central Office for National Security of France (Paris)*

Fond 1k, 1883–1940. 13,892 storage units.

The Central Office for Public Safety was established in 1791 as part of the French Ministry of the Interior. During 1899–1903, the Central Office was joined with the Cabinet of the Minister of the Interior and was not, in that period, an independent institution. By a law of 31 March 1903, the Central Office once again functioned independently within the French Ministry of the Interior. The office repeatedly altered its internal structure (1907, 1910, and 1920s). The most important reorganization of the Central Office for Public Safety took place in 1934 in connection with heightened international tension and a drastic worsening of the internal political situation. It was renamed the Central Office for National Security. On the eve of the German occupation, the structure of Sûreté Nationale included the office of administrative police and general information, the office of police for territorial control and surveillance of foreigners, the directorate of services of territorial surveillance, the main inspectorate of administrative police services, and the main inspectorate of criminal police services.

The collection is catalogued in 82 inventories.

Documents contained in the collection can be classified, according

---

* With the exception of 200 files from inventory 2, this collection was transferred to France during the period 1993–2000, and is currently located at the Center for Contemporary Archives (Centre des archives contemporaines), Paris. Microfilms are available at RGVA. For a comprehensive description of this collection, see http://www.archivesnationales.culture.gouv.fr/chan/index.html.

to their nature, into three groups: files opened by the French police on government and political figures, persons suspected of political unreliability or espionage, and persons having committed criminal acts and the like; general recordkeeping documents of the Central Office for National Security of France; and documents of the central services for the issuance of identification papers and passports.

The collection contains dispatches and reports on the activities, leadership, and personnel of various Jewish organizations active in France. It contains correspondence with police prefects and the Ministry of Foreign Affairs on the activities of Jewish organizations on French territory: the Committee to Aid Refugees, the League of Friends of Jewish Workers in Palestine, the Committee to Aid Victims of the Hitlerite Regime, the French Committee to Defend Persecuted Jewish Intellectuals, the National Committee to Aid German Émigré Victims of Antisemitism, Poale Zion, the Association of Jewish Youth (Paris), the Jewish Union of Supporters of the Labor Party in France, the Vladimir Medem Jewish Youth Union, the Jewish Workers' Hearth, Machazikei Hadas, the Society of Friends of the Jewish People in the USSR, the Union of Palestinian Action, the Jewish Public Union, the Union of Jewish Communities of France, the Committee for the Defense of the Rights of Jews in Central and Eastern Europe, the Association of Polish Jews in France, the National Union of Jewish Patriots, the Federation of Jewish Communities of France, the Association for the Preservation of Jewish Tradition in France, Jewish Renaissance, the International League Against Antisemitism, the League to Defend Persecuted Jews, the Society to Aid Russian Jews, the Jewish Workers' Bund, the Society of Supporters of Jewish Colonization in the USSR, and the Association of Russian-Jewish Intelligentsia in Paris.

There are documents on the political trustworthiness of various persons: M. Zimmerman, O. G. Schwarzbach, I. Saffer, I. Fusch, I. Ribashovsky, M. Jurblum, Zilberstein, E. F. Braunstein, Nachum Sokolow, A. Feferkorn, V. Gordon, G. Goldemberg, G. Friedland, V. Gersohn, Menahem Ussishkin, Genrikh Sliozberg, I. Levin, L. Hufnagel, R. Aaron, and Israel Efroykin. There are also documents on the 1936 Geneva constituent conference of the World Jewish Congress, and on meetings of the Jewish Agency for Palestine.

The documents are in French.

INDIVIDUALS

Rotshil'dy – rodovoi fond

Rothschild family*

Fond 58k, 1827–1940. 132 boxes.

[No RGVA descriptive information is available on this collection.]

* Returned to France in 1994, 2000, and transferred to the Rothschild Archive, London. Accessible via the Rothschild Archive, London.

GREAT BRITAIN

OGRANIZATIONS AND INDIVIDUALS

Rotshil'dy – venskie bankiry

Rothschild Family and the Rothschild Bank, Vienna*

Fond 637k, 1769–1939. 419 storage units.

The Rothschild dynasty of financial magnates was founded by Mayer Amschel Rothschild of Frankfurt-on-Main. Most of the collection's documents relate to the Rothschild branch that settled in Vienna. In 1816, M. A. Rothschild's second son Salomon Mayer (1774–1855) moved to Vienna, where he founded a bank in 1818. He was friendly with Metternich and was made a member of the nobility in 1822. His main achievements included financing the construction of the first Austrian railroad and establishing the Österreichische Creditanstalt, which later became the state Bank of Austria. Salomon Mayer's successor was Anselm Salomon (1803–74), who received a seat in the Austrian parliament in 1861. He was succeeded by his son Albert Salomon (1844–1911), who gained fame as a philanthropist and patron of the arts.

By the end of the nineteenth century, the Rothschild family's position in the financial market of Austria-Hungary had weakened substantially. After Albert Salomon, the Vienna banking house was headed by his two sons Alphonse Mayer (1878–1942) and Louis (1882–1955). Louis was arrested two days prior to the Anschluss of Austria in March 1938. After a year spent as a hostage, he was freed — for ransom, and due to pressure from international banking circles.

---

* Transferred in 2001 to Great Britain, and currently located in the Rothschild Archive, London. Microfilms are available at RGVA.

The collection's contents are catalogued in two inventories. The inventories are arranged by subject.

The collection includes documents related to Mayer Amschel Rothschild's appointment to the office of court factor (1769), the granting of credit to M. A. Rothschild, the accounts on the Frankfurt bank (1797–1807), and the Rothschild brothers' acquisition of an estate in the vicinity of Frankfurt-on-Main. The collection contains legal documents, financial statements, minutes of meetings, correspondence, and various documents on the estates of the Rothschild family, including estate maps.

The collection contains diverse documents on the Rothschilds' financial activities: contracts, financial documents, business correspondence, income statements, copies of state papers, and letters from government and political figures. These include documents on business cooperation between members of the Rothschild family (contracts and agreements); on the activities of the Rothschild family's banks in Paris, Vienna, Frankfurt, and London (financial statements, accounting documents, and audit reports); on providing credit to the Esterházy princes, Count von Henckel-Donnersmarck, and Prince E. von Hohenlohe; on the issuance of loans to the governments of Austria, Hungary, Belgium, the Netherlands, France, Germany, Sweden, and others; on acquiring real estate in Paris (notarized documents); on purchasing stock; and on purchasing and liquidating enterprises. The collection includes experts' reports and documents on the appraisal of property; a list of Salomon von Rothschild Bank securities; and reports on the financial situation and gold reserves of European countries.

There are extensive documents on the Rothschilds' philanthropic activities: deeds of gifts; contracts; financial statements of, and reports on the activities of, various Rothschild-sponsored institutions; lists of donations; petitions; letters of thanks; documents on the construction of a synagogue in Frankfurt-on-Main, the Brünn [Brno] Polytechnic Institute, and a women's hospital in Vienna; and documents on charitable contributions from the estate of Anselm Salomon Rothschild.

The collection also contains documents related to appointments to offices, promotions in rank, and the conferral of honorary titles and citizenship. These include certificates and copies of certificates of merit and commendation, including certificates from Landgrave Wilhelm I, Tsar Alexander I, Emperor Franz, and others. Also included is correspondence of a formal nature (invitations, congratulations, and condolences); and correspondence with the "Goethe" lodge of B'nai B'rith.

There are extensive materials of a personal, family nature: Rothschild family members' personal correspondence (personal correspondence of Clarice, Alphonse, and George Rothschild); personal documents of Adolf Rothschild (identification papers, citizenship applications); marriage contracts, wills, photographs, birth and death certificates; a genealogy of the Rothschild family; reports of personal and family expenses; and accounts of trips.

The collection also contains photo materials, books, pamphlets, newspaper clippings, and articles; an alphabetized catalogue of documents in the family archive; a catalogue of the art collection of Nathaniel Rothschild (London); and a biography of Mayer Amschel Rothschild compiled by S. I. Cohen (1813).

The documents are in German, French, English, Hebrew, and Yiddish.

THE NETHERLANDS

ORGANIZATIONS

Evreiskie religioznye organizatsii i uchrezhdeniia Gollandii

Jewish Religious Organizations and Institutions of the Netherlands*

Fond 1432k, 1778–1943. 1,025 storage units.

The Dutch-Israelite Congregation (DIC) and the Portuguese-Israelite Congregation were officially founded in 1870. The Dutch-Israelite Congregation consisted of representatives of the "central synagogues" of twelve regions of the Netherlands, each of which had its own chief rabbi. Everyday operations were managed by a permanent committee of three (later five) members, most of whom represented the Jewish community of Amsterdam. The best-known leader of the DIC was the main Amsterdam synagogue's president Abraham Carel Wertheim, who led the DIC over the course of several decades. Rabbi J. H. Dunner served as chief rabbi of the Amsterdam synagogue, as well as head of the Dutch Israelite Seminary, between 1874 and 1911.

The collection's contents are described in one inventory. Documents in the collection are not systematized, although many files have been grouped together by theme.

The collection contains charter documents of the Jewish religious community of Amsterdam and of the Netherlands: the charter of the main synagogue of Amsterdam, rules of procedure for meetings of the Jewish

---

* Transferred to the Netherlands in 2003. The collection has been divided: most is currently held in the Amsterdam Municipal Archives, parts are held in The Hague Municipal Archives and Utrecht Municipal Archives. Portions are available on microfilm at RGVA.

religious community of Amsterdam board of directors, regulations on the conduct of weddings in the main synagogue of Amsterdam, regulations on procedures for burial at the Jewish cemetery, and the charters of Jewish religious schools and the Jewish religious seminary.

The collection also includes documents on the construction of the main synagogue of Amsterdam and on the celebration of Jewish holidays, and sheet music for synagogue cantorials. There is information on the academic curricula of the Jewish religious seminary and curricula of religious subjects at Jewish schools; documents containing information on leaders of the Jewish community of Amsterdam and on individual members; references, attestations, and certificates issued by the main synagogue of Amsterdam and by the permanent commission on general affairs of the Dutch Jewish religious community to community members.

Also featured in the collection is financial documentation of the administration of the Dutch Jewish religious community (reports and surveys on intra-community tax payments, documents on the purchase and sale of plots of land, etc.); information on the financing of Jewish community, religious, and educational institutions in the Netherlands; financial accounting information of local Jewish communities of the Netherlands; and analogous documents.

The collection contains extensive correspondence: of the Dutch Jewish religious community's permanent commission on general affairs with leaders of the main synagogue of Amsterdam; of local Jewish religious communities (memoranda, circulars, congratulations, bulletins on education, etc.); and of leaders of the Dutch Jewish religious community with international Jewish and Zionist organizations (including Keren Kayemeth LeIsrael) — and with private individuals on personal matters.

The collection contains photographs, cards, newspapers, journals, pamphlets, blueprints, posters, placards, sheet music, and stamps.

Also deposited in the collection are documents reflecting the realities of how the Jewish community functioned under the conditions of the Nazi German occupation of the Netherlands; and documentation on the deportation of Dutch Jews to Nazi concentration camps. There are German Order Police announcements informing the Amsterdam Jewish Council of executions and deaths of Dutch Jews in concentration camps.

The documents are in Dutch, English, German, Hebrew, Yiddish, and French.

INDEX

INDEX OF
PERSONAL NAMES